PITTSBURGH THEOLOGICAL MONOGRAPH SERIES

Dikran Y. Hadidian
General Editor

35

ORIENTATION BY DISORIENTATION

Studies in Literary Criticism
and Biblical Literary Criticism

ORIENTATION by DISORIENTATION

Studies in Literary Criticism
and Biblical Literary Criticism

Presented in honor of
William A. Beardslee

Edited by
Richard A. Spencer

THE PICKWICK PRESS
Pittsburgh, Pennsylvania
1980

Biblical quotations in chapters 5, 6, and
15 from the Revised Standard Version of
the Bible, copyrighted© 1946, 1952, 1971,
1973 by the Division of Christian Education of the National Council of the
Churches of Christ in the U.S.A., are
used by permission.

Grateful acknowledgement is made to the
University of Chicago Press for permission to quote from Paul Hernadi, "Literary Theory: A Compass for Critics", published in *Critical Inquiry*, Vol. 3, No. 2,
Winter 1976.

Grateful acknowledgement is made to the
Society of Biblical Literature for permission to reprint an abridged and revised version of John Dominic Crossan,
"It is Written: A Structuralist Analysis of John 6", published in *Society of
Biblical Literature: 1979 Seminar Papers*,
edited by Paul J. Achtemeier (Missoula:
Scholars Press, 1979), 2:197-213.

Library of Congress Cataloging in Publication Data
Main entry under title:

Orientation by disorientation.

   (Pittsburgh theological monograph series ; 35)
   Bibliography: p.
   Includes index.
   1. Bible--Criticism, interpretation, etc.--Addresses,
essays, lectures. 2. Beardslee, William A.
I. Beardslee, William A. II. Spencer, Richard A.
III. Series.
BS511.2.O74   220.6   80-21842
ISBN 0-915138-44-1

Copyright© 1980 by
THE PICKWICK PRESS
5001 Baum Boulevard
Pittsburgh, PA 15213

CONTENTS

Part I: Toward Defining Literary Criticism

Part II: A Discipline in Ferment

This collection of studies is presented to honor William A. Beardslee on the occasion of his sixty-fifth birthday. The particular topic of this volume was chosen (as opposed to other areas of study to which Will has been a significant contributor, such as process studies, Hellenistic studies, or studies in Wisdom) owing to the healthy state of ferment in which literary criticism and biblical studies exist today, and the fact that Professor Beardslee is widely appreciated for his pioneering work in the dialogue between literary criticism and biblical studies.

Orientation by Disorientation is more than a collection of essays on varied topics donated by friends and former students of the honoree. It was decided that a Festschrift in honor of Professor Beardslee would be most truly an expression of esteem if it would accomplish two things: first, that it further the enterprise which has been so much a part of his own work (that of drawing lines of communication between literary criticism and biblical studies), and second, that it make a useful contribution to that enterprise. This volume has been designed and prepared with those two objectives in view. Consequently, the contents include essays on the definition and history of literary criticism and biblical literary criticism (PART I: TOWARD DEFINING LITERARY CRITICISM), description and analysis of various aspects and methods of literary criticism (PART II: A DISCIPLINE IN FERMENT), and the application of literary analysis to biblical materials (PART III: LITERARY ANALYSIS OF BIBLICAL MATERIALS).

Subscribing contributors to this work was itself a rewarding experience. The widespread respect for Will Beardslee which was the generating factor in this effort was articulated with increasing frequency as the responses of acceptance came in and as encouragement and gratitude for this exercise were repeated from many quarters. The contributors were selected not for the range of relationships to Will which they represent (though two are former students, others are colleagues and professional associates, and Will's Doktorvater Amos N. Wilder has graciously provided a Foreword), but because of their expertise in and engagement with literary or phenomenological analysis, biblical studies, or both.

Paul Ricoeur, who had begun an article, had to withdraw, owing to health problems. Nevertheless, he has joined us in honoring Will by providing a title for the work. In speaking of the transmutation of human existence which is effected in the parables and proverbs of Jesus (as shown by Robert Funk and Will Beardslee, respectively), Ricoeur states that this "is accomplished in the proverb by the strange strategy which I will call *re-orientation by disorientation*" ("Biblical Hermeneutics," *Semeia* 4 [1975]: 114). In recent studies (see, e.g. "Saving One's Life By Losing It," *Journal of the American Academy of Religion* 47 [March, 1979]: 57-72) Will has developed his discussion of the challenging of vision and recomposition of vision which is effected in Jesus' proverbs. In so doing, he has adapted Ricoeur's phrase to "orientation by disorientation", using it to great advantage for employing a process hermeneutic in the literary study of biblical materials. This phrase, then, with its own proverbial ring is most suitable for gathering up various significant moments of Will's work. It is used here with the kind permission and hearty encouragement of Professor Ricoeur.

I am indebted to many people for their help in making this work become a reality. Naturally, my gratitude is due principally to the contributors who eagerly accepted their respective charges and met deadlines with dispatch, and to Mr. Dikran Hadidian and the Pickwick Press for constant assistance and encouragement. Professor Robert Detweiler's suggestions, penetrating critique, and enthusiasm for this work have been greatly appreciated. In the initial stages of preparing Professor Beardslee's Bibliography, my graduate assistant, Mr. Joseph C. Tuttle, provided me with much assistance. Mrs. Jo Philbeck of the Southeastern Baptist Theological Seminary Library was often helpful with reference matters so indispensible to editing. To Mrs. Evelyn Carter I owe special thanks for her untiring assistance and expertise in typing and preparing the manuscript. *Orientation by Disorientation* is presented as the accomplishment of many people who know and respect Will Beardslee, as a tangible expression of our gratitude for his many personal and professional contributions to religion and life.

Richard A. Spencer
Wake Forest, North Carolina
January, 1980

FOREWORD

Both as regards the study of the biblical texts in their
ancient setting and the study of their modern import, William
Beardslee occupies a strategic place in our changing discipline. So far as concerns our older tools and methods he knows
how to honor these, but also to employ them in conjunction
with newer strategies and in wider contexts so as to further
their yield. But these more refined operations also help us
to clarify the continuing claims of the biblical witness at a
deeper level, thus enabling a more effective dialogue with our
contemporary culture.

By way of illustration I would point to three areas of
his interest in which on the basis of scholarly exploration he
has been able to carry out far-ranging observations which have
their bearing not only on primitive Christianity but on modern
theological issues. In each case it has been thanks to the
wide humanistic and literary character of the approach that he
has been able to open up the significance of the form or texts
in question. His study of proverbial Wisdom in the Gospels
has served as a useful corrective to certain over-emphases in
the theology of the Synoptics, and links up with that insistence on "concrete existence" which Beardslee sees as a perennial trait of the Gospel. His recurrent attention to New Testament apocalyptic and its differentia underlies his important
discussions of the phenomenology of hope in its modern versions, as for example in the theology of liberation and in
process theology. His interest in narrativity in the New
Testament, shared indeed with many others but focused especially on the Christ-story, provides him again with support for his
theme of "concrete existence", particularly as disallowing an
all too familiar existentialist reduction of that story.

Common to all these literary-rhetorical probings of early
Christian forms is the effort to relate them to comparable
ancient genres and usage but also to language phenomena generally. This literary procedure does not absolve the scholar of
rigorous historical-critical responsibility, rather the contrary. In his *Literary Criticism of the New Testament*[1] Beardslee compares his approach with that of Northrop Frye and Erich
Auerbach. His own approach "will be more concrete...and will
attempt to concentrate on how the form is related to the reli-

---

[1]Philadelphia: Fortress Press, 1970.

gious function". The original function of the New Testament books "was religious, and an understanding of their function in their religious setting...is fundamental to a grasp of their impact".[1] But such understanding, of course, requires the scholarly disciplines.

To study the New Testament texts in the light of these wider considerations of language and literature, as I have said, can render a double service. The writings themselves, their forms and functions at the time of their origin, are better understood. How the language "worked", with the signals of its various genres and symbols, is better grasped than when this historical task was carried out with the older methods. It is true that those methods went beyond narrowly philological operations and sought to deal with the meaning and message of the texts. But, lacking adequate rhetorical and linguistic resources, these strategies were inadequate to the task. Both the processes by which the writings emerged and their import were construed in too rationalistic a way and with those limiting assumptions about cultural and religious movements which governed both liberal and dogmatic historiography. Even the existentialist approach which sought to overcome this superficiality, whether in biblical criticism or in hermeneutics, suffered from similar limitations.

The literary-rhetorical procedure furthers the historical reconstruction with respect to both form and substance. But its double contribution appears as we note that beyond this, barriers are broken down between the ancient literature and our modern situation and apperception. At the fundamental level of language, as evident in some of its perennial modes such as story, gnome, oracle and myth, with their dynamics, continuities appear between past and present such as are blocked at other more discursive levels, ideological or dogmatic. At all stages of its operation, historicism must be "de-constructed"--its moves re-opened--by a more fundamental act of recovery, a more adequate episteme.

A basic issue as regards Beardslee's work and, indeed, all literary study of the New Testament, can be highlighted when we recognize the essentially secular character of this approach. Some of the resistance to it no doubt arises at this point: like phenomenological or structural tools, those of the literary student are seen as alien to the canon of revelation, or as merely aesthetic or external or faddist,

---

[1]Ibid., pp. 11-12.

if not heretical. But the point to make here is that if the Bible is human in the sense that God here is thought to speak to our nature universally, then its meaning will only be fully disclosed in interaction with all our categories, structures, scenarios and the imaginations of our hearts. The literary study of Scripture like that earlier of the higher criticism or like the challenges of Wisdom in the Book of Job—precisely as secular and humanistic—presses the sacred tradition to disclose its universal import. But this is always to some extent to take the sacred deposit out of the hands of its recognized authorities.

It is no accident therefore that we can find Beardslee at times departing from prevailing views in our field. It was already untoward that he should assign such importance to the aphoristic material in the Gospels. Though on the basis of comparative studies he identifies the generic peculiarity of the proverbial element in the Synoptics, he yet insists on the importance of this sapiential strain over against the kerygmatic. By their roots in the mundane, the proverb and the beatitude set limits to the open transcendence of the eschatological sayings. So also in his discussion of the parables, he sees not only a shock to our accustomed stance in life but also fundamental orientation, a "finding or deepening of the place" of our existence.

> The Pauline-Lutheran type of piety has always felt a certain uneasiness with the Synoptic Gospels and with the parables—for in them the indicative is one which bundles together the gifts and the activity of man in a way which frustrates the Pauline concentration on *sola gratia*. Here the action, indeed the interaction of man, remains part of the datum, part of the world which is offered by the parable, and does not allow the clear-cut subordination of the imperative that Paul effects.[1]

In this connection Beardslee notes the "progressive reduction of 'world'" in the modern, individualistic interpretation of the parables from Jülicher on through Bultmann and later in-

---

[1]"Parable Interpretation and the World Disclosed by the Parable," *Perspectives in Religious Studies* 3 (Summer, 1976): 138.

terpreters, and finds here an argument not only for a more adequate literary approach to them, but for a process theology which safeguards the worldly character of such stories.

At the time when Beardslee was engaged on his doctoral thesis at Chicago, later revised and published with the title, *Human Achievement and Divine Vocation in the Message of Paul*,[1] a number of us from the schools in that area were engaged in a project for the Study Department of the World Council of Churches devoted to the subject of Natural Law. Papers on this theologically suspect topic were prepared covering various periods and texts running from the Old and New Testaments through the Church Fathers to the Eighteenth Century. Especially because of the neo-orthodox wave of the time all this represented a highly sensitive agenda.

Beardslee's original interest in non-dogmatic and universally human ingredients in Christian experience and its texts, as evident in his dissertation, so it seems to me, goes back in part to this setting and these concerns of some of his teachers. Certainly his theses as to human agency, work, growth and participation in the advent of the Kingdom ran counter to then dominant views of the Christian life. In any case there has been a consistent line of development in his work from that beginning, concerned as he has been with the full humanizing of our understanding of the operations of grace and the Gospel.

In this scholar's books and articles one finds him at work along the whole line which extends from the original texts of Scripture to their modern implications for theology, ethics and literary criticism. Both in his writing and in his editorial roles in our Societies he has made a notable contribution to the changing front in New Testament studies today and their significance for our contemporary dilemmas in church and culture.

As a former teacher of Will Beardslee, as an older colleague and friend, as one closely associated with him in various teams and activities, and in deep personal appreciation of both Will and Kit--in which Mrs. Wilder joins me--I rejoice in this honor done him by the editor and the contributors, which is at the same time a reflection of the vigor and many-sidedness of his contributions to our common labors.

Amos N. Wilder

---

[1]*Studies in Biblical Theology*, No. 31 (London: SCM Press, 1961).

A BIOGRAPHICAL SKETCH OF WILLIAM A. BEARDSLEE

William Armitage Beardslee was born on March 25, 1916, in
Holland, Michigan. A member of the Reformed Church in Ameri-
ca, he was ordained by the North Classis of Long Island on
May 26, 1941. He maintains ministerial membership in the
Classis of Queens (the governing body which succeeded the
North Classis of Long Island).

In 1937 Will received the A.B. degree, magna cum laude,
from Harvard University. New Brunswick Theological Seminary
awarded him the B.D. degree in 1941. From 1941 until 1945 he
served as minister of the Reformed Church of Queens Village,
N. Y. In 1948 he received the M.A. degree from Columbia University and Union Theological Seminary. At the University of
Chicago, Will wrote his doctoral dissertation entitled "Man in
History in the Thought of Paul" under the direction of Amos N.
Wilder. He received the Ph.D. degree in 1951, and several
years later published a revised version of the dissertation,
entitled *Human Achievement and Divine Vocation in the Message
of Paul* (1961).

A scholar whose brilliance and productivity have not gone
unnoticed, Will has been the recipient of various academic
honors. He is a member of the Phi Beta Kappa society. He was
awarded the Colver-Rosenberger Prize in 1953 by the University
of Chicago for his dissertation. From 1961 until 1962 he
studied at the University of Bonn on a Fulbright Senior Research Grant. In July, 1973 he was a Summer Fellow at the
Institute for Ecumenical and Cultural Research in Collegeville,
Minnesota. Most recently, the Society of Biblical Literature
provided him with a Claremont Center Research Grant (1976-
1977).

In hearing Will speak of his wife, either in personal
conversation or in the exercise of academic dialogue, one is
made aware of how profoundly he has drawn from her in learning
of the important matters of life which underlie scholarly endeavor. Will first met Kathryn Q. Walker when they were studying abroad for a year. During his undergraduate studies at
Harvard University, Will spent the year 1935-1936 at Lingnan
University in Canton, China. It was there that he met Kit, a
Swarthmore College student who was also studying oriental culture. The relationship developed, and on June 14, 1941 Will
and Kit were married. This union proved to be not only inter-
collegiate, but also interdenominational, as Kit was a Quaker
by background. Kit holds the M.N. degree from the Yale School

of Nursing and has worked as a visiting nurse for the Community Service Society in New York, N. Y. In Atlanta she served
for many years as a permanent supply teacher on the staff of
the Glenn Memorial Methodist Church Kindergarten, and for a
while as Acting Director. The Beardslees now make their home
in Decatur, Georgia.

Will and Kit are the parents of two children, a daughter,
Joy, who passed away in 1975, and a son, William R., who is a
child psychiatrist on the staff of the Boston Children's Hos-
pital. William's wife (nee Barbara O'Brien) works as a social
worker in a child guidance clinic in Framingham, Massachusetts.
William and Barbara have one child, Elizabeth O'Brien Beardslee.

Religion and education have played an important role in
the lives of the members of the Beardslee family. Will's
father, John W. Beardslee, Jr., was Professor of New Testament
at New Brunswick Theological Seminary from 1917 until 1949,
and President of that institution from 1935 until 1947.
Will's father was his first New Testament teacher. At present, Will's brother, John W. Beardslee, III, is Professor of
Church History at New Brunswick Theological Seminary. Another
brother, David C. Beardslee, is Director of Institutional Research at Oakland University in Rochester, Michigan. A sister, Ellen B. Mellen, is a librarian in the public school system of Chelmsford, Massachusetts. Another brother, Frank P.
Beardslee, now deceased, served as minister of several churches
of the Reformed Church in New Jersey and New York.

Since 1947 Will has taught at Emory University in Atlanta,
Georgia as Assistant Professor of Bible (from 1947 until 1952),
Associate Professor of Bible and Religion (from 1952 until
1956), and Professor of Religion (from 1956 to the present
time). In addition to his teaching responsibilities at Emory,
he has served as Director of the Graduate Institute of the
Liberal Arts (from 1957 until 1961), Acting Dean of the College of Arts and Sciences (from February until June, 1958),
and Acting Chaplain to the University (during the spring and
fall of 1967). He has also taught as Visiting Professor at
Pomona College (in Claremont, California, during the spring of
1969), and Visiting Instructor of Theology at Columbia Theological Seminary (in Decatur, Georgia, in the winter of 1973).

Professor Beardslee has contributed to biblical studies
and religious studies not only by his own writings, but also
by the series of editorial responsibilities which he has main-
tained. He was associated with *The Journal of Bible and Religion* as a member of the Editorial Committee from 1958 until

1960 and as Associate Editor from 1961 until 1966, and its
successor, the *Journal of the American Academy of Religion* as
Associate Editor from 1967 until 1969 and as a member of the
Board of Editorial Consultants from 1970 until 1976. From
1970 until 1974 he was a member of the Editorial Board of the
Society of Biblical Literature Monograph Series. From 1974
until 1979 he functioned as Editor of the Semeia Supplement
monograph series, becoming Associate Editor of that same series in 1979.

In other professional connections, he has been President
of the Southern Section of the Society of Biblical Literature
(1957-1958), a Corresponding Member of the Institute for Antiquity and Christianity in Claremont, California (1970 to the
present time) and a member of the Revised Standard Version Bible Committee of the National Council of Churches (1973 to
date).

As a biblical scholar, Professor Beardslee has been engaged primarily in the task of building bridges or drawing
lines of communication between three areas of study: Hellenistic studies, literary criticism, and process theology. From
his father who was a learned classicist and from Frederick C.
Grant, Will gained an appreciation for the rich tradition of
New Testament and classical studies. A formative figure in
his appreciation of literary criticism was his teacher and
director of his dissertation study, Amos N. Wilder. From this
poet and biblical scholar Beardslee learned much about the
power of the imagination and the fruitful interaction between
Christian commitment and the search for insight and spiritual
depth to be found in other areas of our culture. His process
hermeneutic has been developing over a long period of time,
and has been influenced and informed significantly by his
long-time friend and former colleague, John B. Cobb, Jr. His
turn to process thought was made in the hope of finding a more
holistic alternative to the fragmenting existentialism of New
Testament studies which came about under the influence of Rudolf Bultmann. It is tempting to draw further details at this
point; but, John Cobb has done that in his article, and Amos
Wilder has drawn lines of connection and development in Will's
work in his Foreword to the present work. It would be easy to
mention many other friends, only a few of whom are represented
in this collection of essays, who have influenced and worked
with Will, and who in turn have profited by association with
him. Many of these appear in the Bibliography of Will's writings, for they have collaborated with him in producing text-
books on biblical studies, ethics, and theology, or in co-
ordinating symposia on timely and provocative topics.

It has been my happy privilege on behalf of all who have worked with Will Beardslee as teacher, colleague, or student, and on behalf of all who deeply appreciate his keen insights into and profound contribution to biblical scholarship, to organize this work in his honor. The creativity, imagination, and foresight in exploring uncharted terrain which have marked his career have benefited us all.

While this work is presented to Will in proximity to a traditional anniversary for a Festschrift (his sixty-fifth birthday), it is not intended to commemorate but to celebrate the significant work of this creative biblical scholar. The variety and extent of his bibliography (which continues to grow) speak for the vigor of his scholarly pursuits. In addition, his influence reaches beyond the pages he has written, in the form of the growing company of students who have profited from his teaching, direction, and personal association. Everyone who knows Will personally or who knows him through his writings anticipates from him many further developments both in the areas in which he has already made important and unique beginnings (such as process theology and biblical literary criticism) and in other areas as yet unexplored. As a teacher, colleague, and scholar, his congeniality, optimism, quickness of mind, and creativity are the tools which in his hands have not become dull but rather have sharpened with consistent use.

Richard A. Spencer

BIBLIOGRAPHY OF THE WRITINGS OF
WILLIAM A. BEARDSLEE
COVERING THE PERIOD 1949-1979

Books

1956   *Reading the Bible: A Guide.* Englewood Cliffs,
N.J.: Prentice-Hall, 1956. Second edition,
1964. Co-authored with Ellis H. Rece.

1961   *Human Achievement and Divine Vocation in the Message
of Paul. Studies in Biblical Theology*, No. 31.
London: SCM Press, 1961.

1962   *Truth, Myth, and Symbol.* Englewood Cliffs, N.J.:
Prentice-Hall, 1962. Co-edited with Thomas J.
J. Altizer and J. Harvey Young.

1967   Editor, *America and the Future of Theology.* Philadelphia: Westminster Press, 1967.

        *Faith to Act: An Essay on the Meaning of Christian
Experience.* Nashville: Abingdon Press, 1967.
Co-authored with Jack Boozer.

1970   *Literary Criticism of the New Testament.* In "Guides
to Biblical Scholarship", edited by Dan O. Via,
Jr. Philadelphia: Fortress Press, 1970.

1972   *A House for Hope: A Study in Process and Biblical
Thought.* Philadelphia: Westminster Press,
1972.

1978   Editor, *The Poetics of Faith: Essays Offered to
Amos Niven Wilder*, Part 1: *Rhetoric, Eschatology, and Ethics in the New Testament*, Part
2: *Imagination, Rhetoric, and the Disclosures
of Faith. Semeia* 12 and *Semeia* 13. Missoula,
Montana: Scholars Press, 1978.

Articles

1953   "The Vision of Puritanism." *Emory University
         Quarterly* 9 (October, 1953): 129-40.

1956   "Identifying the Distinctive Features of Early
         Christianity." In *A Stubborn Faith: Papers
         on Old Testament and Related Subjects Presented
         to Honor William Andrew Irwin*, pp. 144-54.
         Edited by Edward C. Hobbs. Dallas: Southern
         Methodist University Press, 1956.

        "Was Jesus More Optimistic Than Paul? A Study in
         Teaching the New Testament." *Journal of Bible
         and Religion* 24 (October, 1956): 264-68.

1959   "Natural Theology and Realized Eschatology." *The
         Journal of Religion* 39 (July, 1959): 154-61.

1960   "The Casting of Lots at Qumran and in the Book of
         Acts." *Novum Testamentum* 4 (1960): 245-52.

        "Frontiers in the Interpretation of Religion."
         Religion in Life 29 (Spring, 1960): 228-38.

1961   "The Dead Sea Scrolls and the Teaching of the New
         Testament to Undergraduates." *The Journal of
         Bible and Religion* 29 (January, 1961): 44-47.

        "The New English Bible: New Testament." *The
         Chicago Theological Seminary Register* 51
         (November, 1961): 7-12.

        "Scholars and Saints." *The Journal of Bible and
         Religion* 29 (October, 1961): 277-79.

1962   "Antiochians", "Candace". In *The Interpreter's
         Dictionary of the Bible*, vol. 1, pp. 148-49,
         498. Edited by George A. Buttrick. Nashville:
         Abingdon Press, 1962.

        "James." In *The Interpreter's Dictionary of the
         Bible*, vol. 2, pp. 790-94. Edited by George A.
         Buttrick. Nashville: Abingdon Press, 1962.

        "Lucius", "Lysias, Claudius". In *The Interpreter's
         Dictionary of the Bible*, vol. 3, pp. 178, 193.
         Edited by George A. Buttrick. Nashville:
         Abingdon Press, 1962.

"Truth in the Study of Religion." In *Truth, Myth, and Symbol*, pp. 61-75. Edited by Thomas J. J. Altizer, William A. Beardslee, and J. Harvey Young. Englewood Cliffs, N.J.: Prentice-Hall, 1962.

1963   "Conscience", "Judging, Ethical". In *Dictionary of the Bible*, pp. 173-75, 541-42. Edited by James Hastings. Revised edition by Frederick C. Grant and H. H. Rowley. New York: Charles Scribner's Sons, 1963.

"Revelation, Book of." In *Encyclopaedia Britannica*, vol. 19, (1963): 237-39.

"Salaries and Freedom." *The Journal of Bible and Religion* 31 (January, 1963): 1-2.

"Theology in the Modern University." *Emory University Quarterly* 19 (Summer, 1963): 84-94.

"The Theology of Rudolf Bultmann." *Emory University Quarterly* 19 (Spring, 1963): 8-13.

1966   "The Background of the Lilly Endowment Study of Pre-Seminary Education." *The Journal of Bible and Religion* 34 (April, 1966): 98-105.

1967   "The Wisdom Tradition and the Synoptic Gospels." *Journal of the American Academy of Religion* 35 (September, 1967): 231-40.

1968   "A Comment on the Theology of Dr. Altizer." *Criterion* 7 (Spring, 1968): 11-14. Reprinted as "Dialectic or Duality". In *The Theology of Altizer: Critique and Response*, pp. 58-67. Edited by John B. Cobb, Jr. Philadelphia: Westminster Press, 1970.

1969   "The Motif of Fulfillment in the Eschatology of the Synoptic Gospels." In *Transitions in Biblical Scholarship*, pp. 171-91. Edited by J. Coert Rylaarsdam. Chicago: University of Chicago Press, 1969.

1970   "Hope in Biblical Eschatology and in Process Theology." *Journal of the American Academy of Religion* 38 (September, 1970): 227-39.

"John Woolman." Foreword to the Garrett Press reprint of the first edition of his *Works*, pp. iii-xiii. New York: Garrett Press, 1970.

"Uses of the Proverb in the Synoptic Gospels." *Interpretation* 24 (January, 1970): 61-73.

1971   "New Testament Apocalyptic in Recent Interpretation." *Interpretation* 25 (October, 1971): 419-35.

"New Testament Perspectives on Revolution as a Theological Problem." *The Journal of Religion* 51 (January, 1971): 15-33.

1972   "Hope in the Crisis of Faith." *Religious Education* 67 (September-October, 1972): 351-55.

"Proverbs in the Gospel of Thomas." In *Studies in New Testament and Early Christian Literature: Essays in Honor of Allen P. Wikgren*, pp. 92-103. Edited by David E. Aune. Leiden: E. J. Brill, 1972.

"Teaching and Preaching: The Problem of Place." *Religion in Life* 41 (Spring, 1972): 59-68.

1973   "Openness to the New in Apocalyptic and in Process Theology." *Process Studies* 3 (Fall, 1973): 169-78.

1974   "Introduction." In *Theology and Body*, pp. 7-11, 72-73. Edited by John Y. Fenton. Philadelphia: Westminster Press, 1974.

1975   "De facie quae in orbe lunae apparet (Moralia 920A-945D)." In *Plutarch's Theological Writings and Early Christian Literature*, pp. 286-300. Edited by Hans Dieter Betz. Leiden: E. J. Brill, 1975.

"Narrative Form in the New Testament and Process Theology." *Encounter* 36 (Fall, 1975): 301-15.

1976   "Introduction and Annotations to *Ecclesiasticus*." In *The New English Bible With the Apocrypha: Oxford Study Edition*, pp. 115-75. Edited by Samuel Sandmel, M. Jack Suggs, and Arnold J. Tkacik. New York: Oxford University Press, 1976.

"Parable Interpretation and the World Disclosed by the Parable." *Perspectives in Religious Studies* 3 (Summer, 1976): 123-39.

"Sex: Biological Bases of Hope." In *Religious Experience and Process Theology: The Pastoral Implications of a Major Modern Movement*, pp. 175-94. Edited by Harry J. Cargas and Bernard Lee. New York: Paulist Press, 1976. Reprint of chapter one of *A House for Hope* (1972).

1977   "Christology in Scripture and Experience: The Case of Process Theology." In *Scripture in History and Theology: Essays in Honor of J. Coert Rylaarsdam*, pp. 343-55. Edited by Arthur L. Merrill and Thomas W. Overholt. Pittsburgh: The Pickwick Press, 1977.

1978   "Amos Niven Wilder: Poet and Scholar." *Semeia* 12 (1978): 1-14.

"De garrulitate." In *Plutarch's Ethical Writings and Early Christian Literature*, pp. 264-88. Edited by Hans Dieter Betz. Leiden: E. J. Brill, 1978.

"Parable, Proverb, and Koan." *Semeia* 12 (1978): 151-77.

1979   "Whitehead and Hermeneutic", and "Saving One's Life By Losing It". *Journal of the American Academy of Religion* 47 (March, 1979): 31-37, 57-72. Professor Beardslee served with David J. Lull as guest editor of this issue of the *Journal*.

Book Reviews

1949   Scott, Ernest F. *St. Paul's Epistle to the Romans*. *Review of Religion* 13 (1948-49): 429-31.

1951   Pierce, Alfred Mann. *Lest Faith Forget: The Story of Methodism in Georgia*. *Emory University Quarterly* 7 (October, 1951): 188-89.

1956   Bowman, John W. *The Drama of the Book of Revelation.* *The Journal of Religion* 36 (October, 1956): 300.

Pierce, C. A. *Conscience in the New Testament.* *Review of Religion* 21 (1956-57): 102.

Preiss, Theo. *Life in Christ.* *The Journal of Religion* 36 (January, 1956): 60.

1958   Van Doren, Mark. *Don Quixote's Profession.* *Emory University Quarterly* 14 (October, 1958): 189-90.

Parker, Pierson. *Inherit the Promise: Six Keys to New Testament Thought.* *The Journal of Bible and Religion* 26 (January, 1958): 72-74.

Trocmé, Étienne. *Le "Livre des Actes" et l'histoire.* *The Journal of Religion* 38 (April, 1958): 133-34.

1959   Giet, Stanislas. *L'Apocalypse et l'histoire: Étude historique sur l'apocalypse Johannique.* *The Journal of Religion* 39 (January, 1959): 68-69.

1961   Bruce, F. F. *The English Bible: A History of Translations.* *Chicago Theological Seminary Register* 51 (November, 1961): 22-23.

Crownfield, Frederic R. *A Historical Approach to the New Testament.* *Journal of Bible and Religion* 29 (October, 1961): 340-42.

Dentan, Robert C. *The Design of the Scriptures.* *The Journal of Religion* 41 (October, 1961): 316-17.

Minear, Paul. *Images of the Church in the New Testament.* *Chicago Theological Seminary Register* 51 (November, 1961): 21-22.

1962   Montague, George. *Growth in Christ: A Study of St. Paul's Theology of Progress.* *Journal of Biblical Literature* 81 (September, 1962): 296-97.

1963   Meland, Bernard E. *The Realities of Faith: The Revolution in Cultural Forms*. *Religion in Life* 32 (Spring, 1963): 307.

Niles, D. T. *As Seeing the Invisible: A Study of the Book of Revelation*. *The Journal of Religion* 43 (July, 1963): 248-49.

1964   Bultmann, Rudolf. *The History of the Synoptic Tradition*. *Christian Advocate* 8 (April 9, 1964): 17.

1965   Barth, Markus. *Conversations With the Bible*. *Christian Advocate* 12 (June 3, 1965): 19-20.

Jones, Geraint Vaughan. *The Art and Truth of the Parables*. *Journal of Bible and Religion* 33 (July, 1965): 268-70.

Kümmel, Werner Georg. *Introduction to the New Testament*. *Christian Advocate* 9 (December 30, 1965): 16.

1967   von Rad, Gerhard. *Old Testament Theology*. Volume 2. *Journal of the American Academy of Religion* 35 (September, 1967): 302-03.

1968   Cullmann, Oscar. *Salvation in History*. *Religious Education* 63 (May-June, 1968): 241.

Furnish, Victor P. *Theology and Ethics in Paul*. *Christian Advocate* 12 (September 19, 1968): 20-21.

Wuellner, Wilhelm H. *The Meaning of "Fishers of Men"*; Martin, R. P. *Carmen Christi: Philippians 2:5-11*. *Religion in Life* 37 (Spring, 1968): 154-55.

1969   Martyn, J. Louis. *History and Theology in the Fourth Gospel*. *Religion in Life* 38 (Spring, 1969): 150.

Nineham, D. E. *The Gospel of St. Mark*. *Encounter* 30 (Winter, 1969): 65-66.

1970   Achtemeier, Paul J. *An Introduction to the New Hermeneutic*. *Encounter* 31 (Summer, 1970): 292-93.

Ellis, E. Earle, and Wilcox, Max, eds. *Neotesta-mentica et Semitica: Studies in Honor of Matthew Black*. *Journal of Biblical Litera-ture* 89 (June, 1970): 243-44.

Légasse, S. *Jésus et l'enfant: "Enfants", "pe-tits", et "simples" dans la tradition synop-tique*. *Journal of Biblical Literature* 89 (September, 1970): 383-84.

O'Gorman, Ned, ed. *Prophetic Voices: Ideas and Words on Revolution*. *Journal of Ecumenical Studies* 7 (Summer, 1970): 607-08.

1971   Harvey, A. E. *Companion to the New Testament: The New English Bible*. *Interpretation* 25 (October, 1971): 514-15.

1973   Bloch, Ernst. *Atheism in Christianity*. *The Review of Books and Religion* 2 (April, 1973): 7.

Doty, William G. *Contemporary New Testament Inter-pretation*. *Journal of Biblical Literature* 92 (March, 1973): 158-59.

Schwartz, Hans. *On the Way to the Future*. *Reli-gion in Life* 42 (Autumn, 1973): 424-25.

Wells, David F., and Pinnock, Clark H. *Toward a Theology for the Future*. *Journal of Ecumeni-cal Studies* 10 (Spring, 1973): 411-12.

1974   Smith, Morton. *The Secret Gospel: The Discovery and Interpretation of the Secret Gospel According to Mark*. *Interpretation* 28 (April, 1974): 234-36.

1975   Holifield, E. Brooks. *The Covenant Sealed: The Development of Puritan Sacramental Theology in Old and New England, 1570-1720*. *Candler Review* 2 (January, 1975): 40.

Lee, Bernard. *The Becoming of the Church: A Process Theology of the Structures of Chris-tian Experience*. *Religious Education* 70 (July-August, 1975): 452-54.

Strauss, David Friedrich. *The Life of Jesus Crit-
        ically Examined.* Edited by Peter C. Hodgson.
        Journal of the American Academy of Religion
        43 (June, 1975): 427-28.

1976   Cobb, John B., Jr. *Christ in a Pluralistic Age.*
        Religion in Life 45 (Autumn, 1976): 385-86.

        Donahue, John R. *Are You the Christ?* *Interpreta-
        tion* 30 (January, 1976): 96.

1977   Crossan, John Dominic. *Raid on the Articulate:
        Comic Eschatology in Jesus and Borges.*
        Parabola 2 (Winter, 1977): 119-20.

        Patte, Daniel, ed. *Semiology and Parables: Ex-
        ploration of the Possibilities Offered by
        Structuralism for Exegesis.* *Journal of the
        American Academy of Religion* 45 (June, 1977):
        261-62.

        Pittenger, Norman. *The Divine Triunity.* *Religion
        in Life* 46 (Winter, 1977): 511-12.

1978   Bennett, Curtis. *God as Form: Essays in Greek
        Theology with Special Reference to Christianity
        and the Contemporary Theological Predicament.*
        The Journal of Religion 58 (January, 1978):
        70-71.

        Pregeant, Russell. *Christology Beyond Dogma:
        Matthew's Christ in Process Hermeneutic.*
        Process Studies 8 (Spring, 1978): 51-56.

1979   Latourelle, René. *L'Accès à Jesus par les évan-
        giles: Histoire et herméneutique.* English
        translation by A. Owen, *Finding Jesus Through
        the Gospels: History and Hermeneutics.* *Reli-
        gious Studies Review* 5 (October, 1979): 300.

        Metzger, Bruce M. *The Early Versions of the New
        Testament: Their Origin, Transmission, and
        Limitations.* *Interpretation* 33 (January,
        1979): 94-96.

        Theissen, Gerd. *Sociology of Early Palestinian
        Christianity*; Daly, Robert J. *The Origins of
        the Christian Doctrine of Sacrifice*; and Childs,
        James M., Jr. *Christian Anthropology and Eth-
        ics.* *Religion in Life* 48 (Spring, 1979): 126-27.

Zeller, Dieter. *Die weisheitlichen Mahnsprüche bei den Synoptikern. Journal of Biblical Literature* 98 (September, 1979): 441-42.

Translations

1965   Strecker, George. "A Report on the New Edition of Walter Bauer's *Rechtgläubigkeit und Ketzerei im ältesten Christentum.*" *Journal of Bible and Religion* 33 (January, 1965): 53-56.

1967   Pannenberg, Wolfhart. "Response to the Discussion." In *Theology as History*, pp. 221-76. Edited by James M. Robinson and John B. Cobb, Jr. New York: Harper and Row, 1967. Professor Beardslee served as principal translator, with Thomas Oden and Carol Fellows.

Tapes

1975   "Literary Criticism and the New Testament: Interview with William A. Beardslee." *Catalyst* VII, 4 (April, 1975).

        "The Church and Contemporary Ethical Concerns." *Catalyst* VII, 6 (June, 1975).

1977   "The Normatively Human in Biblical Thought." *Catalyst* IX, 3 (March, 1977).

        "The Normatively Human in Process Thought." *Catalyst* IX, 9 (August, 1977).

Other Writings

1960   "Index of Book Reviews and Reviewers, Vols. I-XXV."
        Journal of Bible and Religion 28 (January,
        1960): 51-147.

1964   "Politics: Participation and Protest." *The Inter-
        collegian* 82 (October-November, 1964): 3-5.

        "Editorial Preface." *Emory University Quarterly* 21
        (1965): 217. Professor Beardslee was also edi-
        tor of this issue of the *Quarterly*.

1966   "The National Endowment for the Humanities." *The
        Journal of Bible and Religion* 34 (July, 1966):
        195-96.

1967   "The Undergraduate Professor of Religion: Stabili-
        zer or Prophet?" *Bulletin of the American
        Academy of Religion* 4 (Summer, 1967): 7-10.

1973   "Sermon in the Form of a Fable." In *Experimental
        Preaching*, pp. 141-52. Edited by John Killin-
        ger. Nashville: Abingdon Press, 1973.

CONTRIBUTORS

THOMAS J. J. ALTIZER is Professor of English and Religious
    Studies at the State University of New York at Stony
    Brook.

HENDRIKUS BOERS is Professor of New Testament at the Candler
    School of Theology, Emory University in Atlanta, Georgia.

MARTIN J. BUSS is Professor of Religion at Emory University in
    Atlanta, Georgia.

JOHN B. COBB, JR. is Ingraham Professor of Theology at the
    School of Theology at Claremont in Claremont, California,
    Avery Professor of Religion at the Claremont Graduate
    School, and Director of the Center for Process Studies.

JOHN DOMINIC CROSSAN is Professor of Theology at DePaul Uni-
    versity in Chicago, Illinois.

ROBERT C. CULLEY is Professor of Old Testament Studies in the
    Faculty of Religious Studies, McGill University in Mon-
    treal, Canada.

CHARLES T. DAVIS, III teaches in the Philosophy and Religion
    Department of Appalachian State University in Boone,
    North Carolina.

ROBERT DETWEILER is Director of the Graduate Institute of the
    Liberal Arts and Professor of Liberal Arts at Emory Uni-
    versity in Atlanta, Georgia.

WILLIAM G. DOTY is Associate Professor of Human Development at
    Hampshire College in Amherst, Massachusetts.

LEANDER E. KECK is Dean of the Yale Divinity School and Wink-
    ley Professor of Biblical Theology at Yale University in
    New Haven, Connecticut.

EDGAR V. McKNIGHT is Professor of Religion at Furman Univer-
    sity in Greenville, South Carolina.

NORMAN R. PETERSEN is Acting Chairman of the Department of
    Religion at Williams College in Williamstown, Massachu-
    setts.

ROBERT M. POLZIN is Associate Professor in the Department of Religion at Carleton University in Ottawa, Canada.

RICHARD A. SPENCER is Associate Professor of New Testament at Southeastern Baptist Theological Seminary in Wake Forest, North Carolina.

ROBERT C. TANNEHILL is Fred D. Gealy Professor of New Testament at Methodist Theological School in Ohio in Delaware, Ohio.

DAN O. VIA, JR. is Professor of Religious Studies at the University of Virginia in Charlottesville, Virginia.

AMOS N. WILDER is Hollis Professor of Divinity Emeritus at Harvard Divinity School in Cambridge, Massachusetts.

PART I

TOWARD DEFINING LITERARY CRITICISM

AFTER THE NEW CRITICISM:
CONTEMPORARY METHODS OF LITERARY INTERPRETATION

Robert Detweiler

It is customary to sketch the modern history of literary criticism in the West, especially in the United States, by tracing the growth and decline of the New Criticism.[1] What was new about the New Criticism was its focus on the literary text as the object for scrutiny in terms of its formal properties of texture and structure, in contrast to the "old" criticism that concerned itself with the cultural, historical, moral, and other dimensions of the literary work. Thus one names the persons and trends in the early decades of the twentieth century who represent the repudiation of the "extrinsic" approaches and embrace the "intrinsic" method and shows how the New Criticism gradually attained predominance by the decade of the Thirties. Henry James, T. E. Hulme, Ezra Pound, Joel Spingarn are among the acknowledged progenitors of the New Criticism; T. S. Eliot, I. A. Richards, the Agrarians, F. R. Leavis, William Empson, René Wellek are a few of its heroes. One acknowledges that extrinsic approaches such as the biographical, historical, philosophical, and sociological survived and that others such as the archetypal and psychological even flourished, but that the first four of these were seen as valid mainly when they supplemented intrinsic readings and the last two were judged not quite respectable because of the excesses indulged in by their practitioners.

The moments leading to the New Criticism's decline are, in such a recital, harder to fix, but they appear to consist of events like the delayed effect of Sartre's existential-phenomenological criticism finally striking the English-speaking literary world in the Fifties, Northrop Frye's archetypal approach in the late Fifties that could be disparaged but not ignored, the cumulative effect of respected critics like Edmund Wilson, Lionel Trilling, Alfred Kazin, and Irving Howe who extended the text's implications into extra-literary dimensions, and the innovations of younger critics such as Hillis Miller who combined close reading with Continental philosophical methods such as those introduced by the critics of consciousness. By the mid-Sixties the New

Criticism was being challenged by structuralism (especially dramatically in the Gallic context in the strife between Raymond Picard and Roland Barthes), but by the mid-Seventies the structuralist vogue, the most glamorous critical fashion since post-war existentialism, had subsided and was being replaced by--or expanded into--movements such as the new sociological criticism provoked by the Frankfurt School and its latest avatar Jürgen Habermas, the reception aesthetics of the Constance School, the narratologists' theories, and above all the anti-criticism of Jacques Derrida.[2]

Although such a rehearsal immediately slips into caricature, it has the typical value of distortion: it leads us to consider what we have exaggerated and to seek a more balanced view. This recital first, as do most histories of modern criticism, overstates the exclusiveness of the New Criticism even during its time of greatest prominence. For although it is true that the New Criticism was for a good three decades the leading mode of interpretation, and although it is also true that for many American professors of literature it served as the single method to be taught to their students, it is misleading to portray it as the only method that flourished during the thirty years between 1920 and 1950. Where the older historical approach merged with the new sociological method, for example, a powerful kind of extrinsic method appeared that challenged the New Criticism and that, in the dress of Continental Marxist criticism, shows no sign of fading at a time when the New Criticism is on the wane. Taking another example, we can argue that even though psychological criticism did not gain respectability in the Twenties and Thirties because its Freud-oriented advocates took it to ludicrous extremes, it nonetheless functioned as a popular approach and then found legitimacy in the writing of expert scholars such as Kenneth Burke, Lionel Trilling, F. L. Lucas, and André Malraux.

One could demonstrate further that other critical methods, such as the philosophical and the biographical, also co-existed with the New Criticism and were by no means constantly dominated by it; but, these illustrations should suffice. A second important qualification of our caricature-sketch of the history of modern criticism is that the New Criticism itself did not hold exclusive rights to the intrinsic mode or the formalist method. Russian and Czech formalism were developed, in the first quarter of the century, apart from the origins of the New Criticism, as were the German philological approach and the French *explication de texte*; and in the United States the "Chicago School", or the neo-Aristotelian approach emerged that disputed the New Criticism on its own premises. I do not mean to say that these other "formalisms" precisely duplicated

the effort of the New Criticism; indeed, each of them in one
way or another distinguished itself from the New Criticism.
R. S. Crane, a leading proponent of Neo-Aristotelianism,
argued, for instance, that the New Criticism lacked an adequate aesthetic-theoretical base and paid too little note to
generic distinctions; consequently Crane sought to create as
his "mimetic" approach a philosophically-aware criticism that
would ground intrinsic analysis on sound formal (in the Aristotelian sense) doctrine--an endeavor that the New Critics
rejected as already going outside the literary work and establishing a language of criticism on non-literary concepts.[3]
The point to be made, however, is that the New Critic was not
the sole proprietor of formalist methodology. Rather, he
represented one group--a most influential group--of text-
oriented interpreters.

A final qualification of my sketch is that the New Criticism was not, contradictory as it sounds, always and completely an intrinsic method. The most rigorous and thoughtful New
Critics have regularly gone beyond the text or have arrived at
the text from some outside vantage point. John Crowe Ransom,
R. P. Blackmur, and Allen Tate, for example, in the process of
defending the New Criticism as a method derived from the nature
of literature and the literary experience, called upon established philosophical terms and categories to state their cases.
Insofar as the New Critics have tried to establish a theory to
support their method, they reveal their dependence on something that is not literature and demonstrate the weakness of
a position (a mistaken notion of apodicticity) that claims the
sufficiency of intrinsic analysis.

Thus, a revised version of the history of modern criticism
that tries to correct the distortions represented above might
look like this: it is not the case that in the last two decades, with the decline of the New Criticism, we lost the unity and focus of a single dominant critical method and as a result are struggling with the chaos of multiple and competing
methods. It is also not the case that the New Criticism
thrived as the single "right" mode of analysis because it was
the one that most respected the nature of literature and the
language of literary-critical discrimination. Rather, the
multiplicity of methods has been with us since the early years
of the century, at least, but many of us persisted in the view
that the other modes were at best supplementary to the New
Criticism and hence not worth taking very seriously, or at
worst, antagonistic to the New Criticism and hence not to be
taken seriously at all. The past two decades, rather than producing critical chaos, have been the temporal setting for a
liberation of critical pluralism of great fecundity that has
(paradoxically, from the New Critical perspective) brought

about more clarity on the formal elements of literature than the preceding generation of formalist scholars. In fact, the past twenty years have shown us that the intrinsic/extrinsic distinction, while helpful, is deceiving if taken as absolute.

It is valuable to begin with such a caricature of modern criticism and then offer a revised and, one hopes, more accurate if more complicated version because the current state of literary criticism can best be comprehended against the background of multiple methods that have been nurtured in the earlier twentieth century. Along with arranging the many kinds of contemporary critical methods into tentative groupings, in the remainder of this essay I shall trace the antecedents of these methods and show the continuity of present-day criticism with that of the previous decades.

Since we have been orienting ourselves according to the fortunes of the New Criticism, it is appropriate to begin this next stage of our over-view with a description of the formalist methods that seem to have grown out of the New Criticism. In 1966 Geoffrey Hartman in "Beyond Formalism" accused a leading New Critic, Cleanth Brooks, of not being formalist enough, and "an avowed antiformalist, Georges Poulet", of being more formalist than he believed.[4] Hartman's implication obtains today; formalist criticism is not and has not been limited to the practice of the New Critics, and a good deal of criticism labeled as something else is in key ways formalist. We may oversimplify for the moment and state that virtually any method that remains text-centered and explicatory is somehow formalist. If this is so, then we can consider recent studies of narrative form, of metaphor, and of "intertextuality" as extensions of formalism that are supplanting the old New Criticism.

The New Critics directed their efforts largely to the poetic text; its brevity and concentrated form were more congenial to their attempts to identify meaning through form than was prose narrative. Or one could say that the poem as a compact literary object lent itself more readily to the disinterested pose of the formalist, borrowing from the empirical attitude of the scientist, than did the often unwieldy and intractable novel that seemed to belong more to the world of unfolding consciousness than to the realm of the articulate image. As a result, the New Criticism fashioned a theory of the poem to accompany the close reading of the poetic text; but, it did not develop a theory or vocabulary of the novel or story. Recent formalist and "post-formalist" criticism have tried to redress this omission and pay attention precisely to "narratology" or the theory and criticism of narrative. As one would guess, the current formalists are less dependent

on the model of the objective scientist as they scrutinize the
text, are more aware of the intricacies of subjective involve-
ment in interpretation, and thus one often finds formalist
critics engaged in narrative studies in transition from a
thorough-going intrinsic approach to an inclusion of extrinsic concerns.

Wayne Booth's *The Rhetoric of Fiction* (1961) is one of
the first studies of narrative to present a sophisticated discussion of the formal components of story such as types of
narration and authorial voice; Barbara Hardy's *The Appropriate
Form* (1964) is an examination of mainly nineteenth and twentieth century novelists (James, Hardy, Lawrence, *et al.*) to
discern how narrative structure shapes and embodies the art-
ists' sense of reality, and her 1975 *Tellers and Listeners:
The Narrative Imagination* does essentially the same thing.[5]
Hardy's writing is an example of the best current application
of the New Criticism that does not venture beyond it. Robert
Scholes and Robert Kellogg in *The Nature of Narrative* (1966)
broaden and deepen the definition of narrative by identifying
elements of narrative not only in the story but in other
genres such as folktale, allegory, and satire and then describing three formal narrative components (character, plot,
point of view) as they function in this expanded context.[6]
The Nature of Narrative was a strategic book for narrative
studies, for it freed the analysis of narrative from its narrow focus on the novel and encouraged the creation of a general lexicon for narrative--a task the New Critics ignored.
Thus, although Susan Sontag could write in 1964 that "what
we don't have yet is a poetics of the novel, any clear notion
of the forms of narration", by the late Sixties such a poetics
was emerging.[7]

Four collections of critical essays on narrative published
during the Seventies illustrate the progression of narrative
theory from a formalist to a broader orientation. *The Theory
of the Novel: New Essays* (1974), edited by John Halperin, is
heavily oriented toward New Criticism, but displays, if somewhat ingenuously, an awareness of post-formalist alternatives
thriving on the Continent, those practiced by the structuralists and critics of consciousness. *Towards a Poetics of Fiction* (1977), edited by Mark Spilka, is a somewhat more knowl-
edgeable anthology. A few of the essayists such as Robert
Scholes ("Formalism, Structuralism, and Fiction Theory") reveal a willingness to engage the issues of narrative theory
raised by the post-formalists. Yet on the whole the essays,
published between 1967 and 1976 in the journal *Novel: A Forum
on Fiction*, are aligned to the old intrinsic concerns and betray the tenaciousness of the New Criticism. A dramatic difference is seen in the Winter 1976 issue of *New Literary His-*

tory, "On Narrative and Narratives". Although the issue is
older than Spilka's collection, the essays offer a variety of
approaches to narrative study that take formalism seriously
yet all, in one way or another, go beyond it. For example,
Roland Barthes' well-known "An Introduction to the Structural
Analysis of Narrative", included here, is a structuralist
classic that nonetheless employs formalist categories, and
Seymour Chatman's imposing "Towards a Theory of Narrative"
combines a "formalist-structuralist theory" with phenomenological, semiotic, and genre approaches to construct an encompassing view of narrative that moves beyond a consideration of
prose fiction alone. The fourth collection, *Interpretation of
Narrative* (1978), edited by Mario J. Valdés and Owen J. Miller,
goes a step further by identifying formalist and hermeneutic
criticism of narrative as two central approaches and attempting to effect a reconciliation between them.[8] It is clear
that by now the critical discussion of narrative is no longer
dominated by New Critical texts such as Brooks' and Warren's
Understanding Fiction.[9] Instead, the formalist method and attitude have been incorporated into a broader and more ambi-
tious endeavor to describe the nature and structure of narrative discourse.

Just as indicative of the movement beyond the New Criticism that still includes the formalist concern is the recent
increase in attention paid to metaphor. The study of metaphor
was a favorite New Critical occupation, yet it was generally
conducted in a way that comprehended metaphor merely as a
literary device, albeit an important one, and hence the notion of metaphor as a primary epistemological element of discourse could emerge only as the limiting New Critical context
lost its force. For all of the incisive work on metaphor done
by scholars such as I. A. Richards, William Wimsatt, Monroe
Beardsley, and Philip Wheelwright, the New Critical discussion
of it rarely ventured beyond cautious literary-aesthetic description of its properties and potential.[10] Even though the
New Critics were the ones who insisted on the recognition of a
special poetic language which is at heart metaphoric rather
than literal, and even though this metaphoric language was
said to generate critically desirable effects such as tension
(Allen Tate), irony and paradox (Cleanth Brooks), or ambiguity
(William Empson), the formalist treatment of metaphor remained
aligned to an objective view of language and reality that de-
pended, however uneasily, on the human ability to organize experience systematically, unequivocally, and rationally.[11]

Some of the more recent critics, in contrast, have *begun*
with concepts such as paradox and ambiguity inherent in metaphor and have treated them as elements of discourse indicating
our *in*capacity for ordering experience altogether coherently

and rationally. These critics declare that if metaphor comes to fruition in the literary text and provides us with original versions of wholeness there, it also breaks down in the self-conscious act of interpretation, for in deconstructing metaphor we discover not an ontological foundation, as Ransom had claimed, but an epistemological dilemma: the logical thought structures for interpreting metaphor are found to be themselves fictions, and hence the critic is caught up in a game of interpretation that has rules but no referee.[12] This loss of the autonomy of underlying logic for interpretation has caused the post-New Critical treatment of metaphor to travel in three directions. One is the position of Max Black, Nelson Goodman, and others that metaphors have cognitive functions and truth value as do literal statements.[13] The second is the structuralist effort to make language itself the new ontological authority. The third is Derrida's endeavor to turn the metaphoric suspension itself into an ontological condition.

The position taken by Black and Goodman provides metaphor with analytical philosophical significance, raises it to a status that it did not have as a literary or rhetorical device, and strengthens the ontological foundation that Ransom projected. This position represents a philosophical articulation and reinforcement of a view of metaphor defended not very successfully by New Critics such as Ransom. I know of no critic who has tried to elaborate this position into a literary theory of metaphor, and it is not surprising if none has, for it would be difficult to establish the cognitive status or truth value of a metaphor in a literary text, quite apart from the fact that the current temper shows more signs of effort to challenge rather than to prove the cognitive status and truth value of any component of language. Nevertheless, a number of writers in the Autumn 1974 *New Literary History* issue, "On Metaphor", refer to Black or Goodman as orienting points, and still more do so in the Autumn 1978 issue of *Critical Inquiry* on metaphor, often in the process of developing tentative new views of metaphor out of the formalist perspective.[14]

The second direction of the post-New Critical treatment of metaphor is by now more familiar. This is the structuralist effort based at least in part on Roman Jakobson's linguistic distinction between metaphor and metonomy, whereby metaphor represents language creating sense out of combinations of discrete elements and metonomy stands for language making sense via contiguity, or the association of similar elements.[15] Transposed into literary criticism, this distinction helps to explain the structuralist interest in discovering and developing the "deep structure" of a text, for this structure becomes known through the interplay of metonomy and metaphor--through the discovery of paradigmatic patterns embedded in the syntagm of the surface discourse. Roland Barthes, Tzvetan Todorov, Paul de Man (by no means a card-carrying structuralist), and Jonathan Culler are among those who have employed and explained metaphor, post-New Critically, in this manner.[16]

The structuralist stress on playing with discrete elements is taken to its extreme in the work of Jacques Derrida. The prolific Derrida, who one could argue is both the ultra-formalist and the nemesis of formalism, has been the most alluring critic in recent years and the subject by now of hundreds of essays and reviews. As his emphasis on "difference" suggests, Derrida wishes to take metaphor to its self-destructive limit and to demonstrate not only the impossibility of language (and hence the human mind) ever to state unambiguously and exhaustively an intended meaning but also the impossibility of escaping the tension of metaphor. In the effort of interpreting metaphor through "generalizing" language--which inevitably reduces or "destroys" metaphor and necessitates new metaphor--is the productive frustration of modern humankind incessantly reaching to embrace more than can be embraced.[17] Derrida's philosophy-criticism is so influential because he, no matter how idiosyncratically, expresses the post-formalist groping for a way to cope with the experience of a language at once capricious, inadequate, and yet inexhaustibly rich, and with the reality reflected in this language.

Not only Derrida's influence but just as much the French flair for elegant games with language has produced a late-formalist and post-formalist kind of criticism that is at this point as much fashion as substance but deserves mention. It is a critical activity called "intertextuality" and is defined by one of its proponents, Jeanine Parisier Plottel, as an approach that treats a literary text in terms of its dependence on other texts and on the literary and cultural tradition reflected by the reader.[18] Plottel cites Derrida's dictum to the effect that "every script (*l'ecriture*) is a script of another script (*l'ecriture d'une ecriture*)...in a sense, all writing is a collage of other writing, of language, and of tradition".[19] One could call the method the critical version of our post-modern fiction that plays with the narrative tradition (illustrated by writers such as Beckett, Nabokov, Borges, Reed, Handke, etc.). Just as the contemporary experimental novel or story uses the conventions of narrative ironically, distorting them to surprise the reader's expectations, so too the intertextual critic intensifies the techniques of the New Criticism (and other methods) beyond the point of its attempts to shape a balanced analysis, and instead transforms the critical endeavor into a commentary on current themes in literary theory.

One has the impression that the intertextualists are extremely self-conscious critics familiar with a plurality of
approaches yet committed to none, trying to offer meaningful
statements in a context devoid of the older critical norms yet
also lacking new surrogates. In a way, intertextuality is the
revenge of the New Criticism on itself. The text is its own
interpretation and critical end and reveals itself as insufficient for *serious* analysis, so that one turns to playfulness
with the text as a way of encountering it; one plays with the
text to draw in other dimensions and expand its significance.
I do not view this effort as critical bankruptcy, fatuous as
it can easily become (Hayden White would certainly include it
under his category of absurd criticism).[20] Rather, I think
that it recalls for us the delight ("the pleasure of the text",
in Roland Barthes' phrase) that literature and its interpretation should inspire.[21] The legacy not only of Derrida but of
Georges Bataille, Jacques Lacan, and Barthes, deriving in turn
from Freud, is apparent here. One takes perverse joy in un-
covering, or creating, a meaning for the text that is original,
at the boundary line of credibility, and yet compelling.
Through intertextuality Derrida's vision of a metaphoric
criticism finds incipient realization.

My overview thus far has paid increasing notice to structuralism as a contemporary critical method, and it is appropriate to discuss structuralism now as an influential approach
evolving from and in some ways superseding formalism. I could
have just as well dealt with the recent flourishing of narratology in the context of structuralism, for it has been the
structuralist literary critics such as Barthes, A. J. Greimas,
Todorov, Gérard Genette, and Julia Kristeva who have been mainly responsible for shaping viable theories of narrative out of
the prior studies of Russian formalists such as Viktor Shklovsky and Vladimir Propp, and who have laid the groundwork for
the next generation of narrative analysis.[22] Unlike formalism,
however, structuralism strives toward acting as far more than
a literary-critical method. The largest group of structuralists (who do not necessarily agree among themselves), those
oriented toward linguistics, define their effort as a study of
the synchronic organization of whatever aspect of culture they
have chosen as their field of research. This study begins with
a conscious suspension of the historical (diachronic) dimension
in order to disclose a system somehow analogous to the structural view of the system of language. One could also describe
the structuralists' project as a concentration, in the context
of the structural linguistic theory of the arbitrary sign, on
the signifier rather than the signified--on the actualizing
component of a cultural entity rather than on the historical
evolution of that entity. One recognizes here the influence of
formalism; added to the formalist concerns are certain linguis-

tically-derived "laws" such as those determining binary opposi-
tions and inter/intrasystemic transformations. The influence of
structuralism has been immense in the Seventies decade, and even
those critics who reject it have found it necessary to take issue with it. Among the most helpful texts by American and English critics on structuralism as a literary method are Robert
Scholes' *Structuralism in Literature* (1974), Jonathan Culler's
excellent *Structuralist Poetics* (1975), and Terence Hawkes'
Structuralism and Semiotics (1977), which concludes with a fine
chapter on the relationship of structuralism to the New Criticism.[23] Even the more staid literary journals are publishing
structuralist criticism these days; but, a few newer ones exist
that are fundamentally oriented toward it: *Tel Quel* from Paris,
Structuralist Review, *Sub-Stance*, and *Glyph* are examples.[24]

The structuralist vogue inspired the broader study of
sign systems called "semiotics" which has currency especially
in the Soviet Union (Jurij Lotman is the leading scholar),
where it has been much enhanced by the work of information
and systems theorists and students of cybernetics. Hawkes'
Structuralism and Semiotics and *The Tell-Tale Sign: A Survey
of Semiotics* (1975) edited by Thomas A. Sebeok provide a sound
overview of the field (it is more than a method) that promises
to gain popularity in the United States.[25]

Structuralism and Soviet semiotics, obviously, have close
connections to Marxist criticism--in the work of writers like
Lucien Goldmann the two are inseparable--and in some ways
structuralism has made an otherwise unpalatable Marxism at
least accessible to non-socialist cultures such as the United
States. We cannot linger here on the complicated history of
Marxist criticism: on its evolution out of the ideology of
the October Revolution of 1917 or the relations of dialectical
materialism to socialist realism in literature, or the Maoist
version of Marxist literary criticism in the People's Republic
of China, but we should not forget, at least, that Marxist interpretation represents the largest and probably most influential kind of criticism world-wide. In Western Europe and recently in the United States, the origins of the neo-Marxists
Goldmann, Walter Benjamin, Theodor Adorno, Jürgen Habermas,
and of Georg Lukács, the Marxist aesthetician with a problematic relationship to Marxism, have been particularly influential.[26] A main difference between the criticisms generated by
these writers and the more doctrinaire Eastern European Marx-
ists is that Lukács and the neo-Marxists are more resolute in
their examination of literary forms and structures as they relate to socialist concerns, rather than using literary texts
to render socialist dogma and practice attractive. Adorno's
transformation of dialectical materialism into literary-critical categories, for example, has done much to persuade non-

socialist critics that Marxist approaches are worth learning.
Not incidentally, in Adorno's teleological treatment of the
dialectical method, where he distinguishes between the apparent and the essential, is reinforcement for the structuralist
dialectic of the surface structure and deep structure.[27]   It
is also through structuralist narrative theory that Marxist
criticism is entering the United States discussion through the
back door.   Few American critics have realized that the presuppositions of narratology adopted from the French structuralists cannot be separated from their Marxist rationale, and thus
we must anticipate an eventual coming to terms with this ideological source.   Fredric Jameson's *Marxism and Form* (1971) is
still the best American-composed overview of contemporary
Marxist literary analysis, and his last chapter, "Towards Dialectical Criticism", is an especially incisive treatment of
post-modernism in America from a Marxist point of view.[28]

Our discussion of structuralism leads to a rehearsal of
other approaches with strong social emphases, and we should
take this direction to its current endpoint and sketch the
current state of sociological literary criticism.   Sociological criticism in the surveys of criticism is often merged with
historical criticism, but it need not be.   Employing sociology
categories to illuminate areas of literary study is not the
same as using the language of historical criticism, although
the two have been closely associated especially on the Continent, where the discipline of sociology grew out of the nine-
teenth-century obsession with history.   We tend to forget that
some prominent critics (Erich Auerbach, *Mimesis*, 1946; Ian
Watt, *The Rise of the Novel*, 1957; Irving Howe, *Politics and
the Novel*, 1962; Harry Levin, *The Gates of Horn*, 1963) have
included the sociological perspective in their literary analyses for years without borrowing sociological terminology.[29]
More recently, anthropologists and sociologists such as Clifford Geertz, Victor Turner, James Boon, and Robert Coles have
applied their social science methods to literary study to produce provocative analyses of literature in relation to culture
that other approaches have not accomplished.[30]   Among the so-
ciologically-inclined contemporary literary critics themselves
two other emphases are appearing that seem to hold healthy potential: socio-criticism and the sociology of knowledge.   Two
proponents of socio-criticism distinguish it from sociological
criticism and sociology of literature and state that it "seeks
a definition as a *poetics of sociality*, inseparable from a
reading of the ideological in its textual specificity".[31]   The
writers using the method are influenced by formalism and structuralism, and seem to wish to find the ideological expression
of a political-social identity in the very texture of the literary work (a curious inversion of the New Critical task) but
also to locate such expression in systematic form in the deep

structure of the text. The 1976 *Sub-Stance* issue on "Socio-Criticism" contains representative essays by such stellar scholars as Fredric Jameson and Jacques Leenhardt, and Gerald Graff's *Literary Ideas in Modern Society* (1979), at least because of its censure of both the New Criticism and post-formalism for their disregard of external factors influencing the text, could be labeled socio-critical.[32]

The sociology of knowledge has a more substantial history, having risen out of the classical sociology of Max Weber, Emile Durkheim, and Karl Mannheim on the one hand and out of Max Scheler's phenomenology on the other. It would appear to hold great promise as a mode of literary analysis; Wellek and Warren in their *Theory of Literature* call attention to its possibilities as well as its faults, and Fokkema and Kunne-Ibsch advertise its advantages in *Theories of Literature in the Twentieth Century*.[33] The concern of the sociologists of knowledge, as described by Peter Berger and Thomas Luckmann in *The Social Construction of Reality* (1967), is to examine the connections between social situations and human thought according to a dialectical process comprised of the interacting moments of externalization, internalization, and objectification.[34] Hans Robert Jauss of the University of Constance is the most prominent critic currently engaging the approach.[35] One expects that the number of its practitioners will increase.

Another major area of criticism related to the rise and fall of the New Criticism is that concerned with consciousness and the unconscious—although this area includes a number of approaches such as the psychological, archetypal, and phenomenological that are related by the object (better said subject) of their study rather than by a common method. The psychoanalytical approach inspired by Freud and his followers arose about the same time as the New Criticism and shared with it a dependency on the scientific method of isolating and categorizing the parts of the research object. Yet, whereas the New Critics turned this intense scrutiny to their advantage in close reading, the psychoanalytic critics too often produced exaggerated interpretations that distorted both the literary text and Freudian theory. Fortunately, Freudian thought has been too original and powerful to have been totally discredited in the literary-critical context, and in the Sixties and Seventies it has, merged with the other post-formalist modes, gained new vigor. The inventive uses of Freud by the French scholars such as Jacques Lacan, René Girard, and Derrida, and the combined use of Freud and Marx by Goldmann have received considerable attention, but in the United States equally valuable psychoanalytical criticism has been undertaken by Lionel Trilling, Simon O. Lesser, F. J. Hoffmann, and, more recently, by Norman Holland, Frederick Crews, and Jeffrey Mehlman.[36]

Both French and Americans have been involved in rereadings of Freud, resulting for the French (including Mehlman as a translator and advocate of the Gallic situation) in new interpretations of the Oedipal complex, the concept of "trace", the deceptions practiced by the unconscious, etc., and for the Americans in reconsiderations of the psychology of reader reaction to a text and the dangers of Freudian reductionism.

Archetypal criticism, largely Jungian-based, is a version of the psychological approach that is almost as popular as the revived and revised Freudianism these days and is still more suspect to many critics unfriendly generally to the psychological method. Curiously, some of the best archetypal criticism has been written by a literary scholar not strictly Jungian-- namely Northrop Frye in texts such as *Anatomy of Criticism* (1957) and *Fables of Identity* (1963), but another critic who is Jungian, Joseph Campbell, has also written voluminously and skillfully in the archetypal mode in works such as the four- volume *The Masks of God* and *The Hero with a Thousand Faces*.[37] It is hard to say, on the other hand, whether Leslie Fiedler's *Love and Death in the American Novel* (1960) has helped or harmed the reputation of this mode, for it is both a brilliant and willfully eccentric reading of American culture and literature according to underlying archetypal forms and ritual practices.[38] Quite recently, the Jungian analyst James Hillman has put the method to work in a stimulating fashion by relating dreams, concepts such as animus/anima, the need for ritual expression, the modern presence of myth to the human story- telling impulse in books such as *The Myth of Analysis* and *Re- Visioning Psychology*.[39]

Whereas psychological and archetypal criticism are aligned to a study of the unconscious, phenomenological criticism fo- cuses on consciousness, although sometimes in ways that deny the efficacy of the psychological approach. Grounded in the work of the phenomenological philosophers Husserl, Heidegger, Merleau-Ponty, and Sartre, phenomenological literary criticism views literature as a representation of consciousness intending and apprehending itself and its "life world" and involves a complicated reductive technique providing the interpreter with a relatively unbiased attitude toward the text, in contrast to what the phenomenologist considers the prejudiced approach of the empirical scientist.[40] It would seem, then, that phenomen- ology and the New Criticism would be totally incompatible, since the New Criticism grew out of empiricist and even posi- tivist positions, yet one critic, at least, the Polish scholar Roman Ingarden, managed to combine them as early as the Thir- ties in major texts such as *The Literary Work of Art* (1931) and *The Cognition of the Literary Work of Art* (1937).[41] Varieties of the phenomenological approach have been developing on the

Continent since then, for example in the existential phenomenology of Sartre, and in the criticism of consciousness practiced by Georges Poulet, Jean Starobinski, *et al.*, and most
recently in Paul Ricoeur's study of narrative and metaphor.[42]
In the United States an example of excellent recent phenomenological literary criticism is David Halliburton's *Edgar Allan
Poe: A Phenomenological View* (1973).[43] The Winter 1976 issue
of *Boundary 2* contains a number of perceptive essays composed
from a Heideggerian aspect, and Robert Magliola's *Phenomenology
and Literature* (1977) should be mentioned as a reliable over-
view of the evolution of the approach since its genesis.[44] Although phenomenological criticism has not experienced anything
like the heady fortunes of structuralism, it has been steadily
growing as a method sufficiently promising to be worth the effort of learning it, in spite of its complexity, and it may yet
become a major and durable critical force.

Certainly phenomenology has been helped in gaining what
currency it has by the attention paid to hermeneutical criticism and reception theory, the final methods I shall treat.
Both of these have close connections to phenomenology, and in
the recognition they have gained in recent years phenomenology
has also received more exposure. Although hermeneutics arose
independent of phenomenology through Schleiermacher's attempt
to interpret Christianity persuasively to the liberals in the
early 1800's, and then through Dilthey's effort at turning it
into a method of interpretation for the humanities, it became
aligned to phenomenology early in the twentieth century through
Heidegger's appropriation of it and then through the refinements by Bultmann, Gadamer, the "event" theologians such as
Fuchs and Ebeling, and Ricoeur.[45] Hermeneutics is unique among
modern literary-critical methods in that it originated among
theologians and biblical exegetes and later evolved into a
method for the analysis of secular texts. In the United States
as well hermeneutics was known first as an approach for biblical scholars before it was adopted by critics of secular literature. As such, as a method for the interpretation of non-
religious texts, its history is very recent, and even now it
functions as a theory of interpretation, and a theory of how
one understands at all, as much as a practical, critical mode.
Typical of the stress on theory are the essays in the Winter
1972 issue of *New Literary History*, "On Interpretation", the
Autumn 1978 issue of that journal on "Literary Hermeneutics",
and the *Interpretation of Narrative* collection edited by Valdés and Miller.[46] It is harder to find good examples of applied hermeneutical criticism by non-biblical exegetes, but
one of the best is Frank Kermode's *The Genesis of Secrecy*
(1979)--which is, however, a study of the Gospel of Mark from
the hermeneutical perspective of a secular writer.[47] In this
brief and brilliant book Kermode demonstrates how the method

can work valuably by revealing the tendency toward interpretation inherent in the literary text, how narrative contains and
projects its own interpretation, how interpretation is as much
the creation and organization of fiction as it is the exposition of information.

One discovers many more applications to individual texts
in the reception criticism closely related to hermeneutics.
Reception criticism focuses on the act of reading a text and
on the reader's response in the interpretative process, and
has been associated primarily with two professors from the
University of Constance, Hans Robert Jauss and Wolfgang Iser. 48
Iser particularly has taken over the concept of the open text
and of indeterminacy from the phenomenologist Roman Ingarden
and the Czech structuralist Jan Mukařovský and described the
reader's options: because the experience of the text does not
coincide with real life, the reader must insert his own views
into the text or allow the text to alter his view or work with
a combination of the two. Whatever he chooses, the reader
creates meaning through reading as he responds to the text.
Jauss describes the reader's situation in a similar manner,
but he argues that the historical conditions surrounding text
and reader and the fact that the reader is always influenced
by his society are central in determining the text's reception. 49 Thus Iser seems closer to the older formalist approach to the text transformed into the perspective of the
reader's experience, while Jauss represents an orientation
toward history and society in forming the text's significance.

Reception criticism in the United States is relatively
new, although Norman Holland has practiced a psychological version of it in his *The Dynamics of Literary Response* and *Five
Readers Reading* (1975), and Stanley E. Fish has done valuable
work on the reader's interactions with the text in books such
as *Self-Consuming Artifacts* (1972). 50 One anticipates a vigorous American application of the approach in the immediate
future.

We can say, in summary, that the contemporary literary-
critical situation is complicated, and perhaps confusing, but
not chaotic. Irksome as the variety of methods may be, the
situation also reflects the energy of the endeavor to appreciate and comprehend the rich discourse of the literary imagi-
nation--to contribute it to the incessant conversation of
humankind with itself in its attempt to find and create meaning.

18

NOTES

1. For reliable descriptions of the New Criticism cf.
Wilbur Scott, *Five Approaches of Literary Criticism* (New
York: Collier Books, 1962), "The Formalistic Approach:
Literature as Aesthetic Structure," pp. 179-244; and William
K. Wimsatt and Cleanth Brooks, *Literary Criticism: A Short
History* (New York: Vintage Books, 1967), Part IV, pp. 555-
698. In this essay I shall devote more space to literary-
critical methods that are extensions of the New Criticism and
correspondingly less space to methods such as structuralism
and hermeneutics, since these latter are, I assume, better
known to biblical exegetes than are the former. I shall not
discuss theological or religious literary criticism at all,
since these approaches should be fairly familiar to biblical
scholars. For recent surveys of these approaches, cf. Giles
Gunn, "Threading the Eye of the Needle: The Place of the
Literary Critic in Religious Studies," *Journal of the American
Academy of Religion* 43 (June, 1975): 164-84; David H. Hesla,
"Religion and Literature; The Second Stage," *Journal of the
American Academy of Religion* 46 (June, 1978): 181-92; and
Robert Detweiler, "Recent Religion and Literature Scholar-
ship," *Religious Studies Review* 4 (April, 1978): 107-17.

2. Regarding the conflict between Barthes and Picard,
cf. Germaine Bree, "French Criticism: A Battle of Books?"
The Emory University Quarterly 22 (Spring, 1967): 25-35.

3. Ronald S. Crane, *The Languages of Criticism and the
Structure of Poetry* (Toronto: University of Toronto Press,
1953).

4. Geoffrey H. Hartman, *Beyond Formalism* (New Haven:
Yale University Press, 1970), p. 42. The title of the book
and the essay are the same.

5. Wayne C. Booth, *The Rhetoric of Fiction* (Chicago:
University of Chicago Press, 1961). Barbara Hardy, *The Appropriate Form: An Essay on the Novel* (London: Athlone
Press, 1964); *Tellers and Listeners: The Narrative Imagination* (London: Athlone Press, 1975).

6. Robert Scholes and Robert Kellogg, *The Nature of
Narrative* (New York: Oxford University Press, 1966).

7. Susan Sontag, *Against Interpretation* (New York:
Dell, 1969), p. 22.

8.   John Halperin, ed., *The Theory of the Novel: New Essays* (New York: Oxford University Press, 1974). Mark Spilka, ed., *Towards a Poetics of Fiction* (Bloomington: Indiana University Press, 1977). *New Literary History* 6 (Winter, 1975). Mario J. Valdés and Owen J. Miller, *Interpretation of Narrative* (Toronto: University of Toronto Press, 1978).

9.   Cleanth Brooks and Robert Penn Warren, *Understanding Fiction*, 2nd ed. (New York: Appleton-Century-Crofts, 1959).

10.   I. A. Richards, *Practical Criticism: A Study in Literary Judgment* (London: Kegan Paul, 1930). William K. Wimsatt and Monroe C. Beardsley, *The Verbal Icon: Studies in the Meaning of Poetry* (Lexington: University of Kentucky Press, 1954). Philip Wheelwright, *Metaphor and Reality* (Bloomington: Indiana University Press, 1962).

11.   Allen Tate, "Tension in Poetry," in *On the Limits of Poetry: Selected Essays 1928-1948* (Denver: Alan Swallow, 1948). Cleanth Brooks, "Irony as a Principle of Structure," in Morton D. Zabel, ed., *Literary Opinion in America* (New York: Harper & Brothers, 1951). William Empson, *Seven Types of Ambiguity* (New York: New Directions, 1948).

12.   Cf. John Crowe Ransom, "Poetry: A Note in Ontology," in *The World's Body* (New York: Charles Scribner's Sons, 1938).

13.   Max Black, *Models and Metaphors* (Ithaca: Cornell University Press, 1962). Nelson Goodman, *Languages of Art: An Approach to a Theory of Symbols* (Indianapolis: Bobbs-Merrill, 1968).

14.   Cf. for example, F. E. Sparshott, "'As,' or The Limits of Metaphor," *New Literary History* 6 (Autumn, 1974): 75-94; and Donald Davidson, "What Metaphors Mean," *Critical Inquiry* 5 (Autumn, 1978): 31-47.

15.   Roman Jakobson and Morris Halle, *Fundamentals of Language* (The Hague: Mouton, 1956).

16.   Roland Barthes, *S/Z*, trans. Richard Miller (New York: Farrar, Straus & Girous, 1974). Tzvetan Todorov, *Littérature et signification* (Paris: Larousse, 1967). Paul de Man, "The Epistemology of Metaphor," *Critical Inquiry* 5 (Autumn, 1978): 13-30. Jonathan Culler, *Structuralist Poetics: Structuralism, Linguistics, and the Study of Literature* (Ithaca: Cornell University Press, 1975).

17.   Jacques Derrida, "White Mythology: Metaphor in the Text of Philosophy," *New Literary History* 6 (Autumn, 1974):

5-74. For a fine introduction to Derrida, cf. the Translator's Preface to Jacques Derrida, *Of Grammatology*, trans. Ga-
yatri Chakravorty Spivak (Baltimore: The Johns Hopkins University Press, 1970), pp. ix-lxxxvii.

18. Jeanine Parisier Plottel, "Introduction," *New York
Literary Forum*, 2 (1978), issue on "Intertextuality: New
Perspectives in Criticism," pp. xi-xx.

19. Ibid., p. xvi.

20. Cf. Hayden White, "The Absurdist Movement in Contemporary Literary Theory," in Murray Krieger and L. S. Dembo,
eds., *Directions for Criticism: Structuralism and its Alternative* (Madison: University of Wisconsin Press, 1977).

21. Roland Barthes, *The Pleasure of the Text*, trans.
Richard Miller (New York: Hill and Wang, 1975).

22. Cf. Culler, *Structuralist Poetics*, for summaries of
these structuralists, and Fredric Jameson, *The Prison-House
of Language: A Critical Account of Structuralism and Russian
Formalism* (Princeton: Princeton University Press, 1972), for
discussion of Propp and Shklovsky.

23. Robert Scholes, *Structuralism in Literature: An In-
troduction* (New Haven: Yale University Press, 1974). Terence
Hawkes, *Structuralism and Semiotics* (Berkeley: University of
California Press, 1977).

24. *Tel Quel* is published by Seuil, Paris. *Structuralist
Review: A Journal of Theory, Criticism, and Pedagogy* is pub-
lished by Queens College Press in Flushing, New York. *Sub-
Stance: A Review of Theory and Literary Criticism* is pub-
lished by the University of Wisconsin in Madison. *Glyph:
Johns Hopkins Textual Studies* is published by The John Hopkins
University Press in Baltimore. An example of a less adventure-
some journal publishing structuralist material is the essay by
John G. Blair, "Structuralism, American Studies, and the Human-
ities" in *American Quarterly* 30 (1978): 261-81.

25. Thomas A. Sebeok, ed., *The Tell-Tale Sign: A Survey
of Semiotics* (Lisse/Netherlands: The Peter de Ridder Press,
1975).

26. For information on these writers, cf. D. W. Fokkema
and Elrud Kunne-Ibsch, *Theories of Literature in the Twentieth
Century* (London: C. Hurst & Company, 1977).

27. Ibid., p. 133.

28. Fredric Jameson, *Marxism and Form: Twentieth-Century Dialectical Theories of Literature* (Princeton: Princeton University Press, 1971), pp. 306-416.

29. Erich Auerbach, *Mimesis: The Representation of Reality in Western Literature*, trans. Willard Trask (Princeton: Princeton University Press, 1953). Ian Watt, *The Rise of the Novel* (Berkeley: University of California Press, 1957). Irving Howe, *Politics and the Novel* (New York: Meridian Books, 1962). Harry Levin, *The Gates of Horn: A Study of Five French Realists* (New York: Oxford University Press, 1963).

30. Clifford Geertz, *The Interpretation of Cultures* (New York: Basic Books, 1973). Victor Turner, *Dramas, Fields, and Metaphors* (Ithaca: Cornell University Press, 1974). James A. Boon, *From Symbolism to Structuralism: Lévi-Strauss in a Literary Tradition* (New York: Harper & Row, 1972). Robert Coles, *Walker Percy: An American Search* (Boston: Little, Brown & Co., 1978).

31. Claude Duchet and Françoise Gaillard, "Introduction: Socio-Criticism," *Sub-Stance* 15 (1976): 4.

32. Frederic Jameson, "The Ideology of Form: Partial Systems in *La Vielle Fille*"; Jacques Leenhardt, "Toward a Sociological Aesthetic: An Attempt at Constructing the Aesthetic of Lucien Goldmann," *Sub-Stance* 15 (1976). Gerald Graff, *Literary Ideas in Modern Society* (Chicago: University of Chicago Press, 1979).

33. René Wellek and Austin Warren, *Theory of Literature*, 3rd edition (New York: Harcourt, Brace & World, 1956), pp. 107-8. Fokkema and Kunne-Ibsch, *Theories of Literature in the Twentieth Century*, pp. 149-50.

34. Peter Berger and Thomas Luckmann, *The Social Construction of Reality* (New York: Anchor Books, 1967).

35. Hans Robert Jauss, *Ästhetische Erfahrung und literarische Hermeneutik*, I (Munich: Wilhelm Fink Verlag, 1977). Cf. also Fokkema and Kunne-Ibsch, *Theories of Literature in the Twentieth Century*, pp. 174-79, on Jauss and the sociology of knowledge.

36. *Yale French Studies*, No. 48 (1972) on "French Freud: Structural Studies in Psychoanalysis" has the following representative essays: Jeffrey Mehlman, "'The Floating Signifier': From Lévi-Strauss to Lacan," 10-37; Jacques Lacan, "Seminar on 'The Purloined Letter'," 39-72; Jacques Derrida, "Freud and the Scene of Writing," 74-117. René Girard, *Violence and the*

Sacred, trans. Patrick Gregory (Baltimore: The Johns Hopkins University Press, 1977). Lucien Goldmann, *Pour une sociologie du roman* (Paris: Gallimard, 1964). Lionel Trilling, *The Liberal Imagination: Essays on Literature and Society* (New York: Viking Press, 1950). Simon O. Lesser, *Fiction and the Unconscious* (New York: Vintage Books, 1962). Frederick J. Hoffman, *Freudianism and the Literary Mind* (Baton Rouge: Louisiana State University Press, 1957). Norman N. Holland, *The Dynamics of Literary Response* (New York: Oxford University Press, 1968). Frederick Crews, *Out of My System: Psychoanalysis, Ideology, and Critical Method* (New York: Oxford University Press, 1975).

37. Northrop Frye, *Anatomy of Criticism* (Princeton: Princeton University Press, 1957); *Fables of Identity: Studies in Poetic Mythology* (New York: Harcourt, Brace & World, 1963). Joseph Campbell, *The Masks of God*, 4 vols. (New York: Viking Press, 1959-68); *The Hero with a Thousand Faces* (Cleveland: World Publishing Company, 1949).

38. Leslie A. Fiedler, *Love and Death in the American Novel* (New York: Criterion Books, 1960).

39. James Hillman, *The Myth of Analysis: Three Essays in Archetypal Psychology* (New York: Harper & Row, 1972); *Re-Visioning Psychology* (New York: Harper & Row, 1975).

40. For an over-view of the beginnings of phenomenology, cf. Robert Detweiler, *Story, Sign, and Self: Phenomenology and Structuralism as Literary-Critical Methods* (Philadelphia: Fortress Press, 1978).

41. Roman Ingarden, *The Literary Work of Art*, trans. George G. Grabowicz (Evanston: Northwestern University Press, 1973), original publication, 1931; *The Cognition of the Literary Work of Art*, trans. Ruth Ann Crowley and Kenneth R. Olsen (Evanston: Northwestern University Press, 1973), original publication, 1937.

42. Cf., for example, Jean-Paul Sartre, *Saint Genet, Actor and Martyr*, trans. Bernard Frechtman (New York: Braziller, 1963); Georges Poulet, *Mesure de l'instant* (Paris: Plon, 1968); Jean Starobinski, *L'Oeil vivant* (Paris: Gallimard, 1961); and Paul Ricoeur, *The Rule of Metaphor: Multidisciplinary Studies of the Creation of Meaning in Language*, trans. Robert Czerny (Toronto: University of Toronto Press, 1977).

43. David Halliburton, *Edgar Allan Poe: A Phenomenological View* (Princeton: Princeton University Press, 1973).

44. Cf., for example, Stanley Corngold, *"Sein und Zeit:* Implications for Poetics," *Boundary* 2 6 (Winter, 1976): 439-53. Robert R. Magliola, *Phenomenology and Literature: An Introduction* (West Lafayette: Purdue University Press, 1977).

45. For an excellent summary of the development of hermeneutics, cf. James M. Robinson, "Hermeneutic Since Barth," in James M. Robinson and John B. Cobb, Jr., eds., *The New Hermeneutic* (New York: Harper & Row, 1964).

46. Cf., for example, E. D. Hirsch, Jr., "Three Dimensions of Hermeneutics," *New Literary History* 3 (Winter, 1972): 245-61; Peter Szondi, "Introduction to Literary Hermeneutics," *New Literary History* 10 (Autumn, 1978): 17-29; Cyrus Hamlin, "Strategies of Reversal in Literary Narrative," in Valdés and Miller, eds., *Interpretation of Narrative*, pp. 61-77.

47. Frank Kermode, *The Genesis of Secrecy: On the Interpretation of Narrative* (Cambridge: Harvard University Press, 1979).

48. Cf., for example, Hans Robert Jauss, Chapter 6: "Aisthesis: die rezeptive Seite der ästhetischen Erfahrung," *Ästhetische Erfahrung und literarische Hermeneutik*, I, pp. 97-136; and Wolfgang Iser, *Der Akt des Lesens*(Munich: Wilhelm Fink Verlag, 1976).

49. I have summarized this discussion of Iser and Jauss from Fokkema and Kunne-Ibsche, *Theories of Literature in the Twentieth Century*, Chapter 5: "The Reception of Literature," pp. 136-64.

50. Norman N. Holland, *Five Readers Reading* (New Haven: Yale University Press, 1975). Stanley E. Fish, *Self-Consuming Artifacts: The Experience of Seventeenth-Century Literature* (Berkeley: University of California Press, 1972). For an over-view of reader-response approaches, cf. Steven Mailloux, "Reader-Response Criticism?" *Genre* 10 (1977): 413-31.

2

LITERARY CRITICISM IN BIBLICAL STUDIES

Norman R. Petersen

We are in every way children of criticism,
and we seek to go beyond criticism by means
of criticism, by a criticism that is no
longer reductive but restorative.

Paul Ricoeur[1]

The founding fathers of form criticism, whose literary-critical legacy today leads us to reflect on where we are, critically speaking, why we are there, and where we are going, may well have applauded in their time Paul Ricoeur's judgment about our time--that "beyond the desert of criticism we yearn to be called again".[2] Like Ricoeur, the founding fathers sought "to go beyond criticism by means of criticism", to go beyond the disintegrating atomism of source criticism and the historical and religious skepticism it spawned. By means of form criticism and literary history (*Literaturgeschichte*), and with no little demythologizing, the fathers sought to restore the gospel and its proclamatory calling, and for a time they succeeded. But times have changed. Ricoeur speaks for many when he describes our time as a desert of criticism from which we yearn to be called again. Rightly or wrongly, many are finding the critical and theological legacy of form criticism as reductively barren as the desert in which its own call had served as a restorative. And it appears that many would have the new call be a call to literary criticism. In this essay in honor of William Beardslee, I wish to explore the relationships between the old literary criticism in biblical studies, the philological-historical criticism of which form criticism is a product, and the new literary criticism on whose behalf Beardslee was one of the first to speak.[3] My goal is not to assign blame, but to define roles, relations, problems and possibilities.

"To go beyond criticism by means of criticism," says Ricoeur, is the way to a "second naivete" which is the best we "children of criticism" can hope for.[4] An epoch of criticism has cost us an experiential immediacy, a primitive naivete, vis-à-vis texts; and, it is that immediacy which is in need of restoring. Because through criticism we have lost the presumed innocence of a pre-critical naivete, the experience of a second naivete, which is to come "by means of criticism", will be post-critical.[5] I want to revise Ricoeur's historical sequence of pre-critical (primitive naivete), critical, and post-critical (second naivete) by seeing his post-critical stage as a New Critical stage that is dialectically related to an experience of the second naivete, and by speaking of a new literary criticism of the second naivete.[6] This new literary criticism for biblical studies will share some of the traits of its older counterpart in literary studies, New Criticism; but, it will differ from it on the one hand by virtue of its acknowledgment of the results of the epoch of criticism in biblical studies, and on the other hand by virtue of its dependence on the experience of a second naivete in the reading of biblical texts. For these reasons we need to define both the old and the new biblical literary criticisms and the relations between them. Suffice it to say that labeling form criticism as the desert of criticism is entirely too simplistic, not only because form criticism is actually the fertile fringe of the desert, but also because misconstruing it has serious consequences for our understanding of the new literary criticism we seek.

Form criticism is in fact the final and probably supreme development of a literary criticism that emerged at the end of the eighteenth century and in the course of the nineteenth century came to dominate all textual studies, both biblical and other--philological-historical criticism.[7] Successor to the grammatical literalism of the ancient and medieval *sensus litteralis*, which historically was both juxtaposed and opposed to the *sensus spiritualis* or allegorical interpretation, nineteenth century philological criticism divided its literary concerns into two parts. One part, the analytical, was oriented to the intrinsic study of individual texts and is properly called "literary criticism" (*Literarkritik*). The other, synthetic part was textually extrinsic in focus, oriented to the comparative study of texts and to the history of texts, and is properly called "literary history" (*Literaturgeschichte*).[8] Importantly, both parts concentrated on the linguistic dimension of texts and were concerned with lexical, grammatical and stylistic considerations. The foundational conviction of this double-barreled philological criticism was that language is the social vehicle for the individual writer's expression of thoughts and feelings about things in the contingent world of human experience. Through analysis of the language and style of expression the critic gains access both to the thoughts and feelings of writers and to their culture's distinctive ideas and sentiments about life in the world. Texts are the linguistic expressions of cognitive and affective states of consciousness, but they are also conditioned socially (through language) and culturally (through cultural ideas, values, and sentiments). Needless to say, in the course of the nineteenth century philological-historical criticism was influenced by certain understandings of history-- historicism--and of the nature of criticism--positivism--that had a profound influence on the interpretation of philologically-analyzed texts. But these hermeneutical and meta-critical influences are peripheral to our focus on the distinctive roles of philological literary criticism and literary history in biblical studies. For these roles define the era of biblical criticism whose textually-reductive efforts led to the critical desert from which many today seek a restorative calling.

Philological-historical criticism in biblical studies produced two major results, both of which attained their ultimate expression in form criticism, through which they have become philology's discomforting legacy to any new literary criticism at all. On the analytic literary-critical side, the concentration on language and style led to the discovery in many biblical texts of *other* texts. Designed to reveal the integrity of texts, literary criticism actually discovered in them breaks in "continuity, duplications, inconsistencies and different linguistic usage"[9] that collectively demolished any naive sense of textual integrity. These disintegrative features then soon found their explanation in the reductive hypothesis that biblical writers employed other texts as sources for their own texts. Combined with the concern of biblical critics for historical evidence and historical understanding, philological literary criticism's attention tended increasingly to focus on the texts within our texts, and in the process the very meaning of "literary criticism" was transformed to denote *source* criticism, but without a corresponding change of name. Klaus Koch represents a very common present-day, but long-standing view of this transformed literary criticism when he defines it as "the analysis of biblical books from the standpoint of lack of continuity, duplications, inconsistencies and different linguistic usage, *with the object of discovering what the individual writers* [presumably of the sources] *and redactors contributed to a text, and also its time and place of origin*" (Koch's italics).[10] Although Koch recognizes that literary criticism *led* to the identification of sources,[11] he does not seem to recognize that the discovery of sources led to the re-definition of literary criticism itself, one in which the original method is turned upside down! To wit, whereas formerly literary criticism was concerned with textually-integrative features, now it is concerned with textually-*dis*integrative features. At best, the original focus of literary criticism is reassigned to one of the by-products of its application to biblical texts, redaction criticism. That re-assignment already took place in the nineteenth century, although it took until the middle of the twentieth century for it to find a name and a clientele.

Consistent with the re-definition of literary criticism, Koch goes further to maintain for literary (source) criticism an even more restrictive role resulting from the emergence, following source criticism, of form criticism:

> Properly understood, literary criticism
> can now only be considered as a branch,
> along with many others, of form criti-
> cism. It is that aspect of form criti-
> cism which is concerned with the trans-
> mission of books, tracing their develop-
> ment right back to their many written
> sources.[12]

Not spelled-out in this new definition of the role of literary criticism is the rather significant further transformation of it into a literary-*historical* tool; for, what Koch here refers to is the evolutionary theory of biblical literature produced by form critics.[13] In this theory, sources stand at an evolutionary point mid-way between the originally oral state of their parts and the final textual state in which the sources are themselves parts. In the context of the evolutionary theory, literary criticism would, as with Koch, refer to the archeological history of individual texts. His new definition is consistent with the old one, in which literary criticism became source criticism, but the new one also bends the old one in the direction of literary history. That the old one could be bent in this way becomes comprehensible when we recognize that form criticism has both a philologically literary-critical and a literary-historical aspect.

Form criticism's philological heritage is evident in the linguistic and stylistic orientation to texts found in every form-critical study. Analytically, lexical, grammatical and stylistic evidence once more led to a (further) reduction of textual integrity when this evidence was discovered to define the form of textual units within the sources of our texts. Synthetically, on the other hand, comparative literary-historical studies of the forms of these units revealed a small number of formal types that made it possible to classify and analyze the units on the basis of their types (*Gattungen* or genres).[14] Thus, the textually intrinsic and extrinsic comparative evidence led to the hypothesis that the smallest textual units were originally independent oral "texts". From this conclusion it was but a small step to the positing of the evolutionary history of the formally stereotyped oral traditions through a stage of written sources and ending with the redaction of these sources in our present texts. Thus, too, literary history, about which we shall have more to say in a moment, ceased to refer to the history of literature and came to refer to the pre-literary history of the material in individual texts.

Before we turn to the fate of literary history in the philological-historical tradition, it would be well to pause for a moment and reflect on the fate of literary criticism. My concern at this juncture is not with the reductive results of source and form criticism, which I consider to be "archeologically" valid results, but with the philological literary vision that produced source, form and redaction criticism and made their results possible. First and foremost, it is imperative for us to recognize that these three critical orientations are the products of a single methodological approach, that of philology, and that they form a coherent and closed literary system. Sources, formed traditions, and redaction encompass the philologically significant aspects of texts. But philology's exclusive focus on language and style did not require the emergence of source, form and redaction criticism. To the contrary, it was the texts themselves that presented the philological method with empirical evidence which, according to its criteria, was disruptive of textual integrity and in need of explanation. Sources, formed traditions, and redactions are philology's responses to empirical evidence of a linguistic sort. Second, within the history of the philological-historical method in biblical studies, form criticism provided the single most powerful theoretical formulation of the literary insights produced by the method. It did so by extending the method to the archeologically deepest strata of our texts and by providing a comprehensive historical and sociological explanation of the process by which our textual mounds were formed. Third, while in retrospect it seems inevitable that philology's methodological vision would have been acutely sensitive to the linguistic traits of biblical texts, biblical students have not until recently questioned that vision's exclusive focus on matters of language and style.[15] Precisely because literary students outside of the biblical field have also raised such questions of the philological vision in their fields, the resoundingly negative answer biblical philology has given to the quest for the integrity of biblical texts appears to be less definitive than it was. Simply, it is now an open question as to whether the philological orientation to language and style exhausts the possibilities for perceiving textually-integrative features-- even in texts where the linguistic evidence is negative. Fourth, and last, because the orientation of biblical-philological criticism quickly shifted from the integrative to the disintegrative features of our texts, with corresponding shifts of focus from texts to sources and then to *their* sources, our open question may well apply also to the philo-logical-critical tradition as well as to its linguistic and stylistic criteria. That is to say, having ceased to examine the integrative features once disintegrative features were found, the possibilities of literary philology itself may not have been exhausted.

However, despite these questions about the exhaustiveness of biblical philology's literary-critical efforts, I do not want to disparage its results. To the contrary, I want to in-sist on their abiding significance for any new biblical liter-ary criticism at all. With Robert Alter, a noted contemporary literary critic who writes on literary aspects of biblical texts, I acknowledge that *textual compositeness* has been prov-en to be a fundamental condition of biblical literary art.[16] In line with my questions of biblical philology, however, and again in agreement with Alter, I want to go beyond philologi-cal-historical criticism--not merely form and redaction crit-icism--by confronting and critically transcending the condi-tion of compositeness.

Literary history (*Literaturgeschichte*) is the synthetic complement to philology's analytic literary criticism. Also within the linguistic and stylistic horizon of philology, literary history is a fundamentally comparative enterprise in which the individuality of a text is identified in relation to the stylistic form and typological categories (*Gattungen*; genres) of other texts originating before, after and contem-poraneously with it in a relatively closed cultural and his-torical milieu. Literary history could be many things but, as the eminent classicist Eduard Norden claimed, the literary his-tory of texts and the history of style are inseparably parallel histories, the one providing a basis for dealing with the other.[17] Norden's own classic study of ancient artistic prose, *Die Antike Kunstprosa*, is at once a monument to philological literary history and a witness to literary history's contribu-tion to biblical literary criticism. This contribution is re-flected in Norden's approval and support of the earlier con-clusion of the New Testament scholar, Franz Overbeck: When compared with the formal and functional standards of Greco-Roman literature, New Testament writings prove to be non-lit-erary. New Testament writings are at best primitive litera-ture, *Urliteratur*. Christian literature, properly speaking, begins only in the mid to late second century, C. E., when Christians adopted Greco-Roman standards for their writings.[18] Overbeck's conclusion has only been elaborated by subsequent scholarship. For example, Adolf Deissmann, in his *Light From the Ancient East*, self-consciously moved from philological literary criticism to literary history in arguing that the letters in the New Testament are in language, style and form non-literary because, following these criteria, they are most comparable to popular non-literary Greek letters.[19] Similarly, climaxing in K. L. Schmidt's classic essay on the location of the Gospels in general literary history, form critics concluded from literary-critical and literary-historical studies that the Gospels are popular cult-books containing the Christian cult's sacred traditions.[20] Thus, comparative literary-historical study of New Testament writings concluded that they are not literary texts. This conclusion constitutes the second critical condition with which a new literary criticism is confronted.

A further word is in order about the history of philological literary history. As "literary criticism" came to mean something else in the course of its history, so also did literary history undergo a transformation by being assimilated within form history. In literary criticism "literary" came to mean "source", and in literary history "literary" came to mean "form". To be sure, the notion of form has a role to play in literary history, as Overbeck and others have argued. But in form criticism "form" was self-consciously denied any aesthetic connotations in favor of an understanding of form as a sociological product. Indeed, form critics insist that theirs is not a literary but a sociological method in the service of historical criticism.[21] Analytically, one begins by philologically determining the form of a text or textual unit, classifies it according to its ideal type (*Gattung*), and then moves to the type of sociological situation in which such a type was employed. The formal and sociological types then provide a basis for returning to the text in order both to interpret its meaning on the basis of its sociological motivation and to locate it, through comparison with other texts and their typological implications, in social and intellectual history. Form criticism is thus a combined philological-sociological method wedded to the concerns of historiography. Literary history survives only, as indicated earlier, in the form of the "archeological" history of the materials of which our texts are comprised.

An appropriate conclusion to our reflections on the fate of literary concerns in the philological-historical tradition is represented in the history of articles on literary criticism and literary history in the three editions of the monumental reference tool, *Die Religion in Geschichte und Gegenwart*. In it we find that there has never been an entry under "literary criticism", only a paragraph in the articles on biblical criticism, *Bibelkritik*, where it appears after a paragraph on tex-

tual criticism and, in the third edition, before a paragraph
on form criticism.[22] As for literary history, after an enor-
mous essay on *Literaturgeschichte* in the first edition (1912)
by Johannes Weiss, who wrote a highly detailed article on individual texts, the second edition (1929) featured new theo-
retically-oriented essays by Hermann Gunkel and Rudolf Bultmann, both of whom set literary history in a form-critical
context. It is fair to say that their contributions represent
the high point of literary-historical reflection on the results of over a century of philological-historical criticism
in biblical studies. But symptomatic of the success of form
criticism is the two line epitaph to literary history that appears in the third edition (1960): "Literaturgeschichte, biblische————————> Formen und Gattungen".[23] Despite some
still-preserved hopes for literary history, it has ceased to
play a role in biblical studies, just as literary criticism
ceased to play a role when it became source criticism.

From a literary perspective, the epoch of philological
criticism has created a desert that is in literary matters
doubly barren. Literary artifacts have been excluded and
literary methods expunged. Having begun with a bona fide
literary method, the method led first to the disintegration
of biblical texts and then to the denial of their literary
quality. And once these results were achieved, the literary
method was abandoned. The desert is complete.

To move beyond the limits of philological literary criticism while at the same time attending to the conditions it
places upon a new literary criticism, we have a convenient
starting point in the work of a master philological literary
critic and literary historian, Erich Auerbach. Reflecting on
his view of philology and literature, Auerbach unabashedly describes his critical pedigree:

> Our knowledge of world literatures is in-
> debted to the impulse given...by histori-
> cist humanism; the concern of that human-
> ism was not only the overt discovery of
> materials and the development of methods
> of research, but beyond that their pene-
> tration and evaluation so that an inner
> history of mankind could be written....
> The inner history of the last thousand
> years is the history of mankind achieving
> self-expression: this is what philology,
> a historicist discipline, treats.[24]

*Philology, a historicist discipline, treats texts as the self-
expression of the human spirit in its culturally and individ-*

ually contingent modes. Auerbach's famous *Mimesis* exemplifies this orientation by focusing on "The Representation [i.e., *mimesis*] of Reality in Western Literature". In its first two chapters he compares and contrasts some Old and New Testament writings with Greek and Roman literature.[25] Methodologically, linguistic and stylistic modes of representation are examined as expressions of thoughts and sentiments about life in the world under the conditions of historical and cultural contingency. How, Auerbach implicitly asks, do these texts represent and express people's perception of their natural and social world? What in their world is of interest or import to them? What is it--life in the world--all about? In all cases, it is more the style of representation than what is overtly represented that is the subject of Auerbach's attention. The style of expression and representation is all the more important in narrative, whether fictional or historical, because the content of expression and representation--what is expressed and represented--consists of the actions of characters in time and space. In normal, non-narrative discourse, discourse is "saying about things", and what a speaker means (intends) is evident in *what* he propositionally says about what things. Narrative discourse, however, tells us *that* things happened, really or imaginatively, and what the author/narrator[26] wishes to say about the things that happened is revealed in the style of his telling. In narrative, the *how* of expression and representation is the critical index of what is being said about things. What a narrative author (*sic*) means is his story, and story is a peculiar form, a "how", of saying things about things. In this Auerbachian notion of literature as expression we find within philological criticism a means of going beyond the literary conditions inherited from biblical philology without denying those conditions.

Whereas biblical literary history led to the conclusion that biblical writings were unliterary because they deviated from Greco-Roman norms, the notion of texts as expressions of the human spirit in culturally and individually contingent modes both acknowledges and transcends the differences between biblical and non-biblical texts. Auerbach recognizes the differences: "In the last analysis the differences in style between the writings of antiquity and early Christianity are conditioned by the fact that they were composed from a different point of view for different people."[27] He acknowledges, too, a lack of "artistic purpose" in biblical writings, but he does not confuse intent with art. Indeed, Auerbach's distinctive achievement is to have illustrated the artless art of biblical expression and representation, and to have explained it by what it expresses and represents--a vision of the world and of value. Whether or not we like his historicistic explanation is beside the literary point, which is that difference does not preclude, but rather demands, separate but equal literary consideration on a higher analytical level than that in which the differences are focal. Auerbach has thus given us a down-payment on a literary-historical approach to biblical writings that is descriptively valid, because of its inductive procedure, regardless of his explanatory orientation, which is not necessarily wrong simply because it is professedly historicistic.[28] But most of all, Auerbach has demonstrated how wrong-headed it is to measure the literature of one historical-cultural unit by the literature of another, and then to consider the writings of the former unliterary because they do not measure up to the standards of the latter. The door to both comparative and historicist literary-historical study of the Bible is opened by Auerbach.

The literary-critical door, stuck closed by the condition of compositeness, has also been opened, or at least had its hinges well-oiled, by Auerbach's efforts. The lubricant is to be found in his development of the more rhetorical notion of style, as seen in Norden and biblical philologians, in the direction of poetics. Already in Auerbach's notion of *mimesis*, representation, we find a movement beyond linguistics and stylistics, beyond the art of speaking well, to the Aristotelian poetic or compositional categories of action (which is bound up with plot), character, and thought. Representation has to do with the rendering of people, events, and things, even of values, feelings, and motivations. While it is linked to style through the techniques of such rendering, representation has more to do with story, and style with the rhetorical dimension of narrative as discourse.[29] For Auerbach, texts are rhetorical ("uttered") expressions of thoughts and feelings about things, but texts as texts also represent worlds or segments of them. Although not as tidily as perhaps we might desire, Auerbach distinguishes between these textually-represented worlds and the real worlds that express themselves in the representations. Not only does this emancipation of represented worlds from rhetoric and from real worlds signal a poetic advance in philological literary criticism, but it also entails a criticism that anticipates the second naivete heralded by Paul Ricoeur. Ricoeur speaks of an experiential naivete vis-à-vis texts. Auerbach, in developing his ideas in relation to those of Vico, spoke of a decisive "difference between the language of poetic evocation and that of rational communication", and with Vico emphasized the need for "immediate intuition unguided by systematic reason" in the realm of poetic evocation. But against Vico and consistent with a dialectical relationship between a reading and a criticism of the second naivete, Auerbach argued that "The relation between imagination and reason is not one of pure temporal succession; imagination and reason are not mutually exclusive; the two can

work together, and reason can serve to enrich the imagination."[30] Thus, to philological literary criticism Auerbach
adds an appreciation for the poetic (compositional) and
evocatively representative aspects of texts, but also a
sensitivity to the relationship between imagination and reason in the acts of reading and analyzing texts. If in biblical studies philological concentration on the language of
texts led downward through the texts in a textual archeology,
in Auerbach's hands the tools of philology have been employed
to move upwards from the language of texts into the provoca-
tively imaginative worlds that language conspires to create.
In a word, Auerbach's notion of literature extends philology
into the realm of narrativity which, in my judgment, is the
proper literary response to both composite and unliterary
conditions.

However, for us to take the path provided by the notion
of narrativity we also have to pass by Auerbach because he
did not confront the condition of compositeness in a manner
that would be persuasive to biblical critics. He did recognize the lack of unity in biblical texts, and its basis in the
piecing together of older material, but he found an overarch-
ing--or undergirding--unity in "one concept of universal history and its interpretation".[31] The biblical world-view, as
it were, provided unity to composite texts. This solution,
however valid it may be on a comparative cultural level, is
designed to represent the unity of the whole Bible, the Old
Testament and the New, and does not persuasively account for
the more empirical problem of unity in the several extended
texts that comprise the biblical anthology. Methodologically,
Auerbach focused on segments of biblical texts that represented distinctive differences from Greek and Roman texts,
viewed the differences as expressions of the biblical "spirit",
and then used this spirit to explain the unity of the whole
composite biblical anthology.[32] He did not confront the condition of textual compositeness in the Pentateuch (or Tetra-
teuch), the Deuteronomistic history, or the Gospel According
to Mark, from which come the textual segments he discusses.
Thus, too, Auerbach missed the major point of literary concerns in contemporary biblical studies, namely the real question of textual integrity in self-contained or closed texts
like these. The question that remains for us, therefore, is
whether the literary lubricant provided by Auerbach will enable *us* to open wide the literary-critical door. Taking our
lead from narrativity and representation, we have to leave
behind the philological dimension of texts and turn to the
narrative dimension in order to see how we might arrive at
an affirmative answer to our remaining question.

In his *Literary Criticism of the New Testament*, William Beardslee answers the question "What is literary criticism?" in a manner that bridges the promise of Auerbach and the hope of Ricoeur:

> The approach of literary criticism is to accept the form of the work, and the reader's participation in the form, as an intrinsic part of entry into the imaginative world of the work....[Literary criticism's] primary thrust is on what the imaginative world of the work is.[33]

Here the stuck door is represented in the clause, "to accept the form of the work", for the condition of compositeness prevents us from opening the literary-critical door by disallowing our acceptance of the form of the work. Only when the form has been accepted can the reader, by participating in the form, enter into the imaginative world of the work-- wherein one can enjoy the second naivete.

The starting point of literary criticism, Beardslee says, is "to accept the form of the work". The form of the work is a holistic concept requiring us to start with the whole, rather than with the philological and form-critical parts. In principle, starting with the whole meets the condition of compositeness because the condition warns us that vast amounts, perhaps the majority, of textual verbiage is not the original creation of our authors. The authors are, to whatever degree, responsible for the whole. Therefore, to start with the whole makes sense, more sense than starting with parts that may have no authorially intentional function in the whole but be in it only because they were in the author's sources.[34] But the condition of compositeness also warns us that the form of the whole is itself literarily tainted by the composite condition of the text. Form critics grant textual wholeness--the texts have clear beginnings, middles, and endings--but they are exceedingly reluctant to speak about the forms of these textual wholes. The reasons for their reluctance are two-fold, literary-critical and literary-historical. In literary-critical terms, the texts are rather loosely-edited collections (*Sammlungen*) of sources and thus have the "form" of a collection. In literary-historical terms, however, this form belongs to no known category (*Gattung*; genre) of literary form.[35] Texts such as the Gospels, therefore, have a virtually formless form and belong to no literary genre. But form critics have not always been consistent in their discussion of textual form, especially in connection with the Gospels which in New Testament studies have been the principal locus of both methodological and theoretical literary reflection. Form critics predicate the notion of collection on the evidence for compositeness, but they also speak about the Gospels as *narratives* that represent the illusion of history or of biography.[36] That the Gospels possess a narrative form is of course exactly what a naive reading, primitive or second, discloses. Their form may be literarily inelegant because of compositeness and stylistic ineptitude, and it may belong to no known genre, but these detractions do not deny what even form critics have recognized--but have not examined in its own right--namely the narrative form of the Gospels. Similarly with the illusion of history. Concerned to show that the *representation* of history did not correspond to real history, the representation was labeled an illusion. But what from a historical perspective is a pejorative label is from a literary perspective positive, for the illusory representation comprises the imaginative world of the narrative. Thus our Gospels, for example, have a narrative form which can be accepted and an imaginative world into which one can enter. How? By participating in the form of the work.

Surely nothing can seem more strange and objectionable to the philological vision than the ideas of participating in the form of a work or of entering into its imaginative world. Yet, this is what a literary vision both requires and makes possible. In order to comply with the requirement and enjoy the possibility, we who are trained in the philological tradition have to look at our texts in a different way. Having been accustomed to looking at narrative texts as the efforts of authors to say things about things, we must first learn to distinguish between the authors who stand outside of the texts they have created and the *narrators* whose discourse is represented in the texts. Although authors are by definition responsible for the production of texts, what we as readers encounter upon reading a narrative text is philologically the grammatical and literarily the rhetorical voice of a narrator. The nature of the relationship between authors and narrators is, as Wayne Booth has shown, incredibly complex in its potential forms.[37] But literarily, that is, in terms of reading, the most important point is that we attend to the words of the narrator, bracketing questions of authorship as extrinsic to the reading of the text itself. Those questions are relevant for critical activities subsequent to reading but not for the open or naive reading which, like philological reading, must precede them. Be this as it may, placing ourselves as readers in the hands of a narrator is, as Wolfgang Iser has shown, no less complicated than distinguishing between authors and narrators.[38] In most literature we as readers are probably not the original readers whom authors (*sic*) had in mind in composing their texts. Nevertheless, because narrators speak to whoever attends to their words, we can put ourselves in the position of the implied readers, that is, of those to whom the narrator speaks. We can listen to what he says and respond with the ideas and images he evokes. Needless to say, if the text we are reading is in a foreign language or about foreignly past times, we shall need the philological information necessary for us to translate the original language into our own. By the same token, we shall also need to know besides the linguistic code of the text the cultural codes in which the story represented by the text is cast, e.g., the systems of social relations, values, and world views. Philology holds the code books on the basis of which our texts were both encoded and decoded, and by which alone decoding becomes a possibility for us. Our new criticism has to go beyond philology; but, it cannot do so without it.

A literary reading of a narrative text thus begins at the moment when we allow ourselves to be addressed by its textually immanent narrator. That is the first step. All others follow from it. For from that moment on we become participants not only in the form of the work but also in the formation of the work and of the imaginative world associated with it. We participate in the form of the work because, as one is addressed by the narrator until he ceases speaking, we are *with* the narrator both in the time of reading, the time when we allow ourselves to be addressed, and throughout the time of the story he tells. The process of narration, which is also the process of reading, takes place in one time and place, and the story the narrator tells takes place in another time and in another place. Usually almost immediately upon commencing his discourse the narrator shifts from the time of narration to story time, taking the reader with him on a veritable tour of a time past. But unlike real tour-guides who can point to things and scenes the tourist can see, the narrator shows and tells his reader things that the reader must construct imaginatively, thus making him a co-producer of both the narrative work and its world. Having begun in one time and place, the narrator lures the reader into other times and places by perspectively locating himself and the reader in the midst of the scenes and events he describes, enabling the reader to see, hear, and know things he would not have access to without the narrator's guiding voice. Through this device which literary critics call narrative point of view,[39] the reader becomes a participant in the narrative form, which is the processual form of narration. The form of the narrative work is predominantly temporal rather than spatial in character. The *text* is spatial and empirical but the *work* is temporal and, as a result of the work the narrator requires of the reader, imaginative.

The reader is therefore not merely a passive tourist who simply registers what he is told in relation to what he actually sees. Through what he tells and shows, both by commission

and by omission, the narrator evokes images as well as ideas
in the reader's imagination, requiring the reader to see, however determinately, characters and their actions, settings and
movements, and to feel with and about the actors, to make judgments about them and their motives, even to raise questions in
anticipation of answers expected as the narrative process continues to its end.[40] Throughout all of this, the reader's
imagination is controlled by what the narrator says and does
not say, making the act of reading both imaginative and controlled. It is through the control exerted by the narrator,
himself the puppet of an author, that the reader also becomes
a participant in the formation of the work and its imaginative
world. Indeed, we might go further and say that the reader,
by decoding the textual instructions provided by the author,
produces the work which consists of the imaginative world.
The reader's first creative act is the positing of the narrator whom he will follow—for a time.

It is clear, therefore, that as we have distinguished between authors and narrators so also must we distinguish between the text and the work. For a full appreciation of narrative it is necessary to recognize that *all* communications
require participatory work by receivers in order for there to
be any communication at all. In the final analysis the textual aspect of every communication consists of physical (graph-
ic, acoustic, or gestural) tokens which are social conventions
on the basis of which receivers, who know the conventions, complete the tokens and actualize or form the communication—the
work. A bare text is not a communication until it has been
processed by a receiver, who in the process of decoding textual signals produces the communicative work. In writing, for
example, the black spots on the pages comprising texts are con-
ventionally based but authorially-issued instructions requiring
readers to supply other things—words, sentences, ideas,
images, and feelings. A text thus consists, in Saussurian
terms, of encoded signifiers which we, knowing the code, complete by supplying the corresponding signifieds. In narrative
writing such signifieds will consist, for example, of the notion "narrator" when the text presents us at its beginning
with the codal signifier of the grammatical first person singular or with its implied equivalent in third person description. Similarly, to the black spots "and he said", when coming from the narrator's voice, we know on the basis of the
code to imagine someone other than the narrator. And when
that other voice speaks in the first person singular we know
that it is not the narrator's speech but reported direct discourse. So, too, with signals referring to actors and their
actions: the signals evoke more or less determinate images—
not merely ideas—of them.[41] And so on. The point is that
texts define work to be performed by readers and that through

the reader's efforts the literary work is produced.

This is, I dare say, a radical yet common-sensical depar-
ture from the philological way of viewing texts. Whereas the
philological way requires an objectification of the text, in
which the reader looks at it and translates it, the literary
way requires us to go beyond objectification first by recognizing the directorial role of the text vis-à-vis the reader,
and second by enjoining the reader to experience the literary
work from within--by producing it from, as it were, the textual
script. The text is an empirical object that requires the
reader to produce an imaginative object, the work. A literary
reading of a narrative thus differs from a philological reading
by attending also to other than linguistic and stylistic signals in the text. The final word on the integrity of biblical
texts and works will come only when all of the evidence is in
for both sets of signals. But from *prima facie* evidence for
narrative point of view, plot design, and the structural con-
sistency of narrative worlds, i.e., the psychological, sociological, temporal, and cosmic structures of the worlds represented by biblical texts, it would appear that these texts
have a much higher degree of integrity than the philological
method has perceived. In other words, the experience of biblical *works* offers new insights into the integrity of biblical
texts.

Having concentrated on the primacy of the work of reading
in a second naivete, it remains for us to consider the work of
criticism.[42] Although our reading, precisely because we have
read and critically analyzed biblical texts so often, is not
uninformed by criticism, a true participation in the form of
the literary work--one that attends to the textual signals and
follows the words of the narrator--will limit critical reflection by putting it off until the work has been completed.
That is a holistic requirement which we must discipline ourselves to obey. Some readings should intentionally be undertaken with such a restriction in order better to grasp the
unifying and world-shaping features of the author's text and
of the narrator's discourse. Criticism proper, on the other
hand, will, if intrinsic in focus, concentrate on the relationship between what we as readers have perceived as causal signals in the text and the responses or effects these signals
have triggered in us as readers. This criticism will have its
objectivity on the one hand in the textual signals--the encoded black spots on the page--and on the other hand in the
possibility of comparing the stimuli and responses we have experienced with those experienced by other readers and by other
critics. The same objectivity obtains in the case of extrinsic, comparative criticism when we compare and contrast experiences of several texts or of features in them.

In traditional biblical criticism we have proceeded from text criticism (establishing the text) to a philological-historical understanding of the text (translation in the fullest sense) to a consideration of that about which the text speaks (*Sachkritik*).[43] Besides the disintegrative distractions to which this critical procedure is subject, besides its tendency to treat segments of texts atomistically rather than holistically in their contexts, and besides its limiting external standpoint vis-à-vis the text, it, the philological approach, is semantically referential in its orientation. It is concerned with what words and sentences mean (philological semantics) and with the things that they referentially point to (*Sachkritik*). Historically, as Hans Frei has shown, this concern has led to the judging (criticizing) of biblical texts in terms of their value as evidence for the real world events to which they refer.[44] In the new criticism, however, referential real-world concerns will be postponed until the form of the work and the world of the narrative have been comprehended. The new criticism will follow Coleridge in asking for at least a temporary suspension of disbelief until the text has ended, until the narrator has ceased his discourse, and until the last work assigned to the reader by the author and by the narrator has been completed. In the hierarchy of traditional critical activities, the principal change to be brought about by a new literary criticism will consist of the insertion after philological criticism of *literary* criticism, indeed of a literary criticism that is predicated on a literary *reading*. Text criticism, philological criticism, and literary criticism comprise the intrinsic critical activities in the new hierarchy. All other critical activities, which are dependent upon intrinsic criticism, are extrinsic insofar as they deal with textual questions in relation to extra-textual matters—to other texts, to aspects or features of texts, to historical influences and circumstances attending the time of writing, to religious and theological matters, and to questions of truth or enduring meaning. Also dependent upon intrinsic criticism are the synthetic concerns expressed usually in connection with the word "history"—form history, literary history, stylistic history, religious and theological history, and so on.

The literary criticism of the second naivete will enable us children of criticism to go beyond criticism by means of a criticism that is no longer merely reductive but now also restorative. It is naive because it restores to the reading of biblical texts their narrative and poetic dimensions. It is critical because it only permits us to restore what the texts warrant. In its naivete the new criticism moves beyond philology to the phenomenology of reading. In its critical dimension it moves beyond philology toward textual and narrative semi-

otics--to the systems of signals and codes by which signification is possible and by which signification becomes communication. Taken together, these two aspects of the literary criticism of the second naivete comprise what can be called a phenomenological semiotics.[45]

NOTES

1. Paul Ricoeur, *The Symbolism of Evil* (Boston: Beacon Press, 1969), p. 350.

2. Ibid., p. 349.

3. William A. Beardslee, *Literary Criticism of the New Testament* (Philadelphia: Fortress Press, 1970). In the following discussion I shall refer to New Testament scholarship because it is that with which I am most familiar. In principle, however, my comments are equally applicable to Old Testament studies. The limitation of this transfer is in the area of poetry (verse), which plays a major role in the Old Testament and a minor role in the New. My focus is on narrative prose. I should also note that the present discussion has a different focus from my earlier reflections in *Literary Criticism for New Testament Critics* (Philadelphia: Fortress, 1978). There, my concern was with the role of literary criticism in the context of historical criticism. Here it is solely with literary criticism. Accordingly, my focus now is on the philological-literary aspect of the historical-critical tradition, and on the relationship between reading and criticism, neither of which were dealt with in my book, although the issues were latently there. Reflection on what I wrote earlier, and work on "'Point of View' in Mark's Narrative," *Semeia* 12 (1978): 97-121, have contributed to making the latent issues manifest.

4. Ricoeur, *The Symbolism of Evil*, p. 351.

5. On the pre-critical and critical stages of biblical studies see Hans Frei, *The Eclipse of Biblical Narrative: A Study in Eighteenth and Nineteenth Century Hermeneutics* (New Haven: Yale University Press, 1974), Werner G. Kümmel, *The New Testament: The History of the Investigation of its Problems*, trans. S. MacLean Gilmour and Howard Clark Kee (Nashville: Abingdon Press, 1970), Hans-Joachim Kraus, *Geschichte der historisch-kritischen Erforschung des Alten Testaments*, 2nd ed. (Neukirchen: Neukirchener Verlag, 1969), and Edgar Krentz, *The Historical-Critical Method* (Philadelphia: Fortress Press, 1975).

6. I think this revision is consistent with Ricoeur's position, but do not want to attribute it to him because in *The Symbolism of Evil* he was dealing with the hermeneutics of symbols, not with the literary analysis of narrative.

7. Besides the surveys of critical history listed in note 5, all of which refer to Schleiermacher's major philological as well as hermeneutical contribution, special mention should be made of a parallel contribution by one of Schleiermacher's students, the influential classicist Philip August Boeckh. His *Encyclopaedie und Methodologie der Philologischen Wissenschaften* (Leipzig, 1877, but from lectures begun in 1809; 2nd ed., Berlin: Teubner, 1886) is still a reference tool for classicists and many students of literature. Portions of the *Encyclopaedie* are translated in August Boeckh, *On Interpretation and Criticism*, trans. John Paul Pritchard (Norman: University of Oklahoma, 1968). See also F. D. E. Schleiermacher, "*The Hermeneutics:* Outline of the 1819 Lectures," trans. Jan Wojcik and Roland Haas, *New Literary History* 10 (1978): 1–16. F. D. E. Schleiermacher, *Hermeneutics: The Handwritten Manuscripts, AAR Texts and Translations*, was unavailable to me at the time of writing. For classical philology at the end of the nineteenth century, see Friedrich Blass, "Kritik und Hermeneutik," in Theodor Birt, *Kritik und Hermeneutik nebst Abriss des Antiken Buchwesens: Handbuch der klassischen Altertumswissenschaft* 1, 3, ed. I. von Müller and R. von Pöhlmann (Munich: Beck, 1913). Of broader interest for understanding philology, see William Dwight Whitney, "Philology," *Encyclopedia Britannica*, 11th ed., vol. 21, (1911): 414–430. A fine exposition of currently-practiced philological literary criticism in biblical studies is ch. 4, "Literary Criticism," in Robert M. Grant, *Historical Introduction to the New Testament* (New York: Harper and Row, 1963). Peter Szondi's "Introduction to Literary Hermeneutics," *New Literary History* 10 (1978): 17–29, contains a brief description of philological interpretation in the context of the history of literary interpretation. A critical perspective is offered by Hans Robert Jauss in "Literary History as a Challenge to Literary Theory [*Literaturwissenschaft*]," *New Literary History* 2 (1970): 7–37. See also Edward W. Said, *Beginnings, Intention and Method* (New York: Basic Books, 1975), especially ch. 4, "Beginning With a Text".

8. In addition to the references in notes 5 and 7, see René Wellek, "The Term and Concept of Literary Criticism," in his *Concepts of Criticism* (New Haven: Yale, 1963), pp. 21–36, "The Theory of Literary History," *Trauvaux du Cercle linguistique de Prague* 4 (1936), pp. 173–191, and René Wellek and Austin Warren, *Theory of Literature*, new revised ed. (New York: Harcourt, Brace and World, 1956), especially ch. 1, "Literature and Literary Study," ch. 4, "Literary Theory, Criticism, and History," and ch. 19, "Literary History". See also Leo Spitzer, *Linguistics and Literary History: Essays in Stylistics* (New York: Russell and Russell, 1962), for whom linguistics means philology, and the works of Erich Auerbach discussed

below. For criticism see the entries under Szondi and Jauss in note 7, both of which include further bibliography. In dividing literary concerns into literary-critical and literary-historical aspects, I am using terminology that is especially typical of philological-biblical studies. Further discussion of literary history, both older and current, is best found in the journal *New Literary History*, but particularly in the Symposium on the subject in vol. 2 (1970).

9. Klaus Koch, *The Growth of the Biblical Tradition: The Form-Critical Method*, trans. S. M. Cupitt (New York: Scribner's, 1969), p. 70. See, further, "Literary Criticism and Form Criticism," pp. 68-78, and in relation to it Leland Ryken, "Literary Criticism and the Bible: Some Fallacies," in Kenneth R. R. Gros Louis, *et al.*, *Literary Interpretations of Biblical Narratives* (Nashville: Abingdon, 1974), pp. 24-40.

10. Koch, *Growth of the Biblical Tradition*, p. 70.

11. Ibid., p. 69.

12. Ibid., p. 77.

13. See Petersen, *Literary Criticism for New Testament Critics*, ch. 1.

14. Because "form" and *Gattung* are often confused, it is important to remember that for Gunkel, Bultmann, and Dibelius "form" is an empirical category referring to the stylized linguistic composition of texts or of textual units, whereas *Gattung* is the ideal, i.e., classificatory type which comprehends like-formed units. Alternatively, *Gattung* is the general and "form" the particular. Also, *Gattungen*, not *Formen*, belong to equally typical sociological situations, *Sitze im Leben*. The latter are not concrete, historically-defined social moments, but rather typical kinds of situations to which correspond typical kinds of style and form. See especially: R. Bultmann, "Neues Testament. Einleitung 2" (review) *Theologische Rundschau* 17 (1914): 79-90; H. Gunkel and R. Bultmann, "Literaturgeschichte, Biblische," *Die Religion in Geschichte und Gegenwart*, 2nd ed. (1929), cols. 1675-1682; Bultmann, *The History of the Synoptic Tradition*, rev. ed., trans. John Marsh (New York: Harper and Row, 1963). The key element in the form-critical development of philological insight is the notion of style. For the nineteenth century "the style characterizes the man", that is, style was largely seen as the mode of individual expression. But by early in the twentieth century style was understood to be a cultural convention. Thus, Eduard Norden could speak of style in antiquity as a garment--"not the man himself"--that could be changed at will (*Die Antike Kunstprosa*,

2 vols., Leipzig and Berlin: Teubner, 1909, pp. 11-12). In
form criticism, however, the "man" recedes almost out of the
picture. M. Dibelius explicitly denied the connection between
style and the individual in popular writings and termed style
a "sociological product": "...the conception of 'style' is
not meant in the narrow sense which deals only with vocabulary
and construction. Rather under the word 'style' must be understood the whole way of speaking which, at least in the case of
popular writing, is determinative of its category ["Gattung"],
for the lowly people who use this style write according to laws
which are independent of the individual personality. Hence the
style characterizes the category [*Gattung*--note the parody of
"the style characterizes the man"]." See Dibelius, *From Tradition to Gospel*, trans. Bertram Lee Woolf (New York: Scribner's, 1935), p. 7, and pp. 1-8. Style and form are thus virtually synonymous, and both represent types of social expression in popular culture, although Dibelius does admit some authorial intent as well in continuing the paragraph just quoted:
"In certain circumstances also by taking account of the choice
of words, the construction of sentences, the wordiness or brevity, the nature of description, the introduction, and the pero-
ration, we may tell whether the purpose of the author is to
awaken interest or to make converts" (ibid., p. 7).

15. See, e.g., the essays of Erhardt Güttgemanns translated in *Semeia* 6 (1976), but also the essays representing a
variety of perspectives in almost every issue of that journal.

16. Robert Alter, "A Literary Approach to the Bible,"
Commentary 60 (1975): 70-77; the reference to compositeness is
on p. 73. Although Alter writes on the Jewish Bible, his essays are well worth reading by New Testament students. See
also: "Biblical Narrative," *Commentary* 61 (1976): 61-67;
"Character in the Bible," *Commentary* 66 (1978): 58-65; "Biblical Type-Scenes and the Uses of Convention," *Critical Inquiry*
5 (Winter, 1978): 355-368. Alter offers further bibliography.

17. Norden, *Antike Kunstprosa*, p. 1.

18. Franz Overbeck, *Über die Anfänge der patristischen
Literatur* (Darmstadt: Wissenschaftliche Buchgesellschaft,
1954; originally published in 1882). Cf. Norden, *Antike
Kunstprosa*, p. 479, and pp. 479-510, on the literature of
the New Testament.

19. Adolf Deissmann, *Light From the Ancient East*, trans.
L. R. M. Strachan (New York: Doran, 1927; originally published in 1908). Ch. 2 of this book is philological and ch.
3 is literary-historical; and, in the latter, Deissmann identifies his cause with Overbeck's (p. 147).

20. Karl Ludwig Schmidt, "Die Stellung der Evangelien in der allgemeinen Literaturgeschichte," in Hans Schmidt, ed., *Eucharisterion* (Göttingen: Vandenhoeck und Ruprecht, 1923), 2:50-134.

21. See, e.g., Dibelius, *From Tradition to Gospel*, p. 7 (quoting K. L. Schmidt), Bultmann, *History of the Synoptic Tradition*, p. 4, and the full introductions to each of these books.

22. In the first edition (1909) the essay was entitled "Bibelwissenschaft". In subsequent editions, material on critical activities is covered under "Bibelkritik", and "Bibelwissenschaft" represents the history of criticism. In all editions each article has separate Old and New Testament sections, often with parallel topics. In the first edition, (all under "Bibelwissenschaft") Gunkel and Baentsch were responsible for methodologically oriented sections on the OT, while Köhler covered the history of OT research. The NT section by A. Meyer, however, was structured around the history of research. In the second edition (1927) the essays on "Bibelkritik" were by Hans Schmidt (OT) and Martin Dibelius (NT); the essays in the third edition are by F. Baumgärtl (OT) and Erich Dinkler (NT).

23. In the first edition the "literary history" of Israel was covered by Gunkel under "Bibelwissenschaft". The articles on "Formen und Gattungen" in the third edition are by C. Kuhl (OT) and G. Bornkamm (NT).

24. "Philology and *Weltliteratur*," *The Centennial Review* 13 (1969); 4-5 (1-17). See also Auerbach's introduction to his *Literary Language and its Public in Late Latin Antiquity and in the Middle Ages*, trans. Ralph Mannheim (Bollingen Series 74; New York: Pantheon, 1965), pp. 5-24. It should be noted that the 1,000 years in the quotation is the result of the context of that essay. In *Literary Language* he refers to 3,000 years of literary history and includes biblical writings, as he does in *Mimesis*.

25. Erich Auerbach, *Mimesis: The Representation of Reality in Western Literature*, trans. W. R. Trask (Princeton: Princeton University, 1953).

26. On the distinction between author and narrator, see below. For the background of the distinction, see Wayne C. Booth, *The Rhetoric of Fiction* (Chicago: University of Chicago Press, 1961).

27. Auerbach, *Mimesis*, p. 46 (cf. pp. 45-49).

28. Auerbach was so aware of the perversions of historicism that it is hard to fault his own critical version of it. See especially the introduction to *Literary Language*. Also see Hayden White, "Historicism, History, and the Figurative Imagination," in White's *Tropics of Discourse* (Baltimore: Johns Hopkins, 1978), pp. 101-120.

29. The best and most comprehensive discussion of the categories of narrative criticism is in Seymour Chatman's *Story and Discourse-Narrative Structure in Fiction and Film* (Ithaca and London: Cornell University, 1978).

30. Auerbach, *Literary Language*, p. 149.

31. Auerbach, *Mimesis*, p. 17; see also ch. 2, on the New Testament.

32. Auerbach, *Literary Language*, p. 19 (cf. pp. 19-22).

33. Beardslee, *Literary Criticism of the New Testament*, p. 13.

34. That a unit in a text may have no authorially-intentional function, or that an author may not have a conscious investment in everything he writes, are consequences of the condition of compositeness which make much writing on "the Bible as literature" seem pre-critically naive--because the consequences are ignored. See, e.g., the contributions of K. R. R. Gros Louis in Gros Louis, *et al.*, *Literary Interpretations of Biblical Narratives*, and David Robertson, *The Old Testament and the Literary Critic* (Philadelphia: Fortress, 1977). A new literary criticism of the second naivete cannot treat the text as though it were something it is not.

35. See n. 14, above.

36. Bultmann uses the word "illusion" in *History of the Synoptic Tradition*, p. 1, and speaks of narrative as representation frequently in his discussion of the editing of the traditional material and the composition of the Gospels, (pp. 337-367; cf. pp. 368-374). See also Dibelius, *From Tradition to Gospel*, pp. 223-232: Mark's "aim was to narrate"; he transformed "the tradition into a narrative of Jesus' work", p. 223; "he was concerned with a description of would-be history", p. 224.

37. Booth, *The Rhetoric of Fiction*. See also Boris Uspensky, *The Poetics of Composition*, trans. V. Zavarin and S. Wittig (Berkeley: University of California, 1973), and my "'Point of View' in Mark's Narrative" for other references. In addi-

tion to them, see Chatman, *Story and Discourse*, pp. 147-262.

38. Wolfgang Iser, *The Act of Reading. A Theory of the Aesthetic Response* (Baltimore: Johns Hopkins, 1978); see index, s.v. "Reader", and *passim* for a development of the notion of reader and reading in this essay. See also Umberto Eco, *The Role of the Reader. Explorations in the Semiotics of Texts* (Bloomington: Indiana University, 1979).

39. See the references in note 37, above.

40. See especially Iser, *The Act of Reading*, and Uspensky, *The Poetics of Composition*.

41. The role of imagination in reading is evident when we see illustrations of stories or movies based on stories—and object to the characterization or casting because the visual rendering does not match what we imagined in reading. Actors also differ in their rendering of characters, as do directors in their "orchestration" of actors, actions, and settings. The relative indeterminacy of authorial directions allows the reader's imagination a degree of freedom in the shaping of the work and its narrative world.

42. See George Steiner, "'Critic'/'Reader'," *New Literary History* 10 (1979): 423-452 for a provocative discussion of the relationships between criticism and reading. The entire issue of this journal, an Anniversary Issue, is a useful representation of the current scene in literary criticism. See also Thomas Daniel Young, ed., *The New Criticism and After* (Charlottesville: University of Virginia, 1976).

43. See, e.g., Rudolf Bultmann, "Is Exegesis Without Presuppositions Possible," in Schubert M. Ogden, ed., *Existence and Faith* (New York: Meridian Books, 1960), pp. 289-296, and Otto Kaiser and Werner Kümmel, *Exegetical Method*, trans. E. V. N. Goetchius (New York: Seabury, 1967).

44. Hans Frei, *Eclipse of Biblical Narrative*.

45. I do not know whether "phenomenological semiotics" is a new coinage, but it does represent the approaches of the more phenomenological Wolfgang Iser in *The Act of Reading* and the more semiotic Boris Uspensky in *The Poetics of Composition*, which deals with the semiotics of point of view. The unity of these two critical orientations is traceable to Roman Jakobson and is evident in his *Main Trends in the Science of Language* (New York: Harper Torchbooks, 1974). The unity is further developed in Elmar Holenstein, *Roman Jakobson's Approach to Language: Phenomenological Structuralism*, trans. C. Schel-

bert and T. Schelbert (Bloomington: Indiana University, 1976).
See also Robert Detweiler, *Story, Sign, and Self. Phenomenology and Structuralism as Literary-Critical Methods* (Philadelphia: Fortress Press, 1978), and U. Eco, *The Role of the Reader*. I have preferred "semiotic" to "structuralism", as in Holenstein's title, in order to distinguish between text-centered
semiotics and the comparative concern for text-universals in
the tradition of Lévi-Straussian structuralism. In this sense,
I see literary semiotics as a development of intrinsic poetics
and structuralism as concerned with the grammar or logic of
universally human mental operations in relation to cultural
codes on the one hand and to texts (utterances) on the other.

PART II

A DISCIPLINE IN FERMENT

3

THE CONTOURS AND METHODS OF LITERARY CRITICISM

Edgar V. McKnight

Criticism should help a reader make sense of a text. But
today sense has to be made of the chaotic field of criticism
itself before criticism can be used. The lack of an established method of literary study which can bring about "assured
results" of the sort thought possible with the historical approach may be viewed negatively. But this situation is viewed
positively by a growing number of biblical scholars because it
presents the opportunity for the creation of approaches and interpretations which will match the needs of the contemporary
reader and critic.

The first part of this paper attempts to trace the contours of literary criticism in a way which will allow the location of biblical criticism within literary criticism. The
second part suggests some appropriate ways of approaching the
Bible as literature.

I. Literary Criticism

Contemporary literary criticism lacks a universally accepted set of principles and methods; nevertheless, there are
elements of literary study which are recognized by literary
critics, and there is a history of the different coordination
of these elements which may help the biblical critic arrive at
satisfying principles and methods.

THE COORDINATES OF A LITERARY WORK OF ART

A useful way of charting the pattern of criticism is outlined by M. H. Abrams in *The Mirror and the Lamp*. The history
and practice of criticism are illuminated in terms of the dominance of one of the four elements in the comprehensive situa-

tion of a work of art: the work, the artist, the universe imitated in the work, and the audience.[1]

For the classical age, the mimetic orientation was characteristic, Plato and Aristotle being the great exponents of poetry as imitation. Horace's dictum that "the poet's aim is either to profit or to please, or to blend in one the delightful and the useful", united the classical theory of rhetoric (rhetoric being distinguished from poetics in Aristotle) with literary criticism, and pragmatic theories became dominant up through most of the eighteenth century. With romanticism, expressive theories developed, and the literary work of art was seen as the expression of the thought and feeling of the poet or was defined in terms of the process of imagination which utilizes the images, thoughts, and feelings of the poet. Objective theories became dominant in the mid-twentieth century. The literary work became its own world which transcends the facts of composition, the imitated universe, the nature and character of the author, and the effect on the audience.[2]

The four elements form a dynamic system of criticism in which each of the elements is a variable coordinate differing in meaning and function "according to the critical theory in which it occurs, the method of reasoning which the theorist characteristically uses, and the explicit or implicit worldview of which these theories are an integral part".[3] The challenge and the opportunity for criticism today is that no one of the elements is dominant. There is no single pervasive worldview of which one theory could be an integral part and therefore which would be dominant in literary criticism. All of the elements whirl in combinations which defy simple systemization.

CRITICISM AND HISTORY

In the mid-twentieth century, the element of the comprehensive situation of a work of art which became dominant was the work itself, which was seen as transcending the other elements. Abrams, in fact, suggests that while theories centering upon the imitated universe, the audience, and the artist, explored the work of art in relation to those elements, the theories centering upon the work of art "will explain the work by considering it in isolation, as an autonomous whole, whose significance and value are determined without any reference beyond itself".[4]

The beginning of the movement in America which resulted in the dominance of objective theories of literary criticism was a protest of literary scholars to the negation or at least the containment of literary criticism by literary history. In his championing of a new criticism in the 1930s, R. S. Crane drew a sharp distinction between literary history and literary criticism. Literary criticism is understood by Crane as "any reasoned discourse concerning works of imaginative literature the statements in which are primarily statements about the works themselves and appropriate to their character as productions of art". The understanding with which criticism is concerned is not equivalent to "knowing *why* an author said what he said (in a genetic or historical sense)". Rather it is equivalent to "knowing *what* it is he is saying and his reasons for saying it (in the sense of its artistic rationale)".[5]

Crane was very negative in his evaluation of the contribution which literary history makes to literary criticism. He declared:

> If literary criticism is what we want, very
> little of 'the great body of purely genetic
> and historical investigations which have
> absorbed the energies of so many professors
> of literature and the results of which have
> formed the content of so many courses in
> our colleges and universities' is germane.[6]

As a fundamental prerequisite of criticism, literary history is boldly dismissed: "of literary history as such, in its distinctly genetic and narrative aspects, there is seldom need to take account".[7]

René Wellek in the 1940s said that theory, history, and criticism, "implicate each other so thoroughly" as to make one inconceivable without the others. But he also saw a type of literary history which would practically deny the need for genuine literary criticism. Such history sees itself as dealing with verifiable facts and using standards and criteria of the past. It does not need the opinions and judgments of contemporary critics. Such history or historical reconstruction comes to center on the intention of the author. "It is usually assumed that if we can ascertain this intention and can see that the author has fulfilled it, we can also dispose of the problem of criticism. The author has served a contemporary purpose and there is no need or even possibility of further criticizing his work."[8]

Crane, in 1957, after the victory of criticism and the dominance of the New Criticism, spoke of his own activities designed to bring about a new criticism as "rhetorical shock tactics" and lamented that the New Criticism not only revolted

"against the limitations of the older learning" but also
"against the very conception of intellectual method that gave
it its status as a learning".[9] Crane's belated hope might
give direction for the task of biblical critics who are stressing the need for genuine literary criticism of biblical texts:

> there was little reason, once the friends
> of criticism had got a hearing, why they
> should not help to reconstruct university
> literary studies in a spirit of conserva-
> tive reform: carrying on and reinvigorat-
> ing the philological and historical tradi-
> tion, and at the same time, and in this
> context, developing what that tradition
> had been relatively weak in--systematic
> training in the various modes of critical
> analysis and judgment.[10]

"A COMPASS FOR CRITICS"

René Wellek, in a 1963 response to attacks against the
New Criticism, strongly urged that the emphasis of New Criticism upon the literary work of art as "a verbal structure of
a certain coherence and wholeness" did not and could not be
conceived to mean "a denial of the relevance of historical information for the business of poetic interpretation".[11] But
how can we conceive of the literary work of art as related to
external factors such as history and society? Can we organize
the coordinates of literary study in a fashion to do justice
to the work while relating it to external "series"?

Paul Hernadi has provided just such a mapping of the literary field on the basis of his conviction that verbal elaboration is not to be accorded the sole, honored position in literature but that "literature as verbal art relies on the balanced
interplay of expressive intensity, representational coherence,
persuasive power, and verbal elaboration". The traditional coordinates of the comprehensive literary situation are organized
into a field with two axes, the rhetorical axis of communication of messages moving from author to reader and the mimetic
axis of representation moving from language to information.
Critics, then, are to take account of literary works as both
"utterances with potential appeal" and as "verbal signs representing worlds".[12]

The two axes must be defined in a dynamic way to allow for the multitude of actual changes which take place within and between various coordinates in the total literary situation. Along the axis of communication, texts respond to literary and non-literary challenges which in turn influence the reader's response to the text in his day and under his own circumstances. The axis of communication must be extended, then, so that the actual author may be seen against the background of the world as his source of conscious and unconscious motivation. The actual reader, on the other hand, is to be seen against the background of the world as his field of action—not merely purposive action. The mimetic axis of representation moving from language to information is not static, either, and must be extended in such a way that language systems are seen as different ways of utilizing the world as a "reservoir of (not only verbal) signs" and world views are seen as "typical results of employing (not only verbal) signs to represent".[13]

The rhetorical axis of communication includes the implied author and reader who are not unrelated to the actual author and reader. The implied author and reader may be related to the actual author and reader as *parole* (concrete language usage) is related to *langue* (potentiality of language). The authors implied by *The Comedy of Errors* and by *The Tempest*, for example, "are in a sense, fixed, concrete manifestations of the actual author whose permanently shifting potential of manifesting himself in literary works or otherwise was only partially realized between 1564 and 1616".[14] The readers implied by the two plays "are in turn two of many 'roles' which an actual reader may attempt to slip into for the length of time it takes for him to read one work or another".[15] Language is placed directly on the axis of communication through relating illocutionary acts (what we do *in* saying something) to the implied author and reader, and perlocutionary acts (what we do *by* saying something) to the actual author and reader.[16]

The axis of representation is also expanded. The expansion is accomplished by giving attention to different phases of verbal representation. Naming (utterable words or verbal signifiers), signifying (lexically definable meanings or concepts signified), evoking (perceivable characteristics or images evoked) and designating (mental referents or objects represented) are suggested as the phases of verbal representation. It is only by paying due attention to these different phases, Hernadi declares, that criticism can "do justice to the fact that literature's mimetic axis runs all the way from potential signs to representable worlds".[17]

The essential characteristic of literature, according to Hernadi, is the interaction between the rhetorical axis of communication and the mimetic axis of representation. There is a necessary interpenetration of aspects of the two axes: "Just as signs capable of containing information are necessary if one man's motivation is to turn into another man's action, language systems need users if they are to disclose and/or conceal views of the world." The relationship between the two axes is dynamic, for there is a "continuous making and remaking of language systems out of a world-wide reservoir of potential signs as well as the continuous matching and rematching of world views against the available totality of rival views of the world" which takes place in the "on-going processes of communication within (and between) individual speech communities".[18]

Since the key to the question of literature is the dynamic interaction between rhetorical and mimetic acts, "a text is literary to the extent that it invites and rewards the integrated study of the rhetorical acts of illocution and perlocution and the mimetic acts of naming, signifying, evoking, and design(at)ing associated with it".[19] A non-literary text, on the other hand, is one which does not invite and reward such integrated study. The non-literary text invites and rewards "the relatively independent exploration of one or more than one of its various rhetorical and mimetic aspects".[20]

HERMENEUTIC CRITICISM

Traditional literary criticism has stressed that criticism is "reasoned discourse" and "intellectual method". The direct sensory and imaginative appreciation of literary works has not been seen as criticism, although such appreciation is a necessary condition and an important consequence of criticism. The presupposition of traditional literary criticism as to the relationship of appreciation, enjoyment, and understanding to the critical task has been called into question by hermeneutics, which emphasizes that a text has meaning only in relation to its interpreter. The growth of the importance of "understanding" for criticism has implications for the autotelic view of the literary work of art.

Edgar Lohner reflects the new turn in criticism with the question: "How can a critic communicate, in terms that are universally valid, the result of an act of comprehension which can be realized only individually and subjectively?"[21] Lohner reconciles the claims for the autonomy of the literary work

with claims for the cognitive value of the work by a definition of the ontological status of a work of art which includes
the reader. He affirms that "the literary work of art exists
essentially within the triad of poet, work, and reader" and
that the literary work of art "forever remains essentially dependent upon its comprehension by a reader".[22] Because the
work of art involves the reader, criticism must ask about the
mind of the poet and of the reader and about the nature of the
act resulting in the literary work of art and the process of
understanding.

The criticism which includes the insights of poetics and
which may be seen as the proper heir of New Criticism is
termed "revisionist" or "hermeneutic" criticism by Geoffrey
Hartman. It is defined in terms of its major characteristic
of inclusiveness as contrasted with the exclusive tendency of
the New Criticism. In retrospect, Hartman says, the New Criticism's insistence on the autonomy of the literary work and
even the autonomy of criticism itself may be seen as the fu-
sion of a "peculiarly 'American' with a markedly 'English'
prejudice against mixing art with anything, especially with
philosophy".[23] The revisionists, in contrast to the New Criticism, throw open the doors to "foreign elements" imported
from across the Atlantic and from philosophy, theology, linguistics, sociology, and psychoanalysis. These revisionists
have a "methodological faith" that "thinking and writing,
criticism and literature, art and philosophy are creative
modes to be worked through in tandem or in concert".[24] The
genuinely difficult task foreseen by revisionism is the hermeneutic one: "to understand understanding through the detour
of the writing/reading experience".[25]

In forsaking the straight line (the "stigmatic approach")
and seeing the detour (the "wilderness full of ambivalent symbols and indirect signs")[26] as the appropriate hermeneutic
path, revisionism criticizes genealogical or historical reasoning and emphasizes the role of formal genres. This "Fourth
Kantian Critique" is seen as a chief issue in the revisionist
criticism. Hartman stresses two other recurrent issues involved in the hermeneutic detour, both of these having to do
with relationships between factors often separated in traditional literary criticism. The creative and critical, which
seem to be marginal to each other, are viewed as interdependent
and central in their relationship to hermeneutic criticism.
The relationship of interpretation both to the creative and
critical acts of writing and reading and to the will of the
writer and reader is also a central issue. "To an extent,"
Hartman declares, "what is involved is the right to one's own
tongue. We want to have our say despite or within authoritative pressures...."[27]

Structuralism is cited by Hartman as helping to provide the impetus for criticism to cross geographical and disciplinary lines. The structuralist view that linguistic elements are defined by syntagmatic and paradigmatic relationships, and the view of literature and other aspects of the human world as levels of language, provide the rationale for literary criticism to cross all previously determined limits. In hermeneutic criticism, structuralism is not taken as the means for a "supreme synthesis" or a "final knowledge" (although a first wave of literary structuralists saw in Saussure the hope for a solid scientific base for criticism). Structuralism, or structural semiotics (which sees language as only one semiotic system which must be considered along with others in providing a more inclusive semiotics) provides the basis for a "unified field" theory of criticism modeled on the human world in which meaning is finally human and is determined by the reader in relation to the text. The semiotic approach provides a proper place for the text as a statement of the literary past and for the contemporary reader-critic in the creation of meaning. The linguistic-literary competence of the author-reader-critic which is manifested in performance is taken with radical seriousness by structural semiotics.

Structuralism, then, has provided hermeneutic criticism the means of a "reversal of critical perspective" in which what have been considered as "facts" about literary texts are reformulated as "conventions of literature" or "operations of reading". Jonathan Culler calls this a "crucial reorientation" of literary criticism because it (1) relieves the reader-critic of finding some objective property which is unique to literature, (2) gives the reader-critic increased self-awareness and awareness of the way that meaning is produced in literature, (3) allows the reader-critic to see literature as involving various interpretive operations which open challenging and innovative texts to the process of literary reading and criticism, and (4) leads to the kind of interpretation in which the meaning of the work is what it shows the reader-critic about the problem of his condition as a maker and reader of signs.[28]

CONCLUSION

A map of contemporary literary criticism would include the traditional coordinates of a literary work of art but would expand and organize the coordinates into a dynamic field in which the world-wide reservoir of signs and any and all kinds and levels of meaning and meaning-effects impinging upon readers would be involved. The experience, repertoire, and competence (or symbolic capacity) of the reader-critic determines the conceptualization of the field, and each of these is changing. The linguistic-literary competence is evolving through the historical experience of the reader-critic; the repertoire (or specific elements effective within each of the major systems of the field) depends upon both the competence and historical experience of the reader-critic; and the possibility of historical experience depends in part upon the competence and repertoire of the reader-critic.

II. Biblical Criticism

A literary approach to the Bible may be seen as growing logically out of the recent history of biblical criticism. This section shows how literary criticism may be grafted onto historical study and suggests some goals and methods of biblical literary criticism.

A NEW SITUATION IN BIBLICAL CRITICISM

The critical method of Bible study which arose in the eighteenth century was concerned with knowledge and understanding which could be authenticated by the presuppositions and methods of the Enlightenment. A rationalism influencing Christian as well as non-Christian scholars, along with the revolutionary discoveries of geology and Darwinian evolutionary ideas, influenced the development of the historical-critical method. Today, however, the historical confidence or "historicism" which sees the locus of meaning in history is no longer dominant. The historical method and results authenticated by an earlier epoch are not being authenticated in the same way. In addition, historical study of the biblical text has come to see the necessity of genuine literary criticism to complete the historical task. The narratives telling the story of Israel and the early Christian movement have been treated as historical accounts of the events they depict, as collections of traditions reflecting the history of the communities that originated and transmitted them, and as documents which reflect the period in which they were composed. Redaction criticism is concerned with studying the theological motivation of an author as this is revealed in the use of traditional material to compose new material and new forms. In 1976 Norman Perrin declared that conventional redaction criticism was not an adequate method because "it defines the literary activity of the Evangelist too narrowly". The full range of literary activity of the author is missed, not to speak of the injustice done "to the text of the Gospel as a coherent text with its own internal dynamics".[29] Historical criticism needs literary criticism to complete its task. But such criticism is changing the historical approach which gave it birth.

Bultmann's Existential Approach

Long before contemporary developments in redaction criticism, Rudolf Bultmann had approached literary criticism in his use of existential categories to interpret the New Testament. Bultmann began not with traditional literary principles and methods but with poetics, the way that the mind creates story. This sort of approach was set in motion for Bultmann by Hans Jonas who saw the mind as symbolistic, interpreting itself in objective formula and symbols. Since the mind takes a detour by the symbol, the original phenomena hidden in the symbolic camouflage can be reached only through a long procedure of working back to the demythologized consciousness. Although the categories of Heidegger are used to explicate what Bultmann sees as the genuine subject matter of the New Testament, it is in the work of Jonas that a justification and procedure for demythologizing was found.[30]

A literary approach that would attempt to relate itself to the efforts of Bultmann (and to the New Hermeneutic which continued his efforts) must see the limitations of Bultmann's approach. Bultmann's program of scientific investigation which conveys some intellectual content is not inclusive enough to embrace the full range of literary meanings and language functions. The biblical text may *refer* to human existence, but there are functions alongside the referential (or cognitive)--emotive, conative, poetic, phatic, and meta-lingual (to use the categories of Jakobson). The full range of literary criticism and meanings which can be obtained through literary approaches must be appreciated by the biblical critic who would utilize literary criticism.

Bultmann's early attempt to utilize poetics in interpretation should be applauded, but Bultmann's appropriation of Heidegger's existential categories and his wish to emphasize real understanding as arising from the possibilities of human being which are revealed in a work caused Bultmann to overlook some of the possibilities of poetics. Biblical literary criticism will make an important gain in relating itself to contemporary studies in poetics. An approach which unites the creative and critical by relating writing to reading and both of these to interpretation need not begin by defending the Bible as literature on the basis of historical, descriptive criteria. Literary criticism of the Bible may begin with the fact that we can read biblical texts as literature and then see what creative and critical operations are involved in such literary reading.

The multiple value and meaning of myth and other narrative material must be appreciated by the modern biblical critic. Even when theological reflection influences the study of myth, Bultmann's reduction of meaning to existential terms may be questioned today. It is possible, or even necessary, that readers will find in myth realities which can not be expressed completely in logical statements. John F. Hayward finds contemporary value in myth. He suggests that modern man cannot accept the world in which there is no meaning except the "transitory 'meaning' fleetingly bestowed on selected moments by individuals" and he is not satisfied with the transcendence model of "autonomous, scientific man providing successfully, over the passage of time, for his own well-being". Modern man needs myth to speak of his experience of a dynamic process which is "at least as complex and rich in texture as man himself, plus much more which in its ultimate transcendence man knows nothing of".[31]

READING THE BIBLE AS LITERATURE

The reorientation of the critical task whereby the reader-critic is seen as inextricably involved with the text in the creation of meaning gives criticism a new perspective on traditional questions such as "what is literature?" and "what are the aims of literature?" This new orientation is important for rapprochement of critical approaches to the Bible. Literature is what we read as literature, so instead of attempting to define the Bible as literature according to the descriptive and historical criteria, we read the Bible as literature. The aims of the Bible as literature and the purpose of biblical criticism will also be defined in terms of the reader-critic--in community as well as individually, of course. Biblical literature and criticism, then, will not be foreign in any area of the human world. Reading the Bible as literature expands the context from the original context (it does not exclude the original context) into a larger context as broad as the life of man.

Literary Approaches to the Bible

Different and even apparently mutually exclusive approaches to the text are integrated and unified by the reader-critic. Nevertheless, the division of approaches suggested in the history of criticism may be helpful for analysis of the complementary contributions offered by the different approaches.

One group of approaches involves what have been the major concerns of biblical scholars, such as the study of the cultural and historical situations in which the biblical literature developed, the search for sources of biblical materials, and the retrieval of the earliest forms of individual stories. These approaches provide "background information" from the perspective of traditional literary criticism. Such background information will not be viewed as "causes" of the biblical text but as setting the background and perimeters for the meaning of the text. If the critic is determined to think of "causes", he will treat the cultural and historical "background" and the literary-aesthetic "background" as mutually related "causes".

A second group of approaches (forming what Wellek consigns to extrinsic study) seeks to gain some information (in part from the biblical text itself) which can then be applied to the biblical writings. In biographical study, for example, analysis is made of the way that the life of the writer influences his creative works. In historical study, the attempt is made to show how narratives reflect and comment on the social, political, religious, and economic circumstances of the writing.

A third group of approaches attempts the study of biblical texts as "worlds of their own" apart from any extrinsic concerns. Two different types must be distinguished in the study of the Bible as well as in literary criticism in general. One type actually does bring different kinds of knowledge to bear on biblical literature: psychoanalysis, Marxism, existentialism, and myth criticism (appealing to cultural anthropology and the work of Carl Jung). Another type tries to study biblical literature primarily as an aesthetic fact and gives attention to formal poetic devices. The structural tradition going back to the Russian formalists and the Czechoslovak structuralists contains numerous examples of analyses which purport to deal with the grammatical and literary structures of the text independently of outside information. The remarks which Wellek applies to the New Critics who have tried to study the text primarily as an aesthetic fact applies as well to those in the structural tradition: "Even when in appearance

they are inspecting mainly what seem to be poetic devices,...
they aim at a discussion of the general value, coherence, and
maturity of a work of art--values which are human and social."[32]

The concept of literary criticism as involving a dynamic
field or system in which the reader makes sense through the
coordination of the various elements in accord with his own
competence, repertoire, and experience dissolves whatever divisions exist from a historical descriptive perspective: background study *versus* literary criticism as well as extrinsic
criticism *versus* intrinsic criticism.

History and Historical Study in Literary Study of the Bible

An inclusive system of literary criticism does not limit
meanings to those involving the original author and reader,
but it does not deny the legitimacy of attention to the original situation. Attention to the original situation of communication does not abolish the work as literature if the total
range of meaning and meaning-effects impinging upon the author
and reader is considered and if these meanings are not held to
apply only in the original situation. Biblical critics, then,
have the challenge of integrating the various approaches in
such a way as to utilize the vast resources of historical
criticism.

The biblical critic, trained as an historian, might find
it most satisfying and appropriate to continue to use the historical model, giving attention to the original situation of
the text but expanding the concept of "meaning of the text" to
include the totality of meanings and meaning-effects--not just
conscious--which impinge upon man. As biblical scholars integrate the literary approaches they find satisfying in order to
understand and appreciate the original situation more fully,
they will begin to see that the text may move beyond its original situation, that the text may be read as literature in a
fuller way. Study of the motivation of the actual author will
assist in the study of the attitudes and perspectives of the
"implied author". Study of the effect of a work on actual
readers of the text might give assistance in the study of the
moods and insights conveyed to the "implied reader". The
original situation and the history of the interpretation of
the text will be useful for the direction it gives to the
movement of the text to various areas of the world of the
contemporary reader.[33]

The realities to which the reader refers the text, and,
therefore, his literary approaches, will vary. Ideology (Marx-

ism, structuralism, historicism, liberation theology, etc.)
may play a part in the choice of the theory of meaning and the
method to be considered. Serious systematic interest in areas
such as psychology, sociology, ethics, politics, and linguistics will affect the choice. The "practical" uses to which
criticism is to be put will be influential. Whatever the
area or level of meaning and meaning-effect, it may be presupposed that the different meanings and meaning-effects will
be homologous and a multi-faceted literary study will result.
As a multiplicity of meanings--not only conscious--were involved in the original creation, so may a variety of meanings
be discovered and created by the contemporary reader.

Biblical critics are discovering that it is possible to
make sense out of literary criticism, to develop literary approaches to biblical texts which, while not completely objective and scientific, are orderly and rational. The literary
approaches dissolve the distance between the ancient texts and
the modern reader-critic and allow consideration of the multiplicity of meanings and meaning-effects which impinge upon the
modern reader. Such approaches may be found to be satisfying
today because they do not depend upon an unacceptable historicism for justification, yet they allow for integration and
utilization of the rich resources of the historical-critical
tradition.

NOTES

1. M. H. Abrams, *The Mirror and the Lamp: Romantic Theory and the Critical Tradition* (New York: W. W. Norton, 1958). A principal concern of Abrams is the reorientation of criticism taking place in the expressive or romantic theory which compares the mind to "a radiant projector which makes a contribution to the object it receives" instead of to "a reflector of external objects" (p. vi).

2. Ibid., pp. 8-29.

3. Ibid., p. 7.

4. Ibid.

5. R. S. Crane, *The Idea of the Humanities and Other Essays: Critical and Historical* (Chicago and London: The University of Chicago Press, 1967), pp. 11, 16.

6. Ibid., p. 17.

7. Ibid., pp. 17-18.

8. René Wellek and Austin Warren, *Theory of Literature* (New York: Harcourt, Brace and Company, 1942), pp. 30, 33.

9. Crane, *The Idea of the Humanities*, p. 26.

10. Ibid., pp. 26 27.

11. René Wellek, *Concepts of Criticism*, edited and with an Introduction by Stephen G. Nichols, Jr. (New York and London: Yale University Press, 1963), p. 7.

12. Paul Hernadi, "Literary Theory: A Compass for Critics," *Critical Inquiry* 3 (Winter, 1976): 380, n. 20; 369. Comparable charts are to be found in Abrams, *The Mirror and the Lamp*, p. 6 and Roman Jakobson, "Closing Statement: Linguistics and Poetics," *Style in Language*, ed. Thomas A. Sebeok (Cambridge, Mass.: M.I.T. Press, 1960), pp. 353, 357. John Dominic Crossan proposes a field with structural and historical axes in his "Perspectives and Method in Contemporary Biblical Criticism," *Biblical Research* 22 (1977): 45.

13. Hernadi, "Literary Theory," p. 373.

14. Ibid., p. 371.

15. Ibid.

16. Ibid.

17. Ibid., p. 379.

18. Ibid., pp. 373, 379.

19. Ibid., p. 380.

20. Ibid.

21. Edgar Lohner, "The Intrinsic Method: Some Reconsiderations," in *The Disciplines of Criticism; Essays in Literary Theory, Interpretation, and History*, edited by Peter Demetz, Thomas Greene, and Lowry Nelson, Jr. (New Haven and London: Yale University Press, 1968), p. 170.

22. Ibid., pp. 170, 168.

23. Geoffrey Hartman, "Literary Criticism and Its Discontents," *Critical Inquiry* 3 (Winter, 1976): 213.

24. Ibid., p. 214.

25. Ibid., pp. 213, 214, 216.

26. Ibid., p. 216.

27. Ibid., pp. 216, 217.

28. Jonathan Culler, *Structuralist Poetics: Structural Linguistics and the Study of Literature* (London: Routledge and Kegan Paul), pp. 128-130.

29. Norman Perrin, "The Interpretation of the Gospel of Mark," *Interpretation* 30 (April, 1976): 120.

30. James M. Robinson, "Hermeneutics Since Barth," *The New Hermeneutic*, vol. 2 of *New Frontiers in Theology* (New York: Harper, 1964), pp. 34-37. See also Edgar V. McKnight, *Meaning in Texts: The Historical Shaping of a Narrative Hermeneutics* (Philadelphia: Fortress Press, 1978), pp. 70-71.

31. John F. Hayward, "The Uses of Myth in an Age of Science," in *New Theology No. 7*, edited by Martin E. Marty and Dean Peerman (New York: Macmillan, 1970), pp. 70-71, 73.

32. Wellek, *Concepts of Criticism*, p. 309.

33. See Hernadi, "Literary Theory: A Compass," pp. 383-384. Caesare Segre shows the vital relationship between history and interpretation from a structuralist perspective in "Narrative Structures and Literary History," *Critical Inquiry* 3 (Winter, 1976): 271-279. Since the literary message is a "transmission of states of mind, of ideals, and of judgments about the world" as well as a linguistic communication, there are codes of custom, society, and conceptions of the world as well as the code language. "For this reason, the line that conjoins writer and reader is an historical one....If the reader belongs to another age [than that of the writer] he must...complete a series of acts of synchronization and of control which imply a model of historization" (p. 273).

4

PRINCIPLES FOR MORPHOLOGICAL CRITICISM:
WITH SPECIAL REFERENCE TO LETTER FORM

Martin J. Buss

The central task of the present study is to outline
principles for the appropriate study of form. Illustrations
will be derived for the most part from the form or structure
of letters, which furnish convenient examples for several theses to be presented. It will be natural to refer to the writings of Paul, toward an understanding of which the honoree has
contributed in a major way.

First, a word about terminology. The term "form criticism" is difficult to use for several reasons. One lies in
the fact that it has developed three rather distinct meanings:
a systematic or historical study of genres (*Gattungsforschung*
or *Gattungsgeschichte*); a reconstruction of oral tradition
with attention to genres (for some, *Formgeschichte*); and the
examination of a text as it stands (*Formkritik*, according to
Wolfgang Richter).[1] Furthermore, the term is not one used in
ordinary conversation or in writing outside of biblical
studies, so that it does not have the benefit of protection
and clarification by frequent usage. Most seriously, en-
deavors designated by that phrase have often been based on
the view that there is a firm conjunction between linguistic
form, content, and recurring circumstances in oral expression;[2] closely connected with this outlook is a belief that
genres recognized in a given society are clearly separated
from one another. What label shall one use for a study of
forms if these assumptions are not accepted?

An alternative possibility can be found in the term
"morphology", derived from the Greek *morphē* (roughly equivalent to the Latin *forma*). This designation is current in a
number of disciplines; after all, forms appear in many contexts.

In biology, the word "morphology" refers to the shape and
arrangement of organisms or of their parts, examined with attention to the development, functions, and types of such forms.
In geology, it describes rock and land formations, viewed in
relation to the processes which cause their appearance. In

linguistics, it designates inflected word forms, with their use and meaning. In the field of history, "morphological" theories have attempted to combine a holistic treatment of data with a view of organic development, including growth and dissolution.[3] In economics, structural anthropology, and the study of religion, the term has been applied to patterns present in a given culture and subject to classification for comparison with those of other cultures.[4] In theology the same word was employed by E. Stauffer, W. Elert, and E. Schlink for the structure of human existence and expression in relation to God, with attention to verbal genres as embodying dimensions of life and thought.[5]

The expression "morphology" has been used fairly widely in the field of literature, especially--although not only--in regard to genres. Already F. Schleiermacher spoke of the "morphology" of a genre, referring to common features of comparable works. Later, R. G. Moulton presented for biblical and other literature a morphological treatment of the existing text as an "inquiry into the foundation forms of literature", in a manner not unlike Gunkel's. A. Jolles described under such a rubric the general character of basic forms (legend, riddle, etc.) in an insightful manner. R. Wellek and A. Warren used the word to designate the study of genres and of their history. More generally, "morphology" has been employed in Russian and German investigations of fundamental processes and structures of expression (in the 1920s by B. Eichenbaum, H. Pongs, V. Propp, and thereafter by G. Müller). This approach, as an aspect of interpretation, is given a notable place by the Italian E. Betti for the recognition of recurring or "lawful" patterns, including those of major genres.[6]

A distinct advantage, then, of the word "morphology" is its use in many fields, ranging from the physical sciences to the humanities and theology. In fact, the word is often employed to express such a continuity.[7]

Closely connected with this is a further advantage, namely that the term lends itself to an avoidance of an Aristotelian contrast between essence and accidents, as well as of a split between content and (external) form--oppositions which in the past have become associated with the word "form", but which are both problematic now. In medieval Latin, *forma* was used to translate the Greek *eidos*, employed by Aristotle for the essential pattern of an object which is expressed in a definition.[8] The problem with Aristotle's conception lies in a failure to see clearly enough that no one characteristic is necessarily more basic than another. For instance, a rubber ball can be described either as a ball which is, furthermore, made of rubber or as a piece of rubber which is, also, round.

The primacy of one or another characteristic depends on one's purpose, habit, or terminology and is not given--one may hold --in the nature of the object itself. A rejection of objective essence is important for post-Aristotelian nominalism. Extreme nominalism also denies that any form--generality or structure--exists apart from a mind which conceives it. In such a view, form is external, representing an appearance, while true reality itself is individual.[9] In regard to literature, this outlook stresses that genres are conventions which each society can shape as it wishes.

Neither the Aristotelian nor the nominalist perspective is adequate for any of the sciences. Instead, one can envision and recognize a variety of forms interacting with each other. As expressed by Myron S. Allen, "morphology stresses the finding of all possible relationships".[10] A distinction between "deep" and "surface" structure--made in different ways by a number of current theorists must be viewed as relative to a given consideration. Yet relationships can be truly discovered and are not merely imposed by the mind, for the mind is a part of nature. Often they may be described in terms of statistical correlations which can be connected with logically coherent patterns.[11]

If the usage of the term "form criticism" can be purged of certain philosophical and historical assumptions, that phrase may continue to be a convenient one in biblical studies. If not, one may need to adopt another, such as "morphology".[12] Perhaps the expression "the study of forms" can serve as a simple and neutral designation. In any case--whatever term is used--central principles appropriate for such an investigation can be set forth in the following seven theses.

1. *Genres, as they appear in history, are not cleanly divided from one another.* In letter writing, for instance, there is a continuity between private and public letters. As is well-known, A. Deissmann distinguished between "true" or "real" letters, directed to a particular recipient in a certain situation, and epistles which are "literary" in the sense that they are designed for repeated use; writings standing intermediate between these he regarded as "bad letters".[13] In reality, however, all writing participates in both particularity and generality, even though in different degrees and in divergent ways. The medium range between the two poles represents by no means an anomaly, but may furnish some of the very finest expressions. Certainly, it is proper to make distinctions; indeed, in the Hebrew Bible, a difference between a private letter (which may even lead to the death of a bearer who does not realize its content)[14] and an "open letter", in-

tended for circulation (Neh. 6:5-7), is known. Nevertheless, one can usually observe numerous gradations between types and there is no special virtue in standing at one extreme or the other. Furthermore, in most instances, contrasts are not "original", but become sharper over time. For instance, some of the earliest letters known to us, from Greece to China, contain general exhortations and warnings, so that a division between letter and treatise is at that time fluid.[15]

2. *Genres stand within a larger system, within which they are often complementary to one another.* As a society grows in size and complexity, an increasing number of recognized types of expression arise, each with a more or less peculiar function. In Hebrew literature, a distinction was made between priestly transmission of older revelation, with fundamental general directions for life, and prophetic mediation of fresh revelation, relevant especially for particular occasions and showing their relation to the general will of God. These two dimensions together were, in turn, distinguished from a more natural insight, known as Wisdom. The three major aspects were enshrined in the three parts of the Hebrew canon. Similarly, the letters of the New Testament play a complementary role in relation to the Gospels. To a large extent, Christian tradition regarded the Gospel materials (which, like the Pentateuch, include both narrative and ethical words) as fundamental; the letter writers did not seek to replace these, but--like prophecy--directed themselves more especially to particular circumstances, and--like Wisdom--included their own reflection as a subsidiary source of insight. As has already been noted, however, the various differentiations are not altogether sharp. Thus, Paul treated specific issues at such a basic and theoretical level that his writings were worthy of being shared and preserved, as was true of the messages of the great Israelite prophets.

3. *Generic divisions cut across one another, so that they form a multidimensional pattern.* This pattern can be described in terms of a series of distinctions. For instance, a letter can convey a reproof,[16] a warning,[17] or an expression of appreciation and even love,[18] as well as many kinds of information, commands, and requests. These elements of content or thrust form a multidimensional array, reflecting such considerations as emotional tone (positive or negative) and the relative status of sender and addressee. In relation to such factors, the distinction between a written letter and an oral message furnishes an additional contrast independent of, and thus overlapping, the others. Types are then best arranged not hi-

erarchically, with separate subtypes, but in an intersecting fashion.[19]

A corollary of this thesis is that genres cannot be distinguished sharply from other forms. It is true that certain kinds of patterns are often called "genres", while others are not; but, such a division is a matter of tradition and convenience, not one that is adequately justifiable in theory.[20] Indeed, usage of the term "genre" differs widely; it covers such disparate categories as "poetry", "hymn", and "letter". The proper solution to this diversity lies not in creating a definition which one may hope will be accepted by all users, but in recognizing that the classification system for which one chooses to employ that word is only one of several that are possible. For the discussion of the present paper, it would make very little difference if the word "form" is everywhere substituted for "genre".

4. *Genres exhibit various degrees of flexibility, so that their patterns should normally be described in terms of probabilities rather than of rigid standards*. Letter styles form an excellent illustration for this thesis. The flexibility of epistolary forms--despite their formulaic character --has been frequently noted. Thus, in regard to ancient Greek letter style, F. Exler remarks that "so great is the variety in detail, that hardly any two forms are quite alike", and J. White appropriately states that a certain kind of letter "prefers" a given form, or uses it "often" or "sometimes".[21] Variable tendencies, indeed, are a hallmark of most styles and perhaps of all.[22] A major reason for such variability is the fact that a particular expression is affected by a large number of considerations. For instance, a given letter may exhibit the following characteristics: it may be an angry one, written to a brother who is a priest, and concerned with financial matters. Each of the elements mentioned--in addition to others, such as the prior history of the persons involved-- contributes to the form of the expression. Another reason for variety lies in the freedom permitted by tradition or taken by the author. In generic patterns, a high degree of correlation between two features implies a strong press toward regularity in this respect, one which takes precedence over other factors. There is no reason, however, why more moderate tendencies should not operate as well, with allowance for other considerations.

5. *Genres are related to human situations*. This thesis has a negative aspect, namely, a denial of the view that genres

are tightly connected with spatial or temporal settings, for
genres vary greatly in the degree to which they are associated with external occasions. Some expressions are virtually confined to a certain time or place; but others, including
letters, have no such constraint and for many forms (such as
hymns or folk songs) there are preferred, but by no means man-
datory, settings. Often an organization with which a genre is
associated is secondary in relation to the literary form; thus
the post office was created to facilitate the transmission of
letters. Someone who delivers a letter privately is not devi-
ating from an "original" practice, just as someone who sleeps
on the floor does not (secondarily) "imitate" what is now often done on a raised bed. Rather, what is primary is the in-
timate connection of a genre with a human process, such as
communication or rest. This assertion is the positive side
of the present thesis. In the case of letters, the "epistolary situation" is that of physical--and sometimes emotional--
distance, the effect of which the writer seeks to overcome or
at least to mitigate.[23] Writing is employed in this case not
primarily to insure permanence, but to extend the range of a
word which would be given orally if that were possible or convenient.

The specific situation addressed by a document can usually be deduced from the data of the text, especially with the
aid of comparative materials. In part this is so because there
is an inner or logical connection between what is said and what
the speaker seeks to accomplish in a situation presupposed.
Furthermore, a written work is as a rule relatively self-contained, in order to avoid ambiguity for its use in a different
time and place. Some ancient, archaeologically discovered letters lie on the border between written and oral messages; certain items, often even the name of the addressee or sender, are
left to be supplied by the carrier. The letters of biblical
literature, however, all provide the relevant information.
Thus they specify the kind of person who writes or for whom
the message is intended. Some of them describe their address-
ees in quite general terms, with an indication of the condition
in which they are situated; others are more narrowly-focused.
Here it is important to note that, as often in biblical literature, an individual figure stands for others with the same or
similar task or role. Titus and Timothy are pastors; Peter and
others represent apostolic authority.[24] In later times, hand-
books for letter writing headed their samples with descriptions
of the type of situation involved, such as: "Letter to a
Friend in Favour of Another", "To a friend, upon a report of
an unfaithfull dealing", or "From a Young Tradesman to Whole-
sale Dealers, with an Order".[25] Historical and form criticism
have in the past sometimes overemphasized precise circumstances
to an extent not needed for understanding a text and not war-

ranted by its data. More important for interpretation is a
recognition of sociopsychological or anthropological questions
concerning the dynamics of existence.

     6. *As human situations change, genres develop with them.*
Some aspects of human life, it is true, are well-nigh universal, being to a large extent grounded biologically; genres associated with these accordingly evidence relatively little
change over centuries and even millennia. Thus, modern love
poetry is still remarkably like that of the Song of Songs, expressing both the joy of being together and sorrow over absence. Other human experiences, however, are affected much
more deeply by variable conditions. In particular, as social
complexity grows--with an increase in the size of effective
communities--a paradoxical phenomenon occurs. On the one
hand, communication extends to a larger number of persons; on
the other hand, contact with a particular partner who moves to
another area or position in society becomes weaker. The use
of writing, such as in letters, both furthers this development
and becomes desirable in the new circumstances. By facilitat-
ing empire formation, writing contributes to stratification
and social tensions; but the same means was also used to
counteract these tendencies through laws and expressions of
protest. The overcoming of distance in letters exhibits at
once the positive and the negative sides of this condition;
that shows itself in their content,[26] which repeatedly includes a concern with persecution and similar problems.[27] The
limited use of letters in the Hebrew Bible and their heavy use
in the New Testament can thus be seen as connected with important social developments. Christianity, for instance, can
hardly be understood without reference to the existence of an
empire, which creates profound alienation for many groups and
at the same time provides for the easy spread of a faith.
Christianity in part made use of a new genre relevant to such
a political situation: apocalyptic, which expresses a universal perspective and embodies hope in a transcendent salvation
as ordinary social fulfillment becomes impossible for many.
The New Testament's letter style and its strongly eschatological faith are, then related.[28]

     7. *Generic structures are not merely a matter of conven-*
tion, but exhibit a rationale which allows one to recognize
certain elements as appropriate in relation to others. The
format of letters furnishes a number of relevant examples.
Thus, a written communication from one person to another requires, in most instances, an identification of the sender
and of the addressee. The precise phrasing and location of
such data can be largely a matter of convention, but even

these aspects are not entirely arbitrary, for some forms or positions are much more useful than others. A natural place for that information is at the beginning of a letter, since it needs to be known immediately, although the sender's name may be given at the end (also easily noticed) in a gesture of politeness.[29] Furthermore, an initial, or final, greeting cultivates the relationship upon which the letter is based.[30] Especially effective in this regard is word of appreciation for the addressee.[31] That such expressions are not a meaningless formality is supported by the observation that they can be omitted for a number of reasons, including (momentary) anger.[32] Indeed, the nature of greetings is generally closely attuned to the relationship between the parties.[33]

Although the body of a letter can be devoted to a large variety of themes, some topics stand out as especially appropriate for letters. These include the mention of a previous message by either of the parties; such a reference is natural, since a letter is half of a dialogue, according to one of the oldest preserved comments on epistolary style.[34] Similarly, a discussion of past or future travel is relevant to the epistolary situation of physical distance, either in regard to its cause or as a means to abolish it.[35] Inquiries and assurances concerning health and welfare form not only a standard greeting but may constitute a significant element of the communication, for this topic is of major concern in one's relation to an absent friend.[36] Finally, insofar as a letter is designed to reach from a particular person to a specific audience, it is fitting that the personal character of the writer is revealed in the content.[37]

Significant features of letters have been outlined in ancient and modern guides to such writing. To some extent, these guides furnish an introduction to conventions. Much more importantly, however, they seek to point to what is fitting and effective. When they present classical examples, that is done for the most part for the purpose of illustrating commendable characteristics. Modern scholarship can add to these traditional notices a comparison with phenomena in other cultural contexts, in order to establish general and thus possibly integral connections.

If positions or expressions of the Bible are to play a normative role for readers and not merely to function as curiosities, they need to be seen as appropriate in the situations to which they are directed. Such a recognition involves an element of rationality--as has been argued also by William A. Beardslee.[38] Insight into the human significance of the Bible, then, does not stand outside of scholarship, as an afterthought; instead, it lies at the heart of the study of form.

NOTES

1. Wolfgang Richter, *Exegese als Literaturwissenschaft* (Göttingen: Vandenhoeck and Ruprecht, 1971), p. 79; similarly, in part, Gene M. Tucker, *Form Criticism of the Old Testament* (Philadelphia: Fortress Press, 1971).

2. Especially sharply stated by Albrecht Alt, *Essays on Old Testament History and Religion*, trans. R. A. Wilson (Oxford: Blackwell, 1966), p. 87.

3. The most notable historical theory with this name is that of Oswald Spengler, *Der Untergang des Abendlandes: Umrisse einer Morphologie der Weltgeschichte*, vol. 1: *Gestalt und Wirklichkeit* (Munich: C. H. Beck, 1918). In anthropology an outlook close to Spengler's was developed by Leo Frobenius, followed in part by Adolf E. Jensen, *Myth and Cult Among Primitive Peoples* (Chicago: University of Chicago Press, 1963), pp. vii-viii. Such combinations of holistic treatment with the theme of organic change are not, in my opinion, altogether successful. Somewhat differently, Maurice Halbwachs, *Morphologie sociale*, 2nd ed. (Paris: A. Colin, 1946), describes the geographical and biological conditions of social life, in part following earlier French scholarship.

4. Karl Menger, *Grundzüge einer Klassifikation der Wissenschaften* (Jena: G. Fischer, 1899), p. 13 (if one wishes to ground intellectual movements in economic developments, one can find support in the fact that the modern contrast between morphology and historicism was first formulated by K. Menger, who also criticized unfettered capitalism); A. R. Radcliffe-Brown, *A Natural Science of Society* (Glencoe, Illinois: Free Press, 1957), p. 56; P. Chantepie de la Saussaye, *Lehrbuch der Religionsgeschichte*, 3rd ed. (Tübingen: J. C. B. Mohr, 1905), p. 7; Mircea Eliade, *Patterns in Comparative Religion*, trans. R. Sheed (New York: Sheed and Ward, 1958), p. 410, and "Spirit, Light, and Seed," *History of Religions* 11 (August, 1971): 1. Similarly, a contrast between morphology and the genetic dimension is made by Alfred North Whitehead, *Process and Reality* (New York: Macmillan Co., 1929), pp. 334-35, and Hans-Jürgen Hermisson, *Studien zur israelitischen Spruchweisheit* (Neukirchen: Neukirchener Verlag, 1968), p. 34.

5. E. Stauffer, *Grundbegriffe einer Morphologie des neutestamentlichen Denkens* (Gütersloh: C. Bertelsmann, 1929), e.g., pp. 14-16 on the relation of style and thought in genres; Werner Elert, *Morphologie des Luthertums*, 2 vols. (Munich: C. H. Beck, 1931-32); Edmund Schlink, *Der Mensch*

in der Verkündigung der Kirche (Munich: C. Kaiser, 1936), e.g., pp. 20-28, 99, and "Die Struktur der dogmatischen Aussage als oekumenisches Problem," *Kerygma und Dogma* 3 (1957): 251-306 (e.g., p. 299). Schlink presented a fairly sharp criticism of national socialism at a time when that was not easy (*Der Mensch*, pp. 3, 16-17); this observation is relevant here, since the topic of form (*Gestalt*, etc.) was also pursued by Nazis (see, e.g., Klaus W. Hempfer, *Gattungstheorie* [Munich: Wilhelm Fink, 1973], p. 80).

6. Friedrich Schleiermacher, *Hermeneutik*, ed. H. Kimmerle (Heidelberg: Carl Winter, 1959), p. 148; Richard G. Moulton, *The Literary Study of the Bible*, 2nd ed. (Boston: D. C. Heath & Co., 1899), pp. v, ix; André Jolles, *Einfache Formen* (Halle: M. Niemeyer, 1930), p. 1 (this work has repeatedly inspired biblical form criticism); René Wellek and Austin Warren, *Theory of Literature* (New York: Harcourt, Brace & Co., 1949), p. 273; on Boris Eichenbaum, Vladimir Propp, and others, see Viktor Erlich, *Russian Formalism* ('s-Gravenhage: Mouton & Co., 1955), pp. 145, 208, 217; Hermann Pongs, *Das Bild in der Dichtung*, vol. 1: *Versuch einer Morphologie der metaphorischen Formen* (Marburg: N. G. Elwert, 1927); Günther Müller, *Morphologische Poetik: Gesammelte Aufsätze* (Tübingen: Max Niemeyer, 1968), pp. 146-246 (cf. pp. 3-45 for a genre study); Emilio Betti, *Allgemeine Auslegungslehre als Methodik der Geisteswissenschaften* (Tübingen: J. C. B. Mohr, 1967), pp. 213, 341, 419 (for morphology Betti also uses the term *technisch*, derived from the Greek *technē*, "rules of art").

7. An inspiration for stressing the continuity between fields by means of the word "morphology" was furnished by the poet Goethe, who was interested in biology, color, and other regularities. See, e.g., Horst Oppel, *Morphologische Literaturwissenschaft: Goethes Ansicht und Methode* (Mainz: Kirchheim & Co., 1947).

8. E.g., *Metaphysics*, V, 2 (1013a); *Posterior Analytics*, II, 3 (91a); II, 10 (93b).

9. A divorce between content and form proceeded in the theories of G. Agricola (1494-1555) and P. Ramus (1515-1572), with strong individualistic overtones; see, e.g., Walter Ong, *Ramus: Method and the Decay of Dialogue: From the Art of Discourse to the Art of Reason* (New York: Octagon Books, 1974, reprinted from the 1958 edition), pp. 102 (leaving only stylistic elocution for rhetoric), 203, 290. It is probably not accidental that a major work by the nominalist logician Nelson Goodman is entitled *The Structure of Appearance* (Indianapolis: Bobbs-Merrill, 1951). Goodman's work, however, sets forth a quite moderate form of nominalism (called "realistic") which

conceives fundamental individuals as qualities rather than as particulars; a radical nominalism would probably be untenable.

10. Myron S. Allen, *Morphological Creativity* (Englewood Cliffs, New Jersey: Prentice-Hall, 1962), p. 35.

11. For a comprehensive view, see M. Buss, "Understanding Communication," in *Encounter with the Text*, ed. M. Buss (Philadelphia: Fortress Press, 1979), pp. 3-44.

12. I chose the term for *The Prophetic Word of Hosea: A Morphological Study* (Berlin: A. Töpelmann, 1969) in order to express both a continuity with, and a differentiation from, the established tradition of form criticism emanating from H. Gunkel. Since then, the same word has been used, with a narrower range of meaning, by some other biblical scholars. Rolf Knierim, "Old Testament Form Criticism Reconsidered," *Interpretation* 27 (October, 1973): 435-68, e.g., p. 456, employed "morphology" for the linguistic side of a genre. In John Collins, "Towards a Morphology of a Genre," *Semeia* 14 (1979): 1-20, it designates the recurring features, primarily of content, of a genre which is defined in terms of these.

13. Adolf Deissmann, *Bible Studies*, trans. A. Grieve (Edinburgh: T. & T. Clark, 1901), pp. 26, 37 (following Franz Overbeck), 43-44; *Light From the Ancient East*, trans. L. Strachan, 2nd ed. (New York: G. Doran, 1927), pp. 230, 234.

14. 2 Samuel 11:14-17. This motif appears elsewhere in ancient literature, presumably reflecting an assumption either of a low degree of literacy on the part of the bearer or of a protective envelope for the letter (fairly widely used), or both.

15. Adolf Erman, *The Literature of the Ancient Egyptians*, trans. A. Blackman (New York: Benjamin Blom, 1971, reissued from the 1927 edition), p. 205. On the fluidity between private and public productions in antiquity, see, e.g., Hermann Peter, *Der Brief in der römischen Litteratur* (Leipzig: B. G. Teubner, 1901), p. 10; Paul Wendland, *Die urchristlichen Literaturformen* (Tübingen: J. C. B. Mohr, 1912), pp. 344-46; Wilhelm von Christ, *Geschichte der griechischen Literatur*, 6th ed., vol. 2 (Munich: C. H. Beck, 1920), pp. 53-54, 825-26. In China, literary and open letters are very old (since the turn of the era; cf. *Brockhaus Enzyklopädie*, 1967 ed., s.v. "Brief").

16. E.g., Erman, *Egyptians*, p. 203; Jeremiah 29:26-28; Isocrates, Letter 2 (to Philip, I).

17. See, e.g., C. Roetzel, "The Judgment Form in Paul's Letters," *Journal of Biblical Literature* 88 (September, 1969): 305-12; Yigael Yadin, *Bar-Kokhba* (New York: Random House, 1971), pp. 125-28, 137.

18. For pre-Christian Greek and eighth-century Chinese examples, see Christ, *Geschichte*, p. 825, and S. Obata, *The Works of Li-Po* (New York: Dutton, 1922), pp. 151-53.

19. Multiple classification is recognized in the *Excerpta Rhetorica* (appendix on "De epistolis"); William G. Doty, "The Classification of Epistolary Literature," *Catholic Biblical Quarterly* 31 (April, 1969): 197-98; and, in other fields, by Fritz Zwicky, *Morphological Astronomy* (Berlin: Springer Verlag, 1957), pp. 14, 20, and Thomas Munro, *Form and Style in the Arts: An Introduction to Aesthetic Morphology* (Cleveland: Press of Case Western Reserve University, 1970), p. 261.

20. William G. Doty, *Letters in Primitive Christianity* (Philadelphia: Fortress Press, 1973), p. 53, wants to use the word "form" only for small elements, out of which genres are constituted. However, this usage involves problems both in theory and in practice. For instance, thanksgiving can be treated either as a subsidiary element of letters or as a genre which utilizes various expressions; greetings occur in an oral context as well as in letters. Thus, the relative primacy of such forms depends on the particular purpose for which they are viewed.

21. Francis Xavier J. Exler, *The Form of the Ancient Greek Letter of the Epistolary Papyri* (Chicago: Ares Publishers, 1976), p. 133; John L. White, "Epistolary Formulas and Cliches in Greek Papyrus Letters," *Society of Biblical Literature: 1978 Seminar Papers*, ed. Paul J. Achtemeier (Missoula: Scholars Press, 1978), 2:291-92, 312.

22. For flexibility in Near Eastern letters, see, e.g., Edmond Sollberger, *The Business and Administrative Correspondence Under the Kings of Ur* (Locust Valley, New York: J. J. Augustin, 1966), p. 2; Sally W. Ahl, *Epistolary Texts From Ugarit* (Ph.D. diss. Brandeis University, 1973), p. 104. More generally, Pongs, *Morphologie*, p. vii, stressed a combination of law and freedom. Similarly, Everett C. Olson and Robert L. Miller, *Morphological Integration* (Chicago: University of Chicago Press, 1958), pp. 57-83, 268, considered probabilistic "covariance" to be central for form. According to the analysis of Buss, *Hosea*, pp. 61-64, a relative--not absolute--difference obtains between speech in which Yahweh appears in the first person and other statements by the prophet.

23. An extensive discussion of this "letter situation" has been presented by Heikki Koskenniemi, *Studien zur Idee und Phraseologie des griechischen Briefes bis 400 n. Chr.* (Helsinki: Suomalaisen Kirjallisuuden Kirjapaino, 1956). On the overcoming of emotional distance, cf. the letters cited by Adolf Deissmann, *Light*, pp. 188, 192.

24. In Leviticus, instructions given through Moses, the archetypal figure for law, specify those to whom they apply: Aaron (the high priest), Aaron and his sons (i.e., priests), or the people in general. Similarly, psalms for nonclerical individuals are frequently attributed to David. Already Moulton, *Literary Study*, pp. 266-67, pointed out, in a nuanced manner, how modes of address and the contents of what is discussed indicate the situation to which New Testament letters are addressed.

25. P. S. de la Serre, *The Secretary in Fashion*, trans. J. Massinger (London: G. Emerson, 1640), p. 56; anonymous, *A Speedie Post.* (London: W. Sheares, 1625), letter 1; anonymous, *The Letter Writer, or, The Art of Correspondence* (Richmong, Virginia: J. W. Randolph, 1863), p. 7. Among many others, and using the word "situation", cf. William H. Butterfield, *How to Use Letters in College Public Relations* (New York: Harper & Brothers, 1944), p. 144.

26. The content of ancient Near Eastern letters is largely economic, administrative, political, and military; a major category of Greek private correspondence is that of soldiers' letters. In the Hebrew Bible, the majority of recorded or reported letters are by or, in a few cases, to royalty (2 Sam. 11:15; 1 Kg. 21:9-10; 2 Kg. 5:6; 10:2-3, 6; 19:10-13; 20:12; 2 Chr. 2:10-15; 21:12-15; 30:1, 6-9; Ezra 4:11-16, 17-22; 5: 7-17; 7:12-26; Neh. 2:7; Est. 1:22; 3:13; 8:10--some of these perhaps should be classed, like Ezra 1:2-4, as decrees only; but, the distinction is fluid); the rest are similarly political (Jer. 29; Neh. 6:6-7, 17-19; Est. 9:20). Archaeologically discovered Hebrew letters are predominantly administrative, often military, in character; see now Dennis Pardee, *Handbook of Ancient Hebrew Letters* (Missoula, Montana: Scholars Press, 1980). Cultural growth and political expansion as correlates of letter writing have been noted also by Peter, *Brief*, p. 13, and Doty, *Letters*, p. 6.

27. Persecution forms a major theme of ancient Jewish letters (in some from Elephantine and in Ezra, Esther, and Maccabees). Some of Paul's letters were written in prison, a condition from which important modern statements by Dietrich Bonhoeffer (especially on 3 August, 1944) and Martin Luther King, Jr. ("Letter from the Birmingham City Jail", 16 April,

1963) have emanated as well. Exile as a topic or as a situation also occurs frequently (cf. Jer. 29; *Encyclopaedia Judaica*, 1971, s.v. "Letters and Letter Writers", p. 60, referring to communications by Jewish exiles; Herbert A. Giles, *Gems of Chinese Literature*, 2nd ed. [Shanghai: Kelly & Walsh, 1922], p. 80, presenting a letter from the first century B.C.E. exile).

28. In somewhat different--phenomenological--grounds, Klaus Berger, "Apostelbrief und apostolische Rede," *Zeitschrift für die neutestamentliche Wissenschaft* 65 (1974): 207-17, argues that the "genres" of letter, testament, and apocalyptic should not be too sharply separated.

29. In Near Eastern and Greek tradition, both sender and addressee are identified at the beginning, but with a tendency (not a rigid one!) toward placing first the name of the one with higher rank (Robert H. Pfeiffer, "Assyrian Epistolary Formulae," *Journal of the American Oriental Society* 43 [1923]: 26-27; White, "Formulas," pp. 291-93).

30. Various steps toward a "captatio benevolentiae", i.e., to gain an addressee's favorable attention, have been recommended for both oral presentations (Heinrich Lausberg, *Handbuch der literarischen Rhetorik* [Munich: Max Hueber, 1960], p. 277), and letters (Charles Homer Haskins, *Studies in Mediaeval Culture* [Oxford: Clarendon Press, 1929], p. 3).

31. Praise for the recipient appears in the following cases, among others: a letter by an Egyptian priest (Erman, *Egyptians*, p. 200); Sumerian petitions (e.g., James B. Pritchard, ed., *Ancient Near Eastern Texts Relating to the Old Testament*, 3rd ed. [Princeton, New Jersey: Princeton University Press, 1969], p. 382; Plato's seventh letter (the genuineness of which is disputed); Isocrates' letters 5, 7, 8; the Letter of Aristeas; Seneca, *Ad Luciliam epistulae morales*, Nos. 2, 4, 5, 13, 34, 47; New Testament letters; Josephus, *Life*, 365-66 (quoting king Agrippa); later Jewish letters (*Encyclopaedia Judaica*, vol. 11, 1971, cols. 57-58; Franz Kobler, *Letters of Jews Through the Ages* [New York: East and West Library, 1952], pp. 135, 141, 204, 450, 465, 532, 607); an eighth-century Chinese one to a potential patron (Cyril Birch, ed., *Anthology of Chinese Literature* [New York: Grove Press, 1965], p. 233); and more recent Western letters (George Saintsbury, *A Letter Book* [London: G. Bell and Sons, 1922], pp. 123, 141, as advised also by Lillian E. Watson, *Standard Book of Letter Writing and Correct Social Forms*, 2nd ed. [Englewood Cliffs, New Jersey: Prentice-Hall, 1958], p. 30).

32. No praise occurs at the beginnings of Galatians and 2 Corinthians--letters that are fairly critical in tone. Well-wishing is omitted in "sarcastic letters" (Pfeiffer, "Assyrian", p. 27; cf. A. Leo Oppenheim, *Letters from Mesopotamia* [Chicago: University of Chicago Press, 1967], p. 170). There are also other reasons for the lack of a greeting, such as a need for brevity (especially on ostraca) and, it appears, a major difference in rank.

33. As noted by Paul Schubert, *Form and Function of the Pauline Thanksgiving* (Berlin: A. Töpelmann, 1939), pp. 181-3; Otto Kaiser, "Zum Formular der in Ugarit gefundenen Briefe," *Zeitschrift des Deutschen Palästina-Vereins* 86 (1970): 22. For instance, in the ancient Near East a wish for divine blessing often reflected a relatively personal relation, such as between actual or fictive relatives (as noted by Ahl, *Ugarit*, p. 53), and also was especially common--understandably!--when one of the parties had a cultic role or belonged to a priestly family (as observed by Pfeiffer, "Assyrian", p. 34). This distribution is probably related to the usage of the New Testament.

34. Artemon, quoted by Demetrius, *On Style*, par. 223 (perhaps ca. 300 B.C.E.). References to previous messages are very numerous; cf., e.g., Oppenheim, *Mesopotamia*, pp. 96, 103, 135, 137; Lachish ostraca 3, 4, 5, 6 (Pritchard, *Texts*, p. 322); Epicurus to Pythocles (according to Diogenes Laertius, *Lives of Eminent Philosophers*, X, 84); 1 Corinthians 5:9; 7:1.

35. Cf. Plato's letters 3, 7, 11; New Testament epistles (Robert W. Funk, *Language, Hermeneutic, and Word of God* [New York: Harper & Row, 1966], pp. 265-67; and letters from other areas and times (Obata, *Li Po*, pp. 151, 153; Birch, *Chinese*, p. 219; Kobler, *Letters of Jews*, p. 322; Saintsbury, *Letter Book*, pp. 117, 240.

36. Cf. Erman, *Egyptians*, p. 201; Pritchard, *Texts*, p. 490; Joseph A. Fitzmyer, *A Wandering Aramean* (Missoula, Montana: Scholars Press, 1979), pp. 219-26; 1 Maccabees 12:22; 2 Corinthians 1:8-11; 1 Timothy 5:23; 3 John 2; Arthur Waley, *Translations from the Chinese*, 2nd ed. (New York: A. Knopf, 1941), p. 218. To ask about the other's welfare was also standard for an oral meeting (André Lemaire, *Inscriptions hébraiques*, vol. 1: *Les Ostraca* [Paris: Editions du Cerf, 1977], p. 180).

37. As stressed already by Demetrius, *On Style*, par. 227. Personal characteristics and relations are strongly expressed in Paul's letters.

38. William A. Beardslee, "Natural Theology and Realized Eschatology," *Journal of Religion* 39 (July, 1959): 157-58, speaking of "fragments of knowledge". Similarly, for Susanne K. Langer, *Philosophy in a New Key* (Cambridge: Harvard University Press, 1942), p. 238, the "morphology" of feelings, revealed in music, includes their "rationale". Understanding in theology does not rule out paradox, for paradox is appropriate in relation to the ultimate.

5

A MULTIDIMENSIONAL CRITICISM OF THE GOSPELS

Charles T. Davis

The Gospels are an intriguing complexity of language.
An originally oral announcement of God's actions and advent,
after a period of oral transmission, found expression in literary form as four canonical Gospels. Only a multidimensional
literary criticism, sensitive to the dynamics of both the
spoken and the written word of a pre-print culture, can eluci-
date its complexities. Criticism must be prepared to confront
the Gospels as sacred drama and as Canon, taking seriously the
special character of these works as a testimony to the experience of Mystery. Their language challenges the critic to
probe the interrelationships of word to silence, of meaning
to presence, of what is revealed to what is hidden, and ultimately, of his own life to Spirit. This inquiry will explore
the contours of such a multidimensional criticism.

I. HISTORICAL-LITERARY CRITICISM

The appearance of historical criticism was a major
achievement of Christian culture. The philosophic-scientific
proposition that every truth is to be doubted affirms, in
secular form, the monastic experience of the relativity of all
human action and knowledge. The scientific historical criticism that embodied this truth burst upon the Church as a creative explosion whose reverberations are still being felt. The
Reformation and the recovery of an older, more historical order of Christian experience represented in the New Testament
and the first five hundred years of the Church were both the
emerging method's first-fruits and a powerful stimulus to its
further development and refinement. The Medieval Era's dogmatic criticism and superficial historicism were destined to
fall. Men could no longer tolerate a view of history which
sacrificed this world, all human action, and even reason itself to the judgment of the Church. Into deep darkness fall
those who follow only the transcendent. Historical criticism
restored the light of the immanent.

Historical-literary criticism has, however, a darker side. It abandoned the transcendent, failing to realize that those who follow only the immanent fall into darkness too. Historical criticism became, in the hands of the Deists, a weapon against all revealed religion. Building upon this tradition, the French and German Philosophers of Enlightenment employed historical criticism in the fight to oust the "ancient regime" of Church, Pope, and King. The quest for an historical Jesus, the great moral teacher, emerged from behind the NT to challenge the Christ of revelation and Scripture.[1] From Reimarus to Morton Smith, we have witnessed a succession of books reconstructing pictures of Jesus which are manifestly contradictory, yet which share the common purpose of reducing the Christ of the Gospels to a merely mortal teacher. Albert Camus read at least one of historicism's meta-historical intentions well:

> During the two centuries which prepare the way for the upheavals, both revolutionary and sacrilegious, of the eighteenth century, all the efforts of the freethinkers are bent on making Christ an innocent, or a simpleton, so as to annex Him to the world of man,....Thus the ground will be prepared for the great offensive against a hostile heaven.[2]

René Wellek and Austin Warren correctly observe that although historical-literary criticism "may merely attempt to interpret literature in the light of its social context and its antecedents, in most cases it becomes a 'causal' explanation, professing to account for literature, to explain it, and finally to reduce it to its origins".[3] Such a reduction serves to vindicate and to defend the intellectual-political program of the eighteenth century Enlightenment. Only a purely human teacher could vindicate its claim that for seventeen hundred years evil priests had ruled despotically in the name of a Christ Pantocrator of the Church's own fabrication. The "myth" of Enlightenment was thus secured by an unhistorical view of the Christian era.[4] The "imagined" historical Jesus created by Reimarus continues to be a showcase achievement of this methodology of secularism.

Literary criticism must, despite these excesses of the past, continue to utilize historical criticism, but it must cease to absolutize the method. It must allow historical criticism to shed the light of critical doubt on its own meta-historical foundations. With Albert Outler, we can today see signals "of the fading of the special set of cultural presuppositions of the Enlightenment that guided the first pioneers in what has since come to be 'the critical tradition'". Out-

ler is certainly correct in saying: "It is in this new *post-*
Enlightenment context that we must now try to redefine the
present *status quaestionis* of the study of the gospels."[5]

II. INTRINSIC LITERARY CRITICISM

Correctly understood, historical-literary criticism is
an extrinsic criticism properly concerned with understanding
literature by references to its setting, its environment, and
the external forces acting upon it. Its value in preparing
the critic for a study of literary questions is indubitable,
but it is secondary to our main task. To identify biblical
literary exegesis almost solely with a reconstruction of the
history of Christianity, redactors, and/or the *Sitz im Leben
Jesu* is to lose sight of the character of the Gospels as a
text governed by the interplay of rhythm, form, symbolism,
and dramatic presentation. Most of all, it does violence to
the aesthetic mode of language and to the transcendent dimension of reality. It holds to the immanent while letting the
transcendent go. It absolutizes reason and propositional
thought at the expense of vision, intuition, and imagination.[6]
It is thus implicitly hostile to myth, poetry, memory, and all
other genres rooted in the presentational mode of expression.

As literary critics, we must hold to the critical way of
immanence, but we must hold as well to the affirmative way of
transcendence. The beginning of Reality is the Word.[7] Historical questions must eventually give precedence to the
claims of language as the literary critic does justice to its
structures of rhythm, organization, symbol, and world-creating
vision. We shall consider each of these structures in turn.

Rhythm. Rhythm is the musicality of language ranging
from the suppressed and carefully-regulated intervals of scientific prose to the wild, impassioned bursts of lyrical poetry. It is also, to use Stephen Crites's phrase, an aesthetic
reproduction of "the pulse and density of personal time".[8]
The rudimentary musicality of life is aesthetically heightened
in literary activity. Its presence is a reflection of the linguistic structure of Reality. Rhythm--the alternation of silence and sound, activity and passivity, light and dark--is an
intrinsic structure of life and language.[9] This dimension of
the text is thus a major concern for the literary critic.

Organization. Biblical critics have generally been aware
of the importance of formal structure; although they have perhaps been too rigid and analytical in interpreting this dimen-

sion of language. George Kennedy is correctly skeptical of
the prevailing scholastic attempt to bring all Gospels under
a single genre, thought to have been created by Mark, noting
"that there are many examples of classical literature that
conform to no established genre...".[10]

Kennedy is certainly correct in observing that "a gospel
writer's purpose is not literary....If one asks how a gospel
is formulated, however, the answer would seem to be, by proclaiming it (keryssein)...."[11] An essentially oral word has,
as a result of events threatening its existence, been committed to writing. The convergence of oral and written word
in the Gospels suggests that we, perhaps, do best to regard
them as stories seeking to make present the sacred drama of
the acts of God which have produced the new creation. These
acts are the true basis of Christian experience.[12]

The story as a genre exists in oral and written language
and in Jewish, Greek, Roman, and virtually every other culture. It is appropriate to the gospel. Luke declares clearly his intentions to write a narrative in proper order of all
things surrounding the creative acts of God witnessed by the
apostles, the eyewitnesses and the ministers of the Word (1:
1-4).

Stephen Crites has reminded us of the narrative nature
of human experience and offered us two distinctions that are
relevant both to the interpretation of structures in the Gospels and to the interpretation of symbols. The mythopoetic
dimension of the Gospels is what Crites calls the "sacred
story". Such a story is unspeakable. It is subliminal; "for
the sacred story does not transpire within a conscious world.
It forms the very consciousness that projects a total world
horizon, and therefore informs the intentions by which actions
are projected into that world."[13] These stories "orient the
life of people through time, their lifetime, their individual
and corporate experience and their sense of style, to the
great power that established the reality of their world".[14]
This is the invisible reality of the drama of man's confrontation with the Sacred, the Mysterious, the Unnameable Reality.

Crites calls upon us to distinguish the sacred story from
"all stories directly seen or heard".[15] These concrete stories
with their objectifying of the Unnameable through images,
words, scenes, roles, and other narrative devices are but a
human response to the sacred story. They are valiant, but ultimately futile, attempts to articulate the Sacred within the
mundane world. For this reason, they are called "mundane
stories". For this reason too, they will not let us go. Four
Gospels were needed to witness to the one true gospel. Like

all genuine stories, the Gospels have spawned "centuries of interpretation, philosophical, theological, allegorical, psychological, social-class, new critical, structuralist, whatnot".[16] We are called upon again and again to seek to overcome the partiality of our perception and to try once more like Jacob to secure the angel's blessing. Stories call us into the wholeness of a transcendental experience of Reality. Like all true, religious symbols, they must shatter and propel us thereby into the Silence, into the Presence that is Reality.

Symbol. The ultimate incommensurability of the sacred story and the mundane stories is reflected in the symbolic dimensions of literary texts. Symbols, as Tillich reminds us, are concrete objects, but they can make present invisible realities as well. Indeed, religious symbols "are a representation of that which is unconditionally beyond the conceptual sphere."[17]

Historical-literary criticism can illuminate some aspects of cultural symbols. The history of religion has rendered a valuable, but as yet largely unnoticed, service to biblical criticism by collecting, analyzing, and cataloging the major symbolic constellations found in the religions of mankind. Mircea Eliade's *Patterns in Comparative Religion* is a case in point.[18] Such work is, however, not the final answer for the literary critic.

The World Created By The Text. The symbolic dimension of language very quickly forces us to consider the world-creating dimension of all speech. Rhythm, structure, and symbol converge into either a fictional or a theoretical world which is the first-fruit of consciousness. Elizabeth Sewell states the matter well:

> The human organism, that body which has
> the gift of thought, does not have the choice
> of two kinds of thinking. It has only one,
> on which the organism as a whole is engaged
> all along the line...all thinking is the same
> kind....Discovery, in science and poetry, is
> a mythological situation in which *the mind
> unites with a figure of its own divising* as
> a means toward understanding the world.[19]

Theory or poetry, it makes no difference. Our cognitive acts are rooted in the fictional dimension. Carl Jung tells us what should be obvious: "The existence of objects depends entirely on our perception and 'perception' is a psychical act."[20] Neither theories nor literature "describe the abso-

lute beginning of the world, but rather the beginning of consciousness as a second creation".[21] The fictional dimension
is the inner dimension of personhood, the manifestation of
human sublimity. Its literary product is "one of the major
devices by which man communicates his vision of the nature of
reality in concrete terms".[22]

The symbolism of literary texts ultimately forces the
critic to enter into his or her own inner reality. The archetypal symbols of the Unconscious become relevant beyond all
merely historical comparisons.

Linguistically, we can say that the critic is called into
a fictional world presented by the text as the true world.
The text confronts us first on the boundaries of the indicative mood, calling all previous models into question. We are
moved then into the subjunctive mood as language enacts a new
and truer world before us as a vision of what could and ought
to be. It reaches its conclusion as it confronts us with the
imperative--the mood of invitation which calls on us to help
create the future. We are now confronted with the final dimension of the text. We must resolve the power of the words
into action. We must accept or reject the call of the imperative.[23] We can now see clearly Sewell's point: "Language is
to be conceived not as an entity but as activity." Language
is "a moving event, language plus mind, subject to time and
process and change...".[24] All of our theories and stories
are but the figures of a dance through which we move in response to the becoming of Spirit.

To abstract the text into the "timeless patterns"[25] of
apophthegm, legend, parable, and the like; to atomize four
Gospels and then to recombine them into a fifth historical-
critical *Diatessaron* replete with a conjectured history of
the forms and their *Sitz im Leben Jesu* and of the traditors
and redactors of these "forms" is ultimately illusory, as
Frye notes,[26] because it freezes language into an aesthetic
object to be viewed but not heard. It remains at best an extrinsic criticism of language and a proclamation of the "critical myth of Enlightenment"[27] rivaling the sacred story which
produced the Gospels.

Silence. Rhythm, formal structure, symbol, and the world-
creating structure of language are themselves rooted in silence. The literary critic must consider this dimension of the
text before the work is complete. Language arises from and
then recedes into silence. This was obvious in oral-tradition-
al societies. Language could clearly be seen as an act of a
speaker, the incursion of a Power mediated by a person. Out
of silence, the words burst forth into sound and meaning--each

syllable decaying and receding into silence before the next
began. Language was never a text. It was an act of speech,
a proclamation, a bodily activity, and an occasion for awe.
The gospel was clearly such in its origin. It was good news
borne by a messenger. It was a kerygma proclaimed by a herald.
It was sent through men who were called to speak and to embody
the word inseparably. Men were challenged to hear the message
of the King by the person of the herald. Paul makes this
point clearly to the Corinthians: "I was with you in weakness
and in much fear and trembling; and my speech and my message
were not in plausible words of wisdom but in demonstration of
the Spirit and power..." (1 Cor. 2:3-4). Paul is an embodiment of the word.[28] As such, he is the Word.

Once a text was formed, the original character of the
gospel was transformed. The elements of silence and embodiment become far more subtle. The claims of apostolic authorship served, in some part, to preserve the presence of the
apostle. The experience of silence in the presence of the
embodied word is now transmitted by the rhythm of the language
and by the experience of the incommensurability between text
and the sacred acts to which they witness. The inclusion of
four Gospels and the steadfast opposition of the Church to the
Diatessaron were other devices by which the Church preserved
the experience of silence. The four Gospels point to the one
Ultimate Mystery—to that which was uttered as the Word made
flesh; and then only provisionally, for Christ is but the
"image of the invisible God" (Col. 1:15).

Intrinsic literary criticism is sensitive to the structure of language and to its primary, creative relation to reality. It must always be sensitive to the assistance provided
by the extrinsic, historical method. It must be equally aware
that all language is rooted in Silence. It is between these
two boundaries that it finds its proper role.

III. THE MULTIDIMENSIONALITY OF THE TEXT AND THE CRITIC

Origen's observations on scriptural interpretation were
made long before the Canon was closed and they established the
basic model for biblical interpretation prior to the modern
period. Origen recognized a three-fold structure in Scripture
corresponding to the three-fold dimensionality of the human
personality. Man is body, psyche, and Spirit. Scripture,
thus, has an historical body, a symbolic body, and a Spiritual
body. It speaks to the whole man. Is this multidimensional

correlation between the text and the critic valid today? If
so, to what extent?

With Origen, most critics are willing to say that Scripture has an historical body corresponding to the nature of man.
We have indeed, become so exclusively attached to this conviction that we may value little else. We seek, almost desperate-
ly at times, to squeeze from this historical body of Scripture
an even "truer" history to which our times can relate.

Perhaps with Origen we are willing to grant that when the
historicity of the gospel story breaks down, this is a sign
that we must seek intelligibility in the symbolic dimension.
Certainly since D. F. Strauss modern scholars have been open
to this possibility, but they have yet to correlate it with
the psychic dimension of personality. The pervasive tendency
is to rationalize the symbolism. We must yet explore the psychic dimension with the aid of modern psycho-analytic insights.
The intuitive and presentational modes have yet to be valued
properly by criticism.

The most difficult task confronting the modern critic is
the affirmation of the Spirit in Scripture and its correlate,
silence in the critic. It is in the face of the silence of
the text that all methods and human aspirations come to their
proper end. Here we must await the experience in which the
text ceases to be text and becomes instead the unspeakable
mystery of the Presence of God. If we can affirm the presence of Spirit in ourselves as a valid dimension of our personal space, we may yet perceive the movement of Spirit in the
Scripture and in the silence of the cosmos.

The rising post-Enlightenment criticism is, I believe,
prepared to explore the multidimensionality of the critic and
seeks to address the multiple dimensions of texts. Stephen
Crites's distinction of sacred story and mundane story is a
tacit acknowledgement of the role of silence and Spirit in
human speech. He, I believe, is rooted securely in the early
Christian tradition of a multidimensional criticism. He correctly castigates us for the loss of a serious concern with
angels, for, as he tells us, in them "a musical presence enters the story and breaks open the narrative continuity in
space and time".[29] The angel is a concrete, literary figure
proclaiming the reality of the Spirit. Angels cannot be
named. They name us, "That is why they are so terrible and
so liberating."[30]

Crites's observations about the demise of angels in
Western Christianity can also be applied to the fate of the
Gospels. "One wished to express Christian belief in doctrinal

propositions; moral teaching became of central importance, with biblical stories evoked for illustration purposes only...."[31] It is hardly surprising that "there arose a literalism determined to prove by hook or by crook its historical accuracy...".[32] The Enlightenment exhibited an almost paranoiac obsession with historicity, and yet fell victim to its own fantasies of a dark Middle Age in which scheming priests held men in darkness and tyranny under King and Church. It is against this *animus* that much of the "critical tradition" has struggled. Like C. S. Lewis's dwarves in the *Chronicles of Narnia's Last Battle*, we have often taken pride in our delusions, saying that at least among the dwarves there is no humbug. Our fear has led us to limit our personal awareness to the self-conscious rationality in ourselves and to the purely objective surface of experience. We dwell in the scientifically historical like Lewis's dwarves starving in the banquet of eternity.

CONCLUSION

Literary criticism must again become the multidimensional affirmation of the full range of human experience. We must hold to the immanent both externally and internally, but we must hold equally to the experience of transcendence. Historical and intrinsic literary criticism must be wedded and then transcended in the silence before the Spirit. This will constitute a single, whole act of contemplative intelligence.

It is time for what Michael Polanyi calls a post-critical approach to science; for what Albert Outler calls a post-Enlightenment criticism. It is time for a multidimensional criticism. This criticism must do justice to the outer and the inner dimensions of experience. It must acknowledge the power of the proposition and of the presentation. The past must once again be addressed with respect and accorded the assumption of truth and integrity until some evidence to the contrary emerges. Most important of all, this action must acknowledge the nature of the human personality as revealed by depth psychology and do justice to both the tacit and the explicit dimensions of knowing. Only then can we produce a literary criticism capable of responding to the manifold possibilities of rhythms, words, stories, and images--spoken and written--as they arise from silence as an epiphany of Spirit.

NOTES

1. See Charles T. Davis, III, *Speaking of Jesus: Toward a Theology of the Periphery* (Lakemont, Ga.: CSA Press, 1978), pp. 27-56.

2. *The Rebel* (New York: Random House, 1956), p. 35. Albert Outler in the "Introduction: The Colloquy on the Relationships Among the Gospels," *The Relationships Among the Gospels: An Interdisciplinary Dialogue* (San Antonio: Trinity University Press, 1978), p. 28, challenges NT scholarship to confront this issue: "To what meta-historical ends are our historical-literary analyses aimed, given the fact that we *are* engaged in meta-historical judgments, willy-nilly?" René Wellek and Austin Warren in *Theory of Literature* (New York: Harcourt, 1956), p. 9, remind the practitioners of "secular" literary criticism that "no criticism or history is possible without some set of questions, some system of concepts, some point of reference...". Blindness to these often transforms criticism into a new dogmatism.

3. Wellek and Warren, *Theory of Literature*, p. 73.

4. See Eugen Rosenstock-Huessy, *Out of Revolution* (Norwich, Vt.: Argo, 1938), pp. 699-705.

5. "Introduction," p. 20. That historical-literary study has come to an impasse is the judgment of Roland Frye in "The Synoptic Problem and Analogies in Other Literature," *The Relationships Among the Gospels*, p. 87, who observes of NT criticism that: "At this point, coming from outside the 'system', as a representative of literary history in the secular fields, I must observe that few if any of the leading literary historians in secular fields would be comfortable with the widespread assumption among NT critics that it is possible, in the present state of the evidence, to move backwards in time from passages in the extant gospel texts in such a way as to... ultimately...arrive at or near the original life and teachings of Jesus; or that it is possible, through a similar procedure, to explain the Synoptic redactions as we now have them." Such a "disintegrating" criticism is seen by Frye to be a part of the NT scholars' "learned illusions" (pp. 287, 262).

6. Newtonian physics supported this view. Modern physics does not. It vindicates the larger role of vision. Fritjof Capra in *The Tao of Physics* (Boulder: Shambhala-Random House, 1975), p. 186, observes: "Many of the Eastern teachers emphasize that thought must take place in time, but that vision can

transcend it. 'Vision,' says Govinda, 'is bound up with a space of a higher dimension, and therefore timeless.' The space-time of relativistic physics is a similar timeless space of a higher dimension. All events in it are interconnected, but the connections are not causal."

7. See below, pp. 90-91.

8. "Angels We Have Heard," *Religion as Story* (New York: Harper, 1975), p. 29. See also "The Narrative Quality of Experience," *Journal of the American Academy of Religion* 39 (September, 1971): 291-311.

9. "Modern physics, then, pictures matter not at all as passive and inert, but as being in a continuous dancing and vibrating motion whose rhythmic patterns are determined by the molecular, atomic and nuclear structures. This is also the way in which the Eastern mystics see the world. They all emphasize that the universe has to be grasped dynamically, as it moves, vibrates, and dances,..." (Capra, *Tao*, p. 194).

10. "Classics and the Gospels: The Seminar," *The Relationships Among the Gospels*, p. 189.

11. "Classical and Christian Source Criticism," *The Relationships Among the Gospels*, p. 137.

12. See Davis, *Speaking of Jesus*, pp. 71-75, 83-131.

13. "The Narrative Quality of Experience," p. 296.

14. Ibid., p. 295.

15. Ibid.

16. Crites, "Angels We Have Heard," p. 25.

17. Paul Tillich, "The Religious Symbol," *Daedalus* 87 (Summer, 1958): 4-5.

18. New York: Meridian, 1958.

19. *The Orphic Voice* (New York: Harper, 1971), pp. 19-20.

20. "Religionless Christianity," *Journal of the American Academy of Religion* 39 (March, 1971): 45.

21. Ibid.

22. W. F. Thrall, Addison Hibbard, C. H. Holman, *A Hand-*

book to Literature, 3rd ed. (New York: Odyssey, 1960), p.
223. See also James Hillman, "The Fiction of Case History,"
Religion as Story, p. 130: "Both history and fiction can be
narrative stories, one event after another in a time sequence.
But only when the narrative receives inner coherence in terms
of the depths of human nature do we have fiction, and for this
fiction we have to have plot. To plot is to move from asking
the question 'and then what happened?' to the question 'and
why did it happen?' In our kind of fiction (case study) the
plots are our theories."

23. See Eugen Rosenstock-Huessy, *Speech and Reality* (Norwich, Vt.: Argo, 1970), p. 55.

24. Sewell, *The Orphic Voice*, pp. 22-23.

25. Ibid., p. 23.

26. "Analogies in Other Literature," p. 262.

27. See Rosenstock-Huessey, *Out of Revolution*, pp. 699-
705.

28. See Davis, *Speaking of Jesus*, pp. 116-118.

29. "Angels We Have Heard," p. 55.

30. Ibid.

31. Ibid.

32. Ibid.

6

LITERARY AND HISTORICAL CRITICISM OF THE BIBLE:
A CRISIS IN SCHOLARSHIP*

Robert M. Polzin

> *Exegetical scholars are agreed only that
> historical criticism,* the best method of
> discovering the literal sense, *cannot be
> given up.*[1]

> *...we have to conclude that historical
> exegesis is suspect of obscurantism.
> Could it be that its methodological pre-
> understanding is at odds with the con-
> temporary cultural preunderstanding?*[2]

The very first question that today confronts anyone who
attempts to analyze the Bible in a scholarly context is this:
should one's approach be primarily historical or literary?
diachronic or synchronic? Recent claims of some biblical
scholars, especially those employing various versions of literary structuralism emanating from France, tend to cast serious doubt upon the hitherto secure consensus of modern biblical studies concerning the fundamental role of historical
criticism in interpreting the Bible. Thus Patte the structuralist versus Krentz the historian in the above quotations.

The problem is semantic in a double sense: not only is it
a question of which approach best helps us "discover the literal sense", as Krentz puts it, but there is also the problem
of whether a-historical literary approaches to the study of the
Bible may accurately be designated "scholarly". Since recent
structural studies claim not to be based on the findings of
modern historical criticism, and yet claim to be as scientifically rigorous as,[3] or even more rigorous than,[4] their historical counterparts, there appears to be a fundamental dispute as

---

*It is a pleasure to dedicate this essay to Professor
Beardslee, whose work over the years has contributed much toward dealing with the crisis described in the body of the text.

to what constitutes scholarly study of the Bible. On the other hand, the structuralist claim of methodological rigor is contradicted by representative historical-critical statements. For example, we read that "there can be for us no scholarly access to the Bible without a knowledge of the circumstances of its formation".[5]

I would like to spell out in this article my belief that if there is a crisis in biblical scholarship today, it does not consist in the present almost healthy tension between historical and literary criticism of the Bible, but rather in the destructive self image both may mistakenly have concerning their status as scholarly disciplines modeled after the natural sciences. The diachronic/synchronic question of itself presents us merely with a *problem* that in no sense approaches the monumental dimensions of the crisis about which I will speak shortly. As I have stated elsewhere,[6] diachronic and synchronic study of the Bible, historical-critical and literary-critical approaches, possess a complementary relationship to each other. Neither constitutes, *a priori*, the fundamental basis for the other's existence, neither occupies by intrinsic right an academic throne to which the other must bring its conclusions for scholarly approbation, for a scientific *nihil obstat*. (We shall assert below, however, that this complementary relationship does allow an operational priority to literary analysis at the preliminary stages of research.)

The battle which now seems to be increasingly waged in biblical journals and at biblical conferences is similar to that which has been going on for decades among (literary) literary critics ever since the post-war emergence in North America of the so-called New Critics such as Frye, Wimsatt, and Beardsley. Using terminology employed by Said[7] and Krieger,[8] we may say that with the onset of French literary structuralism, these post-war critics are now the "old" New Critics, while modern scholars such as Barthes, Kristeva, Greimas, and Todorov have become the "new" New Critics. How the dispute with the "old" New Critics ran its course may offer some insights for biblical scholars as to what may be the probable outcome of the emerging confrontation between established historical critics and a boisterous, vociferous, but not altogether unified group of younger scholars of the Bible who now appear to be challenging their predecessors.

Within literary circles, one can find a convenient running account of past and present battles between literary *history* and literary *criticism* in the excellent volumes of the journal, *New Literary History*. A helpful analysis of what such battles entail, and how they may be profitably resolved, is Istvan Soter's article on "The Dilemma of Literary Science".[9] The position outlined there offers a number of helpful points concerning the present condition of biblical studies, and represents with some few exceptions the general operational context within which the present essay has been written.

It might be helpful for me now to introduce two assertions that describe the main elements of my synchronic/diachronic assumptions as preface to a third that articulates what I believe to be the real crisis in biblical scholarship today.

1. *A historical-critical analysis of the Bible is necessary for an* adequate *scholarly understanding of what this ancient work means.*

There is no need, of course, to defend such a view before the vast majority of biblical scholars who might read the present pages. For indeed historical criticism is *the* cornerstone of modern biblical studies. But there are some biblical scholars who, influenced by the "old" and "new" New Critics, forcefully proclaim that one need not attend to the historical context of a work in order to discover a whole range of acceptable meanings that a biblical text contains. What Northrop Frye writes of Boehme, many younger biblical scholars might now write of the Bible:

> It has been said of Boehme that his books
> are like a picnic to which the author
> brings the words and the reader the mean-
> ing. The remark may have been intended as
> a sneer at Boehme, but it is an exact de-
> scription of all works of literary art
> without exception.[10]

Since some parts of the Bible may be considered at least in running for the title, "literary art", the question arises as to how important it is to determine by historical means what a biblical author or editor might have *meant* when he wrote or compiled his work. Some structuralists and most New Critics would assert that he who has embarked upon such a quest has fallen prey to "the intentional fallacy".[11]

Perhaps the best known defense of the proposition that the intentional fallacy is itself a fallacy is *Validity in Interpretation*, by E. D. Hirsch.[12] For those who are familiar with Hirsch's thorough discussions, and are in fundamental agreement with his repudiation of the hermeneutical views of New Critics and structuralists alike, the present defense of biblical historical criticism will appear modest--indeed even unnecessary. In any case, I propose to indicate my position without recourse to Hirsch's arguments because I am not entirely comfortable with many of them. As Geoffrey Strickland points out, largely in defense of Hirsch, the latter argues his case mainly "on the grounds of common sense".[13] Now this is precisely the defense to which the biblical historical critics traditionally and mostly implicitly have had recourse; and M. Tsevat's insightful comment about such positions is that "Arguments based on common sense as such have little or no place in the sciences, the humanities included."[14]

I have no space here to develop lines of argumentation that would defend historical criticism's traditional emphasis on extra-textual context, but let me at least indicate what direction such a development would take. First, I would defend such a position by invoking arguments that are drawn from certain positions of modern linguistics, namely those of some who oppose Chomsky's *a priori* ignoring of extra-linguistic context in linguistic analysis. As Robin Lakoff writes:

> ...the notion that contextual factors, so-
> cial and otherwise, must be taken into ac-
> count in determining the acceptability and
> interpretation of sentences is scarcely
> new....But the idea has not merely been
> forgotten by transformational grammar;
> rather it has been explicitly rejected.[15]

Thus, transformational grammar has held in linguistics what the New Critics and some structuralists have proposed in literary criticism: the rejection *in principle* of factors of real-life context in the interpretation of literary texts. It may be that historical critics may not welcome the type of criticism I offer their critics, but I am convinced that this approach is more broadly-based than those put forth by historical critics within biblical studies on the rare occasions that they get down to fundamental discussions of methodological principles.

A second source that could be invoked against the principled rejection of the social context as irrelevant to the interpretation of texts comes paradoxically from certain Russian formalist and sociological literary theorists who have had essential roles in the development of literary structuralism of the Russian rather than the French variety. If a typical historical-critical approach to the study of the Bible can state:

> To hear and understand the witness of the
> biblical books correctly, it is necessary
> to know at what times and in what circum-

stances they came into existence. This involves a knowledge of the history, religion,
and theology of Israel and Judaism, as well
as of the world from which they grew.[16]

a Russian theorist in 1930 can emphasize with italics such
statements as these:

> *The immediate social situation and the
> broader social milieu wholly determine--
> and determine from within, so to speak--
> the structure of an utterance.*[17]

> *Verbal communication can never be under-
> stood and explained outside of this con-
> nection with a concrete situation.*[18]

The impression one gets from reading certain structuralists
is that the first task which the historical exegete feels
obliged to undertake, namely, to use "every linguistic tool
at his disposal to determine the sense the text had for its
writer and first audience (the *sensus literalis sive histori-
cus*)",[19] is a linguistically naive and misguided point of view.
On the other hand, even though the historical critic's impulse
may rightly be termed precipitous, whole schools of modern
semioticians and structuralists would themselves reject the
ignoring of linguistically relevant situations by some of
their colleagues as itself hermeneutically myopic. It is important, therefore, here at the beginning not to group all
structuralists in the same hermeneutical basket.

2. *A competent literary analysis of biblical material is necessary for even a* preliminary *scholarly understanding.*

We may begin by reaffirming Robert Alter's assessment of
modern biblical studies:

> It is a little astonishing that at this
> late date there exists virtually no seri-
> ous literary analysis of the Hebrew Bible.
> By serious literary analysis I mean the
> manifold varieties of minutely discrimi-
> nating attention to the artful use of
> language, to the shifting play of ideas,
> conventions, tone, sound, imagery, narra-
> tive viewpoint, compositional units, and
> much else; the kind of disciplined atten-
> tion, in other words, which through a

> whole spectrum of critical approaches has
> illuminated, for example, the poetry of
> Dante, the plays of Shakespeare, the
> novels of Tolstoy.[20]

The defensive reaction to this article, represented by the
published letters of a number of biblical scholars in a later
issue of *Commentary*, serves to confirm Alter's view that
biblical scholars have little acquaintance with even elementary forms of disciplined literary analysis. Alter's pessi-
mistic opinion is shared by David Robertson,[21] and biblical
critics would do well to listen to such literary critics, especially when the nature and scope of literary criticism, and
its presence within representative biblical scholarship, are
concerned.

The present article assumes that the above assessment accurately represents the state of biblical scholarship today;
it further assumes that this literary lacuna is a primary reason why historical-critical analyses of biblical material have
so often produced disappointing and inadequate results. If
adequate historical studies of literary texts operationally
depend upon the existence of competent literary studies of
such texts, we may have here a plausible reason for a good
number of the failures in historical-critical understanding
of biblical material. It remains now to describe in what
sense literary criticism may be spoken of as having an operational priority over historical criticism.

The question of the sequence of literary versus historical
investigations of literary texts is, of course, one that has
been discussed at great length in literary circles. In the
study of literature, what comes first from a methodological
point of view, a historical (genetic or diachronic) approach
or a descriptive (synchronic or literary-critical) approach?
This is the dilemma of literary science, as I. Soter describes
it.[22] The answer which underlies the viewpoint of the present
essay assumes that scholarly understanding of biblical material
results from a *circular* movement that begins with a literary
analysis, then turns to historical problems, whose attempted
solution then furnishes further refinements and adaptations of
one's literary-critical conclusions. The priority of synchrony
(in the dynamic sense outlined above all by Russian theorists)
over diachrony is not in rank but only in operation. Thus we
are still allowed to call both approaches truly complementary:
each must eventually take the other's conclusions into account.
What is primarily emphasized here is *where one begins*. As Soter writes:

> We must put an end to the dilemma, but
> this is possible only if we start from
> the book as an artistic creation, i.e.,
> we must give priority to critical-aes-
> thetic considerations and only afterwards
> turn to historical problems....Of course,
> 'priority' in this sense is not priority
> in rank, since criticism starting from
> the literary product, and historical re-
> search returning to it, are both secon-
> dary seen from the point of view of the
> book itself.[23]

The reasons for assuming such a sequence in procedures
is admirably and succinctly given by Krystyna Pomorska.[24] She
points out that if we move in the opposite direction, basing
synchronic analyses on historical studies, "we always run the
risk of applying ready-made theories to something not suited
to them".[25] To know one's object intimately (the literary
work), we ought to make it the starting point of our efforts.
But even if we begin with a literary, synchronic analysis,
this does not mean that historical, genetic scholarship is of
lower rank. It is a co-equal partner in research:

> A literary work represents a complex phe-
> nomenon whose *process* is as significant as
> its ontological nature. But it seems im-
> possible to study the process before know-
> ing the nature of the product.[26]

It is impossible, at least, before having a preliminary understanding of the literary composition of the work as *product*.

The great Russian literary theorist, Mikhail Bakhtin,
agrees with the methodological sequence we are describing. In
discussing why he does a literary-critical analysis of Dostoevsky's work before tackling historical questions, he admits that
such a preliminary literary investigation does need to be
deepened by historical perspectives. Nevertheless, "Without
such a preliminary orientation, historical investigations de-
generate into a disconnected series of chance comparisons."[27]

3.   *Both literary and historical criticism of the Bible un-*
     cover hermeneutical principles within the text that ap-
     pear to be at fundamental odds with prevailing views on
     the nature of historical and literary scholarship, views
     based upon the supposed similarity of both disciplines
     to the natural sciences.

      This assertion is in essential agreement with the herme-
neutics of H.-G. Gadamer in his classic work, *Truth and Meth-*
od,[28] and is the basis for my belief that a crisis exists within biblical studies today. My position deals with the contradictory situation scholarship finds itself in when it compares
what the Bible characteristically claims is the road to a correct understanding of God's word and *how* scholarship is supposed to have arrived at its own understanding of these claims.
The "what" and the supposed "how" are paradoxically contradictory, in the sense that scholarly principles of interpretation
reveal a biblical message which denies the validity of many
scholars' self-understanding of the role of interpretation,
at least where the word of God is concerned.

      If the scholar pays attention to the referential aspects
of the biblical text--and it is my conviction that he must do
so in the name of scholarship--he seems forced to make a decision about the hermeneutical principles he will use in his
study. For the scholar who must confront the question of
whether the Bible has some kind of truth-claim on him, any
literary or historical criticism modeled after the uninvolved,
impersonal objectivity of the natural sciences will be seen to
operate according to hermeneutical principles that are in conflict with the message and spirit of the biblical text: *the*
biblical message that this misguided scholarship uncovers would
reject the very method by which it is uncovered.

      A discussion of this assertion is all the more necessary
today, since it is in basic conflict with the usual explana-
tions of the theological significance of "scholarly" (read
here "historical-critical") disciplines of the Bible:

               It cannot be disputed that the Introduction
               to the Old Testament is an auxiliary disci-
               pline of theology....Introduction, together
               with the other historical disciplines, pre-
               pares for an understanding of the scrip-
               tures which will lead to the word of God,
               to which it bears witness, being heard in
               our time.[29]

We are thus led to believe that the better-equipped one is to subject the Bible to the whole array of modern historical disciplines, the better can be one's understanding of what in fact the word of God *says*.

Whether one's ideal be ecclesiastical or scholarly or a combination of both, a basic dilemma is posed by the belief that the primary task of the biblical historian is to hear the Bible's message in the sense it had for its writer and first audience:[30] once one subjects a biblical text to a literary or historical analysis, the conclusion is often inescapable that the typically biblical approach to the word of God it expounds is apparently opposed to such an understanding of the scholarly task. To study the Bible with such an uninvolved and objective stance is still to discover a message that was apparently not meant to be understood in such a way. One can even phrase the dilemma in semiotic style: the result of this kind of decoding of the text is the discovery of an original message that reads, "Do not decode this in the way you have."

But are we not forced to examine the biblical text from a historical-critical point of view if we want to reconstruct what the writer meant and what his audience first understood? Do we not run the risk of interpreting the text in an overly subjective and contemporary way if we ignore the historical-critical approach? As Krentz writes, "Historical study prevents too rapid modernizing."[31]

What is at issue here is whether the *need* one today feels to concentrate one's search for a text's meaning on its author's original situation and intent may not in fact be itself a contemporary and subjective element in the discussion. If this be so, then by trying to avoid contemporary subjectivity in such a way (by this kind of biblical criticism) one has already surrendered to one of the most pervasive of contemporary biases: the supposed greater objectivity of the historical-critical mode of interpretation.

I mean to suggest that the basic arguments for both literary and historical criticism, which were defended above in assertions one and two, are often misused in support of the supposed greater objectivity of a *scholarly* mode of interpretation based upon the natural sciences as models. But what the Bible teaches, and what this view of modern scholarship teaches, about how best to interpret messages as fundamentally assertive as those in the Bible, are plainly at odds with one another. And for all those who view this kind of scholarship as the handmaid of religion or as "the basement and foundation of theology",[32] the clear result of putting this view in practice, by a scholarly application of literary and historical criticism, is to infuse these disciplines with a self-destruct mechanism.

The first two assertions of this essay discuss the two-fold direction of a scholarly understanding of biblical material. The present assertion actually addresses the question of whether much of today's historical and literary-critical efforts is adequate from a biblical point of view. The answer would seem to be "no", and this is precisely what constitutes the present crisis. For so many to believe that they are actually understanding the Bible's claims on its own terms, when in fact they are not, represents a true crisis in scholarship.

There are those who would not dream of asking the question I have just raised. For those who believe that an impersonal, uninvolved scholarship is necessary even to assess the biblical message--necessary at least in the sense that one must first correctly perceive a message before one can assess it--there is no room left for the possibility that biblical messages might justifiably assess such a view of scholarship. Scholarship for these individuals involves a contract which includes a self-justifying clause that reads, "Attitudes toward the Bible that question the fundamental role of an uninvolved, impersonal criticism are critically unacceptable." But critically unacceptable approaches to the understanding of texts are too subjective to be taken seriously. Thérefore one can safely ignore such attitudes. Catch 22. There apparently exists academic as well as religious fundamentalism, scholarly as well as theological dogmatism.

I can illustrate my general position by referring to a specific biblical book. For many, the Deuteronomic History is a literary unity, and the Book of Deuteronomy is its programmatic introduction. As the word of God through Moses, this book is presented as the blueprint according to which the history narrated in the following books is to be interpreted. It might be useful, therefore, to see briefly how various words of God are interpreted by Moses and the narrator in the Book of Deuteronomy.

Moses is portrayed in Deuteronomy as the pre-eminent interpreter of God's words. The story therein describes only one instance of divine speech that was heard by the people of Israel directly, the decalogue of 5:6-21. All the other words of God, even those directly quoted by the narrator in chapters 31, 32, and 34, are not heard by the people, but are transmitted to them through the intervention of Moses primarily and, in a few scattered instances, of the elders of Israel, the Levitical priests, and the narrator himself.

In Deuteronomy, Moses is pictured in his addresses as interpreting speeches that had taken place prior to his interpretative words. As 5:28-31 brings out, Moses carries out this practice as an introduction and as a conclusion to God's "further commands" of chapters 12-26. Thus Moses is pictured as setting the Deuteronomic law code in context by, among other things, interpreting past words, especially those of God's. What is immediately obvious here is the absolutely authoritarian, or at least authoritative, nature of Moses' interpretative function.

It is true that Moses takes care to situate, in time and in space, the past events and speech that he reports:

"The LORD our God said to us in Horeb..." (1:6)

"At that time I said to you..." (1:9).

This practice agrees with that of the narrator whose framing narratives in Deuteronomy situate the words of Moses in time and space: where, when, and in what circumstances Moses spoke the words reported in the book. Indeed, this contextualizing practice of Moses and the narrator helps to create a factual tone in the narrative that invests it with an aura of historicity which must have been as obvious to the book's first audience as it is to us.

When Moses, for example, rehearses in his first address what of importance had been said and done before arriving in Moab, the stated location of Moses' addresses, his audience could supply whatever contextual information was part of their common experience. But what they could not do was to supplement his account with anything that had to do with the *content* of God's words to Moses or Israel, since only Moses is described as having heard these words, with the exception of the decalogue. Moreover, since God had told Moses alone:

> "...I will tell you all the commandment
> and the statutes and the ordinances which
> you shall teach them...(5:31)."

only Moses is pictured as directly authorized by God to *interpret* His words. And more to the point, when Moses in chapter five recounts this authenticating command of God's, no one in his audience is in a position to institute an investigation concerning whether Moses was reporting accurately God's words of authorization; after all, we are told in the book that only Moses heard these words (even though they are reported as agreeing with the previous request of the elders of Israel).

The principal role of Moses, as seen in the Book of Deuteronomy, is hermeneutic: he is the book's primary declarer (*maggid*) and teacher (*m^elammed*) of God's word. He not only declares what God has said, he teaches or interprets what the divine words *mean* for Israel. And he is pictured as doing so in an authoritative manner that was consonant with the status he is pictured as enjoying within the Israelite community.

Even if we confine our illustrative remarks to the Book of Deuteronomy, it is even obvious here at the beginning of the Deuteronomic History that by the end of the book, chapter 34, the narrator has also established *his* authoritative role as *maggid* and *m^elammed* of Moses' words. And the narrator accomplishes the establishment of his authority amazingly enough by remaining mostly in the background of his narrative: the reporting speech of the narrator comprises only about fifty-six verses of the book. He will, of course, come to the foreground with the preponderantly reporting narrative of Joshua-2 Kings. Indeed, what is obvious even on a first reading of the Deuteronomic History is that in the narrator's reporting words, comprising the bulk of Joshua-2 Kings, we have some kind of authoritative interpretation of the words of Moses insofar as they affect the history of Israel subsequent to Moses' time.

In both cases of the reporting of God's words—that is, in the case of Moses' reporting of God's words, and in the case of the narrator's reporting of Moses' words—both the declaration and interpretation of those words are accomplished in an authoritative manner that is completely at odds with the reasoned approach to them that is the result of a natural science type of model within the historical and literary disciplines. This hermeneutical picture in Deuteronomy, admittedly sketched here in too elementary a fashion, has by its very obviousness profound implications with respect of the place of scholarly interpretations of the biblical text.

If the Deuteronomic History tells a story in which certain past events are considered important for men's lives, it follows that when a literary or historical analysis of this work helps us understand, in a more profound way and in greater detail, what that story meant, say, to its original audience, an unavoidable feature of the scholarly retelling of the Deuteronomic story appears to cast a negative light upon an uninvolved scholarship that would retell these stories while deliberately refusing to *apply* them (in Gadamer's sense of application).

The manner in which Moses is described as interpreting God's words in the Book of Deuteronomy, and the manner in which the narrator interprets Moses' words in Joshua-2 Kings, seem to conflict with the manner in which many scholars "interpret" the narrator's words in the Deuteronomic History.

Thus, when Noth, for example, concludes that a gifted individual wrote the Deuteronomistic History in the middle of the sixth century, probably somewhere in Palestine, and when Noth believes that the theme of this author's work was one of unrelieved and irreversible doom, we may say with some accuracy that the words of one so-called historian, the Deuteronomist, have been studied and interpreted by the standard of another historian, Martin Noth.

But suppose we were to reverse the situation--and there appears to be no reason why we should be forbidden to do so-- and ask what would be the case were Noth's historical work to be judged by the hermeneutical standards of the Deuteronomist? This type of reverse question is certainly not original, for most scholars pondering the respective roles of the historical and theological sciences have had something to say on this matter. For example, von Rad wrestles mightily with such a question in the "Postscript" to his great *Theology of the Old Testament*, and both the discomfort and tentativeness apparent there testify to the fact that only on rare occasions has the problem been faced squarely by modern biblical scholars. Such questions most often remain unresolved; the result, I submit, is a genuine crisis within biblical studies today.

If it is true that biblical texts, which themselves most often report and interpret previous discourses to later audiences, do not exhibit the least concern to establish, in any manner that deserves to be called similar to that of an uninvolved and non-applied scholarship, the sense which these previous traditions had for their previous audiences--and we have tried to show that this is, for example, the case with the Deuteronomic History--then of what value is this kind of scholarship as regards to determining the biblical message? For clearly, in such a case, what the biblical message tells such a critic, even insofar as that message is established by the biblical critic, is the relatively useless role of this kind of criticism in dealing with the crucial topics with which the Bible is concerned. Only by a determined effort to avoid such non-involvement will scholars help to resolve the present crisis:

> Both the critic and the historian thus
> emerge from the self-forgetfulness to
> which they had been banished by a think-
> ing for which the only criterion was the
> methodology of modern science. Both find

their true ground in effective historical
consciousness.[33]

NOTES

1. Edgar Krentz, *The Historical-Critical Method* (Philadelphia: Fortress Press, 1975), p. 72.

2. Daniel Patte, *What is Structural Exegesis?* (Philadelphia: Fortress Press, 1976), p. 10.

3. Ibid., p. 19.

4. William G. Doty, "Linguistics and Biblical Criticism," *Journal of the American Academy of Religion* 41 (1973): 119-121.

5. Otto Kaiser, *Introduction to the Old Testament*, rev. ed., trans. John Sturdy (Oxford: Basil Blackwell, 1975), p. 13.

6. Robert Polzin, *Biblical Structuralism* (Missoula and Philadelphia: Scholars Press and Fortress Press, 1977).

7. Edward W. Said, "Roads Taken and Not Taken in Contemporary Criticism," *Contemporary Literature* 17 (1976): 327-348.

8. Murray Krieger, "Introduction: a Scorecard for the Critics," *Contemporary Literature* 17 (1976): 297-326.

9. *New Literary History* 2 (1970): 85-100.

10. Quoted in Geoffrey Strickland, "The Theory of Criticism," *Encounter* 49 (1977): 86-91.

11. For views pro and con, see David de Molina, *On Literary Intention* (Edinburgh: University Press, 1976).

12. New Haven and London: Yale University Press, 1967.

13. Strickland, "The Theory of Criticism," p. 86.

14. "Common Sense and Hypothesis in Old Testament Study," *Supplements to Vetus Testamentum* 28 (1975): 217.

15. "Language in Context," *Language* 48 (1972): 926, n. 12.

16. Krentz, *The Historical-Critical Method*, p. 2.

114

17. V. N. Voloshinov, *Marxism and the Philosophy of Language* (New York: Seminar Press, 1973), p. 86. It should be noted that Voloshinov's teacher, M. Bakhtin, is probably the author of this work.

18. Ibid., p. 95.

19. Krentz, *The Historical-Critical Method*, p. 39.

20. Robert Alter, "A Literary Approach to the Bible," *Commentary* 60 (1975): 70.

21. *The Old Testament and the Literary Critic* (Philadelphia: Fortress Press, 1977), p. 87.

22. Soter, "The Dilemma of Literary Science," pp. 85-100. See note 9, above.

23. Ibid., p. 94.

24. "Russian Formalism in Retrospect," in *Readings in Russian Poetics*, edited and trans. by L. Matejka and K. Pomorska (Cambridge, Mass.: M.I.T. Press, 1971): 273-80.

25. Ibid., p. 276.

26. Ibid.

27. *Problems of Dostoevsky's Poetics* (Ann Arbor: Ardis Publications, 1973), p. 230, n. 4.

28. New York: The Seabury Press, 1975.

29. Kaiser, *Introduction to the Old Testament*, p. 13.

30. Krentz, *The Historical-Critical Method*, p. 39.

31. Ibid., p. 65.

32. Kaiser, *Introduction to the Old Testament*, p. 13.

33. H.-G. Gadamer, *Truth and Method*, edited and trans. by Garrett Barden and John Cumming (New York: The Seabury Press, 1975), p. 305.

7

WILL THE HISTORICAL-CRITICAL METHOD SURVIVE?
SOME OBSERVATIONS

Leander E. Keck

"After three decades of unprecedented growth, biblical study appears to be...." How should the sentence end? "...thriving as never before", "...engaged in grinding the flour repeatedly", "...uncertain of its aims and methods", "...defending its legitimacy once more", "...increasingly passé"? One could make a case for any of these, depending on what phenomena on the current scene were deemed decisive. This essay will not pretend to adjudicate the competing claims of the various discernments; its aims are much more modest--to reflect on certain consequences of the fact that, somewhat to the surprise of its practitioners, the historical-critical method is on the defensive today, pressured this time not from the theological right wing only but also from the critical "left", so to speak. Biblical critics have long since grown accustomed to attacks from the right, and have learned how to legitimate historical criticism in response to charges that it dissolved the authority of the Bible, sacrificed the revealed truth of the Christian religion, and sowed the tares of doubt in the hearts of the faithful. Apart from the recent controversy among Missouri Synod Lutherans and the hint that perhaps Southern Baptists will again be torn by strife over historical criticism, however, the historical-critical method has established itself in even those institutions which were, in part, founded as bulwarks against it--as Lindsell's *The Battle for the Bible* makes clear with regard to Fuller Theological Seminary.[1] How ironic that it should appear that now it is critical chic to disdain historical criticism, or at least to be disenchanted sufficiently to seek alternative modes of criticism.

I.

If there is indeed an undercurrent of malaise beneath the surface vigor of historical criticism, it might be caused by either a failure to make good its initial promise or by too much success. The promise of historical criticism was clear--

it would explain the Bible, both as a whole and in all its parts, by anchoring it in historical circumstances. This explanatory undertaking relied on tracing out genetic relationships as fully as possible; antecedents (or in structuralist jargon, diachronic relationships) were the key. If antecedent texts, traditions, practices, movements, and the like could not be documented, "parallels" would suffice until the missing antecedent capable of explaining the text, or some aspect of it, would turn up. The text was an effect, to be understood in light of its causes. Ever since the Enlightenment, it has become clear that one can explain both the existence of the texts and their contents without regard to divine action, once the Bible was treated like any other book. In the quest for adequate historical causes, scholars have amassed a body of material, and a series of methods, which stagger the imagination and often strike terror into the heart of the beginning student. For New Testament study alone, one is expected to be conversant with antecedent and contemporary Judaism (both Palestinian and Diaspora texts and exegetical traditions), contemporary Greco-Roman culture and religion (from oriental mysteries on the ascendency to Hermetica, and Mandaica as well), early Christian literature (including Nag Hammadi and the Pseudo-Clementines), matters of text-transmission and the history of the canon. For Old Testament, virtually the entire history and culture of the ancient Near East is adduced in one way or other. The achievement is an unprecedented body of information available to students who wish to situate every aspect of the Bible in its proper historical niche in order to understand it as the result of antecedent causes. It is but natural that the study of the Bible has been compared to the excavation of a tell, which only the expert can dig properly.[2]

Still, much of the promise has not been fulfilled, and probably cannot be until even more material is accumulated. Within the bounds of New Testament study, and what pertains to it, one cannot help but wonder what it all amounts to when one discovers that competent scholars cannot seem to agree on so many elemental questions, among them being the following: Did Jesus refer to himself as the Son of Man, and in what sense? Did Matthew indeed use Mark and Q? Is I Corinthians a composite letter? Was early Christianity more apocalyptic than Jesus? Where does one place John in early Christianity? The recent book by the Bishop of Woolwich, unpersuasive though it is, nonetheless reminds us of how slender, and often ambiguous, is the evidence on which the dating of the New Testament books rests,[3] just as Slingerland's history of research on the Testaments of the Twelve Patriarchs shows that we cannot determine whether this text is a Jewish book with Christian additions, or a Jewish Christian book relying on Jewish sources.[4] To be sure, there are answers to all such questions, often advocated as "assured results". Conflicting conclusions are reached by competent scholars, who then charge their peers with neglecting this or that datum, overlooking an article or monograph, or with failure to be methodologically rigorous. Not infrequently, they either ignore contrary judgments or simply register them ("for another view, see...").

Above all, historical reconstructions of Christian origins have, like amoeba, multiplied by division. Heitmüller and Bousset saved us from an over-simplified view of the problem of how to get from Jesus to Paul, for they called attention to the role of Hellenistic Christianity as the key factor between the earliest church and Paul. Now this has been sliced even thinner: not only is Hellenistic Gentile Christianity to be differentiated from Hellenistic Jewish Christianity, but we are to distinguish a Palestinian from a non-Palestinian form of the latter; likewise, we are to distinguish stages in Q, itself an inference from certain phenomena in Matthew and Luke. Moreover, a contemporary scholar claims to understand the theology of Paul's opponents in Corinth better than Paul, and to do so by relying on Paul's own responses to them;[5] careful attention to detail has led some to regard Mark as essentially a veiled polemic against a type of Jewish Christianity.[6]

In short, it is difficult to judge whether the plethora of proposals is a sign that the promise of the historical-critical method--to explain the texts by relating them infinitely to historical circumstances--is a mark of failure or success. Even if the method has failed to produce a consensus on the basic matter--a comprehensive reconstruction of early Christianity which can account for the New Testament we have-- it has succeeded in persuading many people that they cannot really understand the New Testament apart from a historical framework. But this means that the discipline has succeeded in generating a demand for what, apparently, it cannot produce.

Disenchantment with the historical-critical method might also be grounded in a sense that the method has virtually spent itself. It is not simply that one discovers that our forebears in the 18th or 19th centuries often said most of what can be said; it is rather the fact that the whole enterprise appears to be creaking under its own weight. Soaring prices appear not to inhibit scholars from compiling massive footnotes which repeat opinions published (and republished) for virtually a century. Compendious two-volume commentaries summarize, evaluate, and debate a range of opinions and refer the reader to secondary literature available in but a few libraries. Three to five-hundred page monographs are devoted to a few verses. Quite apart from the fact that much of this writing appears to be defensive (i.e., designed to protect oneself against the fiery darts of a reviewer), the fact is that an amazing proportion of what is printed is essentially collated and sifted repetition of what has been argued before; each time the subject is treated, the snowball grows. (I am aware of the dilemma: if one evaluates the secondary literature, one repeats; if one ignores it, one repeats--without knowing it.) So massive is the legacy of critical judgment that it can readily act as a depressant.

At the same time, one might infer that the discipline has exhausted itself from the fact that certain types of scholarly work appear not to be published, at least not in North America. Although text books continue to appear, for decades there has not been published a major critical introduction to the New Testament; likewise, we lack a critical treatment of Jesus or Paul, or early Christianity, though specialized studies abound. The same is doubtless true of courses taught as well--everything but a solid, critical course on Jesus or Paul. There is reason to think that a discipline has exhausted itself when its results inhibit its practitioners from grappling with its central subject matter except in truncated form or as specialized problems.

When Walter Wink pronounced historical criticism bankrupt, he had in view quite different considerations.[7] Paramount for him was discovering that historical criticism did not nourish the inner self, because it put a premium on distancing the student from the text. Biblical criticism "was based on an inadequate method, married to a false objectivism, subjected to uncontrolled technologism, separated from a vital community, and has outlived its usefulness as presently practiced".[8] In earlier years, biblical criticism created distance, and hence freedom from dogmatic Christendom; "Today, however, biblical criticism is the new Establishment. Now, not dogmatic Christendom, but the biblical guild functions as the harsh superego in the self of many exegetes."[9] So Wink indicts the "old" method for failing so to interpret Scripture "as to enable personal and social transformation today".[10] Wink's indictment is to some extent wide of the mark, for the critical method as such was no more designed to transform life than a screwdriver was designed to drive nails. Wink, to be sure, was not the first to argue that the historical-critical method was inherently inappropriate to the subject-matter of the text. Paul Minear's address at the Pittsburgh Festival of the Gospels (1970) pointed out that even if our contemporaries should consult the Gospels for their own hopes (the theme of the Festival: "Jesus and Man's Hope"), they would rarely find help from professional historical critics.[11] Minear called, as he has done repeatedly for most of his career, for exegetes to allow the biblical perception of reality, "superior to our own", to condition the critical method[12]--though he did not specify how that was to occur.

Whereas Wink and Minear drew on religious, existential concerns, Roland Frye and Hans Frei found that the study of literature exposed fundamental flaws in the historical-critical method. At the Pittsburgh Festival, Frye not only likened the whole analytical approach to texts to the by-gone "disintegration" of Shakespeare, but declared that the whole historical-critical study of the Gospels (and hence of the Bible as a whole) was "a highly complex game...with rules as artificial as those of chess", so that the result of applying source, form, and redaction criticisms rigorously is "very rarely anything which would be convincing, at least to leading literary historians in the humanities".[13] Seven years later in San Antonio, at another colloquy on the Gospels, Frye developed his reservations more fully,[14] and concluded:

> And this is what the methodologies in question yield: not sound literary history, but a mass of speculation and conjectures, a labyrinth of pseudo-historical constructs....[Critics' efforts] often do constitute very impressive intellectual exercises, but they are not recognizable as literary history to one who represents this field in secular scholarship.[15]

On a discipline which from the outset prided itself on being rigorously scientific in the reconstruction of literary history, this charge--if true--would have an effect comparable to a sudden cold shower. In both essays, Frye called for treating the Gospels as literary wholes.

Hans Frei's searching discussion of hermeneutics from the Enlightenment onward called attention to the great reversal which historical criticism represents: from being the aperture into reality the Bible became instead a problem to be interpreted into another reality (our own).[16] Frei, too, calls for reading the text as a whole, and as a "realistic narrative". Because the text means what it says and says what it means, one should not seek the "real meaning" outside the text, whether behind it in the reconstructed events inadequately (or inaccurately) reported, or beneath it in more competent ideas. Neither reconstruction of what really happened nor demythologizing into another mode of discourse should displace a realistic reading of the narrative.[17]

It is not clear whether one should include that diverse movement known as "structuralism" among the opponents of historical criticism or not, because at least some of its advocates insist that its role is corrective and complementary. Historical critics can feel threatened by it, nonetheless, because it proposes a consistent, alternate way of reading texts--one which appears not to need historical criticism. Indeed, its articulate advocate among biblical students, Daniel Patte, contends that one must not assess structuralist exegesis in the light of historical exegesis.[18] Just as history is a "field-encompassing field" (Van Harvey), assimilating and ordering a wide spectrum of inquiries and sources of information so that the past can be reconstructed as accurately as possible, so "structuralism" is a "field encompassing field" concentrating on a quite different range of considerations. As Patte puts it, "for the historian man is so predominantly the semantic agent [the 'creator of significations'] that the semantic potentiality of the text is strictly limited to what the author (as an individual or as a group) *meant*".[19] Structuralism, on the other hand, is disinterested in this question. It aims "not at what arises from the author's creativity, but at what imposes itself upon him".[20] It is less what the text says in its particularity and more what permits and inhibits the saying of it at all that interests structuralist exegesis.

Though helpful as a counterweight to historicism, the whole enterprise strikes one as an ahistorical technology of language which "does its thing" with the aid of the text, which is its raw material. The complementarity of methods appears more often to be declared than demonstrated. Be that as it may, one can scarcely avoid the suspicion that the appeal of "structuralism" is proportionate to the sense of intellectual exhaustion of historical criticism, irrespective of the measure of innate compatibility of historical and structuralist analyses.

David Robertson's *The Old Testament and the Literary Critic*,[21] in a way, reinforces Hans Frei's point that in reading biblical narrative one finds the meaning within the story, not outside it, either in that something else to which the text refers (what Frei calls "ostensive meaning")[22] or in what it is to effect (rhetorical considerations, according to Robertson).[23] Robertson is clear: "literary criticism is the disciplinary study of pure literature, just as rhetoric is the methodological study of applied literature".[24] The Bible, as originally written, was applied literature; but, Robertson will assume "that the entire Bible is imaginative literature and study it accordingly". There is a certain ambiguity in Robertson's justification of the method: on the one hand,

there is a tone of playfulness in his acknowledging that declaring the Bible to be what it is not is an arbitrary move
required only by his desire to do so and because "literary
criticism can yield exciting and meaningful results". It is
not better than other approaches, "just different".[25] Since
the method is not being touted as either the inevitable next
self-disclosure of a Geist (Zeit-, Forschungs- or whatever) or
as the discernment of truth made possible only in response to
collapse of culture, we get a hint that this study of the
Bible might actually be enjoyable because so little rides on
it. Who can be against "exciting and interesting results"?
But then Robertson seems to fall victim of the movement of
Geist after all, for literary criticism is a "fourth major
paradigm shift". The previous three? The reading of this
Hebrew literature as Scripture, the reading of it as Christian Scripture, and the reading of it as sources for critical
historiography.

This claim that reading the Bible as imaginative literature is a fourth paradigm shift merits more comment. Robertson claims that "On each of these four occasions the Old Testament was wrenched fairly suddenly and none too gently from
one context into another." Each time, the new is perceived to
be both arbitrary and distorting the true meaning.[26] Here,
historical judgments must be distinguished from historical
warrants. In a brief, popular work like this, one may overlook a certain looseness in historical judgment (that commencing to read Hebrew texts as Scripture represented a sudden
shift, that it was regarded as arbitrary); but, it is difficult to do so when the arbitrary decision of an individual is
legitimated by appealing to paradigm shifts in which faith
communities were reconstituted (the post-exilic community
committed to Scripture in a new way, the church committed to
reading the Scripture through the lens of the Christ-event),
or reformed (biblical criticism's often unstated agenda).
Literary critics might, of course, constitute themselves as
a community; but, what Robertson proposes actually seems to
disregard the relation of the Bible to religious communities
altogether, and might actually be nothing less than a warrant
for reading the Bible seriously at all, though apart from any
prior commitments to it which participation in a faith community usually entails.

The importance of a religious community for reading the
Bible is clear from another angle as well. Robertson himself
points this out when he writes "the Bible as imaginative literature is a very different book from a Bible read as scripture", for as imaginative literature it is "a power to aid
rather than to save" (Robert Frost's word is cited--that a
poem "'ends in a clarification of life--not necessarily a

great clarification, such as sects and cults are founded on, but in a momentary stay against confusion'".[27] At the end of the book, however, we are told that the process of entering the world created by the Bible's words is like religious conversion. When the Bible is read as imaginative literature, as fiction, "it is a word addressed to a hearer and requires an imaginative response...before it can be fully entered into and understood".[28] This sounds like not only Barth's "strange world of the Bible" but like the Christian doctrine of the "inner witness of the Holy Spirit". Still, he points out that the Bible as imaginative literature "is not so powerful as the Bible as scripture" because with regard to the real world, "it can do so little".[29] Why the Bible as Scripture is so powerful is not said; indeed, one may wonder what view of Scripture is at work here. Is it not the case that the Bible has "power" primarily as the canon of a community which it energizes and authorizes?

Just as the importance of canon and community is implied by absence from Robertson's stimulating book, so is the role of historical criticism. This comes clear in chapter 5, which is devoted to the plot of the Bible as a whole, namely, "that the impotence of the prophetic word announcing imminent salvation is compensated for by a striking and momentous development...the prophetic word comes veritably to constitute the event of which it speaks",[30] a process continued in the romantic poets up to Allen Ginsberg.[31] This plot, Robertson points out, is not what "really happened" but is the story which the Bible tells. Actually, it is the story Robertson constructs from selected material conveniently juxtaposed--a procedure not unlike that used by Christians to find Christ in the Old Testament or a plan of salvation or a "progressive revelation" (in both, Jesus picks up at the apex of the Old Testament-- Deutero-Isaiah!). The point is that many would not regard this to be the biblical plot, but a rather imaginative and idiosyncratic one. The point is simply that historical-critical exegesis remains the best way of adjudicating the argument, for it appeals to evidence and warrants, not to individual discernments which are found "exciting and interesting". Or is this type of literary criticism essentially a secularized form of what used to be called "spiritual exegesis", subject to no constraints of historical evidence publically discussed?

Robertson's book is extraordinarily fruitful, partly because it has actually exposed so nicely what happens when the historical-critical method is set aside--the Bible itself becomes something else, and vice versa.

II.

The survival of the historical-critical method and the survival of the Bible as the canon of the community appear to go hand in hand. Given the fact that the church and the synagogue used this literature as canon without historical criticism longer than they did with it, this is a remarkable conclusion indeed. It is not logical necessity that links them but historical circumstance. What Lindsell and other rearguard snipers fail to realize is that the church has so much at stake in the health of historical criticism--despite the foibles and flaws associated with it. Essentially, what makes historical criticism doubly significant today--against the left as well as the right--is precisely that it is historical (in this I include the historical-sociological approach).

To be sure, one ought to eschew all methodological tyranny, including that of historical criticism. The view that one cannot "really" understand a text until one has determined the "original" meaning intended by the author located at a discrete place and time--even if all such matters could be ascertained with complete accuracy--has never been valid. The rise of alternate methods is to be welcomed precisely because they relativize the absolutist claims sometimes put forward on behalf of historical criticism. Conversely, there is little gain in replacing the tyranny of historical criticism with an equally imperious stance on the part of literary criticism (implied by Frye) or structuralism. Methods are, after all, refined tools, modes of inquiry developed in order to learn something in a disciplined way. Methods are inherently complementary because a text is both an event in time (thus eliciting inquiry into genetic relationship--diachronic or historical-critical study) and an internally coherent work with a life of its own (thus eliciting inquiry into internal relationships--synchronic, structuralist or literary study). The real dispute, if there must be one, should be over what it is that we want to know and why knowing it is significant. Consonant with these observations is also the suspicion of any master plan which assigns to each mode of inquiry its proper place, a hierarchical hermeneutic, a "meta-method".

Moreover, the plurality of methods invites historical critics to reconsider the significance of genetic (or diachronic) inquiry, quite apart from curiosity about "what really happened". Since the Bible is after all, and before all, the canon of a community of faith, why should the community know or care about "what really happened", or about what the text meant (or was taken to mean) at the moment of its creation--especially since that meaning cannot be repeated even with deliberate archaizing?

Two responses suggest how one might proceed. (1) Even if the reconstructed past cannot be relived, it does alert the present to analogues. The communities of faith have sensed this repeatedly, though often crudely and intuitively. Otherwise they would scarcely have preserved the highly particular and concrete Jesus-traditions, for instance, when the particulars had long disappeared (one thinks of Caesar's coin, the two brothers' request to sit at Jesus' left and right hand, etc.). The community sensed that what manifests itself in these particulars is not an idea but a perennial problem. Implicit in the movement from memory to tradition to text to Scripture to canon is the fulfilled expectation that the material from the past illumines the ever-moving present, that the past is repeatedly paradigmatic. Historical criticism and the attendant reconstruction of the past can assist the community to perpetuate the process. Historical criticism/reconstruction of itself cannot do this, for it is a matter of discernment. But without historical work, there would be far less to discern. (2) Historical criticism/reconstruction is also a major factor in the community's capacity to come to terms with its own past--precisely in relation to its canon. The "distancing" which distressed Wink can actually be celebrated, for without it there is little likelihood that the community can disengage itself from unsavory elements of its past, such as the "anti-Semitic" dimensions of the Gospels. Likewise, it is historical criticism applied also to the history of criticism that allows us to disallow unsavory elements also in the antipathetic portrayal of Judaism in modern scholarship, just as it is historical understanding which can inhibit us from viewing our own work ahistorically. Historical criticism/reconstruction cannot be confined to the canonical texts but inevitably spills over to the (historical) community and its (historical) understanding as well. Perhaps the most important reason why the communities of the canon have a stake in the health of historical criticism is that this method above all has the capacity to nourish the community's self-criticism. In this light, any turning away from historical criticism to the internal world of the texts or toward fascination with how the text "works" or to perennial deep structures of the human mind will be, and should be, perceived as little short of a flight from history, indeed, as reactionary exegesis, inviting the community to settle for what it is. In short, what is at stake in the survival of historical criticism as a vital factor in the study of the Bible is its capacity to help the community take responsibility for its past.

NOTES

1. Harold Lindsell, *The Battle for the Bible* (Grand Rapids: Zondervan, 1976). "Son of Battle" has now appeared, *The Bible in the Balance* (Grand Rapids: Zondervan, 1979). In a way, the wide acceptance of historical criticism of the Bible appears to be attested by the need to form The International Council on Biblical Inerrancy which Lindsell's more recent book reports.

2. J. Louis Martyn uses the analogy of a tell without antipathy in *The Gospel of John in Christian History* (New York: Paulist Press, 1979), p. 90. On the other hand, James A. Sanders uses the metaphor to express the largely unwanted results of biblical criticism: "Biblical Criticism and the Bible as Canon," *Union Seminary Quarterly Review* 32 (Spring-Summer, 1977): 157-65.

3. J. A. T. Robinson, *Redating the New Testament* (Philadelphia: Westminster Press, 1976). See the extensive review by D. Moody Smith in *The Duke Divinity School Review* 42 (Fall, 1977): 193-205.

4. H. Dixon Slingerland, *The Testaments of the Twelve Patriarchs: A Critical History of Research*, Society of Biblical Literature Monograph Series, no. 21 (Missoula: Scholars Press, 1977).

5. Walter Schmithals, *Gnosticism in Corinth*, trans. John E. Steely (Nashville: Abingdon Press, 1971).

6. See, e.g., Kim E. Dewey, "Peter's Curse and the Cursed Peter," in *The Passion in Mark*, ed. Werner Kelber (Philadelphia: Fortress Press, 1976), pp. 96-114, and Theodore J. Weeden, *Mark--Traditions in Conflict* (Philadelphia: Fortress Press, 1971).

7. Walter Wink, *The Bible in Human Transformation* (Philadelphia: Fortress Press, 1973).

8. Ibid., p. 15.

9. Ibid., p. 29.

10. Ibid., p. 61.

11. Paul S. Minear, "Gospel History: Celebration or Reconstruction?" in *Jesus and Man's Hope*, ed. Donald G. Miller

and Dikran Y. Hadidian (Pittsburgh: Pittsburgh Theological Seminary, 1971), II: 19.

12. Ibid., p. 25.

13. Roland Mushat Frye, "A Literary Perspective for the Criticism of the Gospels," ibid., p. 213. See the response published later by Paul J. Achtemeier, "On the Historical-Critical Method in New Testament Studies," *Perspective* 11 (Winter, 1970): 289-304.

14. Roland Mushat Frye, "The Synoptic Problems and Analogies in Other Literatures," in *The Relationships Among the Gospels*, ed. W. O. Walker, Jr. (San Antonio: Trinity University Press, 1978), pp. 261-302; here, pp. 286ff.

15. Ibid., p. 301.

16. Hans W. Frei, *The Eclipse of Biblical Narrative* (New Haven: Yale University Press, 1974). I reviewed this volume and its sequel, *The Identity of Jesus Christ* (Philadelphia: Westminster Press, 1975) in *Theology Today* 31 (January, 1975): 367-70 and 32 (October, 1975): 312-20, respectively.

17. For Frei, a narrative is "realistic" when the "depiction is of that peculiar sort in which characters...are firmly and significantly set in the context of the external environment....Realistic narrative is that kind in which subject and social setting belong together, and characters and external circumstances fitly render each other." See *Eclipse*, p. 13.

18. Daniel Patte, *What is Structural Exegesis?* (Philadelphia: Fortress Press, 1976), p. 37.

19. Ibid., p. 13, his italics.

20. Ibid., p. 16.

21. David Robertson, *The Old Testament and the Literary Critic* (Philadelphia: Fortress Press, 1977).

22. Norman R. Petersen makes the same point when he writes, "the referential *function* in narrative is to be located in the world created by the narrative, and the referential *fallacy* consists of thinking about this world as though it were a direct representation of the real world, overlooking the conceptual autonomy of the narrative world". See *Literary Criticism for New Testament Critics* (Philadelphia: Fortress Press, 1978), p. 40.

23. Robertson, *The Old Testament and the Literary Critic*, p. 3.

24. Ibid.

25. Ibid., p. 4.

26. Ibid.

27. Ibid., p. 15.

28. Ibid., p. 84.

29. Ibid., p. 85.

30. Ibid., p. 73.

31. Ibid., pp. 82-83.

8

MYTHOLOGICAL ANALYSIS OF NEW TESTAMENT MATERIALS

William G. Doty

The near-bankruptcy of the appeal of traditional historical-critical methods in which most biblical scholars have been
trained cannot help but strike the teacher who is responsible
for "introducing" biblical materials to the college student or
general public. The problems are that the level of required
expertise is so overwhelming, the involuted quality of the
technics--explosively displayed though they may be--so exacting, and the ties of scholarship to theological positions so
elusive and often obscure, that the teacher finds him/herself
constantly admonishing, "Yes, that is an interesting book but
just look at the publisher!...not anything a legitimate [i.e.,
my brand] scholar would take seriously."

Precisely when we are in a position to explain more clearly and in greater detail than ever before, the modes of explanation appear enormously inaccessible to the common reader; and
even the contemporary seminary student often rebels at learning the technical ploys of the games exegetes play.

Certainly one reason so many of us have turned to literary
analysis has been that we have found there a basis for interaction and communication with persons in academe other than
Bible-quoters. Even in such situations, however, tensions continue: in a university course on "Parables", listed in both
Classics and Comparative Literature, I found the classics students, many of whom were religious-studies concentrators, to
be angered when I did not genuflect properly at the theological
nuances beyond the parable-texts, and the complit students
uncomfortable at the mere suggestion that the history of the
Christian tradition was vital to understanding how we come today to any reading of the parables of Jesus.

Ironically, therefore, we know more, but are able to
speak less, in fewer contexts, than ever before. Not a problem I can solve! Nor do I conceive the recent "Bible as Literature" revival as a sufficient way out. Still less is a
"mythological approach to the materials of the New Testament"
an adequate medicine, and yet I want to sketch its contours
here as part of the total range of revisionings that may pro-

vide renewed access to biblical materials, which are increasingly approached within college curricula within the framework
of the history of religions.

In working toward a format for mythological analysis of
biblical materials, I am not proposing that this should become
the new approach, which might guarantee revived interests,
which in turn might be led back to the "real" academic work of
the technician. Resolution of the tensions between technical
academic analysis and non-technical general presentation will
not happen through any one essay, or even any one approach.
But I think it high time that professionals attend to the
problems of conveying the data of their profession more ac-
cessibly (not only in biblical studies, but generally, within
academia).

There is clearly something missing when Chris Popenoe's
massive bibliographic guide to 11,000 books on Inner Development, which I respect, and which has served as a rich source
of references with respect to the current revival of interest
in religion, especially those of non-traditional bent, has no
subsection on "New Testament" in its "Christianity" section,
lists only one book on Paul by a biblical specialist (Schweit-
zer's mysticism book of 1931), and only one general book on
Torah (a guide to weekly synagogue readings--and that listed
in the section on "Jewish Mysticism"!).[1]

Perhaps we have over-specialized ourselves--or our subject matter--out of existence, so intent upon exacting analysis of the texts themselves (shades of New Criticism!) that
we fail to convey the common issues we yet share with the
people who produced the Jewish and Christian Scriptures.
Balancing the past and present, evoking, calling forth and
naming the great human themes which have surfaced in the past,
and which yet surface: we need something of the perspective
of the younger Pliny (*Epist.* 6:21):

> I am the kind of person who admires the
> ancients, yet, unlike some, I do not de-
> spise the talents of our own times.

I am frequently asked how I can resolve the tensions between my background in technical biblical studies and the work
in mythology which has been my primary occupation for several
years now. The question in itself discloses the persistence
of the myth-*versus*-history distinction, applied to "pagan"-
versus-Christian dichotomies for lo these many years.

But of course mythological analysis of NT materials might
seem to be ruled out of court before we begin, if we were to

argue on the basis of the lexeme *mythos* alone: on only five occasions does it appear, four times in Timothy and Titus, and once in 2 Peter (the concordances list only 1 Tim. 1:4, 4:7; 2 Tim. 4:4; Tit. 1:14; 2 Pet. 1:16). In each instance *mythos* appears in contrast to "the truth" of Christianity (so explicitly in 2 Tim.), and therefore is primarily a *negative* concept, translated readily by "tales" ("cleverly-devised tales", 2 Pet. 1:16, New American Standard Bible) or "fables" ("worldly fables fit only for old women", 1 Tim. 4:7, NASB); it is negatively qualified as "Jewish myths" (Tit. 1:14), or linked with "endless genealogies which give rise to mere speculation" (1 Tim. 1:4, NASB). The term is not considered important enough to index in some of the standard reference works (Young's *Analytical Concordance*: entry under "fable", none under "myth"; no entry in Moulton and Geden's *Concordance*, or in several other biblical dictionaries and lexica I consulted).

Our project also appears prohibited by Christian theological polemics, which have consistently argued that Christianity is based upon a historic intervention of deity which is to be contrasted fundamentally with mythological speculation. Such a perspective has doubtless influenced the composition of the reference works; it has certainly exerted its rule over theology and exegetical studies.

However, neither the lexical emptiness nor the theological bias necessarily prohibits an analytic that brings to primitive Christian materials some of the methodologies developed for the analysis of non-Christian mythologies, and I will demonstrate with the example of "Baptism into Death" some of what might take place. Many other possibilities might be focal: apocalyptic materials, hieratic organization, institutional self-concept, images of environment, and so forth. And a longer study might display the anti-myth animus that has been evident in the history of modern NT studies, Bultmann's misleading supernaturalist definition of myth, and recent approaches to mythic "structures" within texts.[2]

We especially need to develop a more adequate, comprehensive definition of myth, which recognizes that there are levels of mythic vitality within any community, as well as competing mythic interpretations of the same image.[3] Heuristically, it would be most instructive to explore two bodies of mythological materials at the same time—the one the NT itself, and the other a canon from a radically different set of cultural suppositions. We might explore how some of the same human issues were perceived and dealt with within each culture area.

Such an approach might go a long way toward a much-needed de-potentiating of the term "myth", for I usually find it necessary to explain that I am in no way speaking pejoratively of dogma or superstition or ideology when I speak of the "myths" of the primitive Christian communities. I am seeking to approach these materials from a stance that finds them exciting, relevant, illuminating, for my own self-perspective. But it is an approach that remains open to and valid within the thoroughly multi-religious atmosphere of the state university and national academy, one which recognizes significance in several communities of human culture, rather than just one. And it is a cross-disciplinary approach that banks very heavily upon recent developments in the anthropology of religion--I think especially of the work of Victor Turner--comparative folkloristics and mythography, and even the re-visioning of early twentieth-century depth psychology, as best represented by James Hillman.

Some aspects of a mythological reading can be illustrated here by seeing how it opens up one NT thematic, "Baptism into Death". The full analysis, prepared as a guest lecture at Wellesley College last year, runs to some thirty pages, so I can present here only parts, mostly in the form of questions that might be asked and omitting references to the rich store of bibliographic tools which are available. The overall questions which guide us:

How does baptism function as *a key symbol* for the primitive Christian community? What secondary symbols does it bring together? With what other symbols is it in tension or complementation?

What *patterns of the religious community* can be recognized from analysis of this key symbol? What sociological consequences follow from this symbol, as contrasted with others?

How does such a key symbol provide *a framework for a metaphysics* or a world view? How do the contexts of the texts in which the symbol is present relate this symbol to other world-founding symbols? What types of myths are involved?[4]

What are *the cross-cultural materials* which provide illumination of our topic? How are similar interests/images presented in other cultures? (Here one moves beyond the range of canonical NT texts to those temporally and conceptually prior to and subsequent to them, and might engage archetypal motifs--and in this instance, should lead there, given the deep significance of the mythemes involved: death, birth, rebirth, initiation, purification through washing, hierophany, *et al.*).

Five aspects may be sketched briefly here, out of a much larger range of possibilities:

1. INITIATION. Baptism as a sign of inclusion in membership, of belonging to a community (baptism *eis to onoma christou* is evidently related to the bank accounts of Hellenistic commerce in that "to the account of" would bear the name of the person who "owns" it). The dialogue in Acts 19:3-5 probably shows the transition from membership in a John-the-Baptist church to the Christ-church; 1 Corinthians 1:10ff. indicates that the lines of membership were much less clearly drawn than we might now assume from our much later perspective; and Matthew 28:19 shows the later NT perspective having become controlling: the churches have become The (trinitarian) Church.

The Qumran community provides examples of the sort of separation and existential transition from identity to identity that was to accompany initiation into a particular religious community; the early catholic Rite of Scrutiny preceding baptism at Easter shows the afterimage. Hebrews 6:1-2 speaks of "instruction about washings", and Philo likewise emphasizes the cleansing, purifying aspects of lustrations: where did this element go in the subsequent history of Christianity?

2. ORIGIN/FOUNDATION MYTH. One of the strong emphases of modern myth research is that myths provide "charters" for communities; we may qualify this a bit to say that *some* myths set out the stories of the original times, which are the specially-powerful times when creative energies are the highest—subsequent ritual enactments seek to reactivate that creativity for the participants. The questions to which an origin myth now gives rise is probably a particularly modern one: no one fully within a myth asks whether it was "really" historically founded. For us, however, the question shapes itself in terms of etiology, the sources of the idea, something that reaches back to the Greeks' concern to name the *prōtos heuretēs*, the "first finder", of a culturefact.

For the subject of baptism, four main sources are primarily relevant:

a) Pre- and Non-Christian. The range of possibilities is almost endless—Eleusinian cults, Bacchic consecrations, Egyptian or Mithraic ceremonies—but few direct parallels seem relevant beyond the image of perishing (going under the water) and ritual lustration (cleansing of individuals or icons).

b) Jewish. Here we see the themes of self-baptism, as well as the hopeful anticipation of Zechariah 13:1 and Ezekiel 36:24f.--which the churches claimed to have experienced as realized.

c) Relationship to John "the Baptist". As part of the pan-Jordanian baptizing movement, John steps out with his once-for-all sacramental purification, not to join the Jewish community, but as a preparation for membership in a future messianic community. (For the present context we will have to ignore the knotty problem of the competition between Baptists and Christians, although I think that is a crucial issue for understanding primitive Christian politics.)

d) Relationship to Jesus. Again a knotty problem: did he or did he not baptize? But Eliade suggests a principle that is as applicable here as it is with respect to the institution of the Eucharist and the Our Father:

> In the eyes of those who perform them,
> initiations are believed to have been
> revealed by Divine or Supernatural be-
> ings.[5]

"Did he or didn't he?" transforms into asking about the necessity to claim that Jesus did institute/found baptism, as well as about the "charter" aspects of such a tradition. Regarding the stories, Norman Perrin, writing in another context, suggests:

> They are, if you will, a mixture of
> mythicized history and historicized
> myth, but the proportion of one to the
> other is not relevant to their func-
> tioning adequacy as foundation myth or
> constitutive history.[6]

3. WATER SYMBOLISM. What I am calling key symbols are radical/central to mythological materials; one indication of the mythological is that its subject matter and imagery touches deep roots, engages master metaphors for segments of the human experience. When such symbols are touched, they resonate, re-sound, not just toward one meaning, but toward many meanings for those who share the same universe of language.[7]

This exposing of the various branches and semantic networks of symbolic resonance I find most exciting of all; but in this restricted context I will have to be content with an inter-relational diagram of the key areas set vibrating (building somewhat upon Victor Turner's masterful study of the symbolism of colors and the *chishing'a* among the Ndembu).[8]

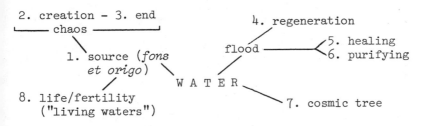

Each term implies another; each aspect gains its effectiveness partly from its position in the whole network; and the total matrix represents the multiplex interweaving of powerful images that allows access through any one of them.

4. DEATH AND REBIRTH. Here we have the themes of Pauline mysticism, as well as typological development of the Exodus motif; but also the revivification of Osiris with Nile water, and the interpretation of Jesus' death as an initiatory baptism, as well as the later "second baptism" of the martyrs. "Living our dying", "dying to life", but "having died, living toward a second death": hence the baptismal font as both tomb and womb in the Syrian liturgy and in Chrysostom. And finally there is the Pauline and neo-Pauline ethicizing of the theme as a sacramental realized eschatology: the rebirth is so powerful that it leads one to regard the world as a *kainē ktisis* in which the old self is now dead, and one belongs (Justin Martyr) to a new "race" of humankind.

5. INSTITUTIONAL DEVELOPMENT. John's eschatological plenary cleansing becomes an official act of the ecclesial institution, and is related to fasting, exorcism, anointing, confirmation, *et al.* An almost magical transformation, along the lines of the non-church mysteries. And then there is the tension between Receipt of the Spirit and Baptism with Water—so we are led into both the Pentecostal narratives and the issues of laying on of hands and authority/tradition.

Beyond these lines of inquiry, which have not even touched the image of "sealing" so important from apocalyptic contexts, the baptism of the pre-christian dead, the question of infant baptism, and many other issues, we can (and perhaps should) move well beyond the Graeco-Roman world to cross-cultural explorations. Eliade's *Patterns in Comparative Religion* and *From Primitives to Zen* collate much relevant material; the sourcebook edited by J. L. Henderson and M. Oakes (*The Wisdom of the Serpent: The Myths of Death, Rebirth, and Resurrection*) is helpful; and we can look at the archetypology of water symbolism associated with the Great Mother, along the lines of Carl Jung and Erich Neumann.

Mythological analysis complements, rather than replaces, historical-critical scrutiny. And to me it holds promise of connections with the material at a level that engages more than just our interest in historicity, which seems to be attenuating rather rapidly today.

Contemporary theologizing might follow; or in the words of Eliade, self-liberation, which seems to me quite enough of an aim:

> To the degree that you *understand* a religious fact (myth, ritual, symbol, divine figure, etc.), you *change*, you are modified--and this change is the equivalent of a step forward in the process of self-liberation.[9]

NOTES

1. Chris Popenoe, *Inner Development: The Yes! Bookshop Guide*, 1979; available from Random House or the publisher: Yes! Inc., 1035 31st Street, N. W., Washington, D. C. 20007.

2. See for instance Daniel Patte, *What is Structural Exegesis?* (Philadelphia: Fortress, 1976), ch. 4, "Mythical Structures and Exegesis"; John Dominic Crossan, *The Dark Interval: Towards a Theology of Story* (Niles, Ill.: Argus, 1975), ch. 2; differently: Charles H. Talbert, *What is a Gospel? The Genre of the Canonical Gospels* (Philadelphia: Fortress, 1977), chs. 2-3.
   From the mass of earlier materials, I will cite only one work, which was stimulating to me even though I often disagree with its conclusions: Geraint Vaughan Jones, *Christology and Myth in the New Testament: An Inquiry into the Character, Extent and Interpretation of the Mythological Element in New Testament Eschatology* (London: Allen & Unwin, 1956).
   Thanks are due to Amos Wilder for sharing some essays with me toward this project, and for his *The Language of the Gospel: Early Christian Rhetoric* (New York: Harper & Row, 1964; reprint ed., Cambridge: Harvard University Press, 1971), ch. 7, "Image, Symbol, Myth".

3. I have taken on the former problem in "Mythophiles' Dyscrasia, or What is Myth and What Does it Do?", 1978, 48 pp., and the latter problem in *Mythography: The Study of Myths and Rituals*, 1977, 357 pp. Neither work has been published as of February, 1979.

4. At present I am working with the following typology of myth-types (with examples): 1. Explicating World-Surround (cosmogonic, cosmological, cosmographic; eschatological, teleological); 2. Providing Origin-Stories (etiological, giving exemplars); 3. Reflecting on Nature (ecology, astrology, technology); 4. Setting Cultural Models (social/familial/sexual patterns; morality; divination; healing); 5. Enumerating Personae (relational roles; hero/ine; religious and political specialists; tricksters); and 6. Developing Metaphysical Concepts (time; theodicy; symbolism).

5. Mircea Eliade, *Rites and Symbols of Initiation: The Mysteries of Birth and Rebirth*, trans. W. R. Trask (New York: Harper & Row, 1958), p. 129. See, more generally on the topic: Wendell C. Beane and William G. Doty, eds., *Myths, Rites, Symbols: A Mircea Eliade Reader*, 2 vols. (New York: Harper & Row, 1975), *passim*.

6. Norman Perrin, *The Resurrection According to Matthew, Mark, and Luke* (Philadelphia: Fortress, 1977), p. 11. Perrin's death occurred just when he was developing a "mythological" approach of some substance; we had many lively discussions about the functional role of myth during the preparation of his *The New Testament: An Introduction* (New York: Harcourt, Brace, Jovanovich, 1974).

7. Mircea Eliade, *Patterns in Comparative Religion*, trans. R. Sheed (Cleveland: World, 1958), p. 189, notes that "The same symbol may indicate or evoke a whole series of realities, which profane experience would see as separate and autonomous."

8. Victor Turner, *The Forest of Symbols: Aspects of Ndembu Ritual* (Ithaca, N.Y.: Cornell University Press, 1967), especially ch. 3 and pp. 296-98.

9. Mircea Eliade, *No Souvenirs: Journal, 1957-69*, trans. F. H. Johnson, Jr. (New York: Harper & Row, 1977), p. 310, author's emphasis.
Having cited Professor Eliade so frequently in this brief paper, I may have given the impression that his work is immediately applicable to NT analysis. It is no more so than the work of other theorists such as Joseph Campbell, Turner, or Claude Lévi-Strauss. Contemporary mythography is itself a field in the process of sorting itself out, so there are no master methodologies at present.

It is a pleasure to submit this essay in honor of Will Beardslee, whose writings and careful, clear-headed criticisms have saved me from many an embarrassing gaffe, while exciting my imagination toward a more truly inter-disciplinary literary biblical criticism--and even, perhaps, toward a mythological criticism!

9

DEMYTHOLOGIZING AS THE SELF-EMBODIMENT OF SPEECH

Thomas J. J. Altizer

I. THE PROBLEM OF DEMYTHOLOGIZING

It might be said that Demythologizing is at once the
center of all truly modern expressions of Christianity and
the primary way whereby and wherein a modern or post-modern
Christianity attempts to integrate its primordial ground in
the Bible with its eschatological goal or end. A truly modern
Christianity is by necessity a radical Christianity, and it is
radical because of its inevitable recognition that it is just
as distant from its beginning in Bible as from its end in
Apocalypse. Such a radical Christianity knows itself as modernity or post-modernity, and knows that the advent of the
modern world issued in a transformation of Christianity even
greater than that effected by its original movement from a
Jewish to a Gentile world. We should not think of Bultmann
and Tillich as the creators of Demythologizing; it would be
more accurate to say that they attempted to accomodate it to
a pre-modern Christianity. For true or full Demythologizing
is by necessity a negation and transcendence of a whole inherited world of faith.

While the pervasive and comprehensive presence of Demythologizing in the modern world is both undeniable and inescapable, its identity and nature remain ever elusive and un-
defined. One essential route into its identity is by way of
an historical and chronological demarcation. Surely its initial expression occurs in the Radical rather than the Magis-
terial Reformation, and it was profoundly effected by it not
expressed in the English, the American, and the French Revolutions. These revolutionary events brought an end to the
ancient world and they might be thought of as marking the
dividing line between a modern and a pre-modern Christianity.
Accordingly, Milton, Blake, and Melville might be thought of
as poets of Demythologizing, and in the succession of their
prophetic epics we can observe the progressive and ever
radicalizing movement of Demythologizing. We can also observe that the Bible is far more deeply and comprehensively
present in their work than it is in that of their less modern

counterparts. From this point of view we can apprehend the historical beginning of our Demythologizing, and also its locus and world, a world which is quite simply the world of modernity. But we cannot thereby apprehend the historical end of Demythologizing, unless we were to judge that modernity came to an end in the Russian and Chinese Revolutions. But that judgment, to say the least, would be premature.

Another essential route into the meaning of Demythologizing is by way of a critical analysis of the meaning and identity of myth. Ever increasingly we have come to see that myth has multiple layers, modes, and dimensions of meaning. For not only is myth integrally related to liturgy and ritual, but so likewise is it to language itself, and most particularly so to the earliest or primal forms or language. No longer can we simply identify myth with the archaic world, however, for it has been reborn in post-modernism, and reborn with such power that it has now become virtually impossible to see the absence of myth in any meaning or identity upon our horizon. Nevertheless, we know full well that mythical meaning has again and again been profoundly challenged and transformed in our history. Two axial points at which this occurred were in the Homeric epics and in the prophetic movement in Israel, and we can understand both not simply as reformations of an archaic tradition but also as revolutionary transformations of consciousness and society. From this point of view, both were movements of Demythologizing, for both negated and transcended an ancient world of myth. A truly new, individual, and interior form of consciousness stands forth in Homer and in the reform prophets, and in each this consciousness breaks forth and establishes itself by negating a world of cosmic sacrality. Consciousness realizes itself in an interior and individual form and mode by distancing itself from a cosmic identity, an original and primordial form of consciousness wherein nature and the sacred were two poles of one continuum.

While we cannot simply identify the mythical consciousness with an original or primordial consciousness, we can see that myth invariably establishes a continuum, a coordination, or a coinherence between the world and the sacred, and a continuum that is either shattered or reborn in the revolutionary moments of our history. Perhaps myth has a singular or common identity in the archaic world, but it certainly does not in our historical world or worlds, and this is so not simply because of the deep differences between historical traditions, but also because of the transformations which occur in particular traditions. Now if we were to identify myth with any order or system that coordinates or integrates nature, consciousness, and the sacred or the ultimate, then we could identify Demythologizing as any genuine uprooting

of that order or system. Furthermore, we could also say that
there are degrees of Demythologizing in accordance with which
a given mythical order is uprooted or assaulted. Is it possible, however, to think of true or pure Demythologizing as
an assault upon all possible mythological order?

Both Homer and the prophets of Israel did deeply assault
everything upon their horizon which was manifest as mythical
order. True, there is something like a mythical order in the
Homeric epics, and to the extent that the Homeric reformation
made possible the advent of Greek philosophy and Greek tragedy
we may speak of these, too, in the above sense, as myth, even
if radically new forms of myth. So likewise the prophetic
reformation of Israel was either originally or soon after-
wards integrated into the cultic and legal traditions of
Israel, and these, too, are clearly mythical. But if Greek
philosophy and literature and the Hebrew Bible are mythical
they are so in a radically new and revolutionary sense. So
likewise if we turn to the great revolutionaries of the modern
world, such as Hegel, Marx, Nietzsche, and Freud, as well as
their literary and other counterparts, we can identify them
simultaneously as Demythologizers and creators or re-creators
of myth. Is it possible, in this context, for the Christian
theologian to identify Jesus and the New Testament as embodying a revolutionary movement of Demythologizing?

Nothing has been more revolutionary in our world than the
advent and development of the modern historical consciousness,
and that consciousness succeeded in establishing a seemingly
uncrossable gulf between our world and the world or worlds of
the Bible. But hand in hand with the progressive development
of a modern estrangement from the Bible there has come forth
a series of modern rebirths of the Bible, and this has occurred not only in literature and the arts at large, but also
in truly modern thinking and politics. Moreover, it is in
revolutionary art, literature, thinking, and politics that the
Bible has been reborn in the modern world. Hegel himself, in
The Phenomenology of Spirit, identified the modern spirit, or
pure self-consciousness, as the comprehensive actualization
and realization of the Incarnation. Blake recreated the
Biblical epics in *Milton* and *Jerusalem*, and thereby made possible what we have come to know as modern literature. Even
Nietzsche re-created the Gospels in *Thus Spoke Zarathustra*,
and could find only in Jesus an historical figure who is free
of the No-saying of *ressentiment*. Modern revolutionary movements, whether in politics, thinking, or the arts, have been
apocalyptic, although apocalyptic in both positive and negative modes, and thereby have clearly been rebirths of the New
Testament. Indeed, the apocalyptic identity of Jesus and the
New Testament was discovered by modern literature and philos-

ophy long before it was unveiled by New Testament scholarship.

Yet each of these modern revolutionary movements negated and transcended the Bible even while making possible its re-birth in our world. And therein lies a fundamental identity of Demythologizing for us. We must never lose sight of the fact that Kierkegaard, our greatest modern religious thinker, could only consistently fulfill his thinking by engaging in a violent assault upon Christendom. It might well be said that it is precisely when faith becomes wholly impossible, in a Kierkegaardian sense, that it is most actual and real. A paradox of this order can lead us to realize that modern De-mythologizing is wholly positive and negative at once and al-together in its relation to the Bible. Bultmannianism, with its Kierkegaardian ground, clearly illustrates this truth. Here, the subjective or existential actuality of faith is realized only by way of a negation of the objective meaning and world of the Bible. It could almost be said that it was only by way of modern historical scholarship that a comprehen-sively distant and alien meaning and identity of the Bible could be established, a truly negative identity which is sub-ject to radical negation. From this point of view we could see that the distinctively modern identification of the Bibli-cal God as all alien God is an essential prerequisite for a full Demythologizing movement of faith. And now we know full well that Kierkegaard's discovery or re-discovery of subjec-tivity or faith was inseparable from his realization of the alien and totally judgmental identity of God.

When the Bible and the Biblical God appear in an alien and negative form even to faith, then faith can be fully realized only by engaging in a Demythologizing of the Bible itself. But something like this occurred in the prophets, who proclaimed the end of ancient Israel, and who looked for-ward to a remnant, a new covenant, or a new community of faith. We can observe full parallels to this negative and individual movement of faith in the Homeric reformation, in Confucius and Lao Tzu, and in the Buddha and the Upanishads. So far from being other than faith, Demythologizing is an expression of faith, the expression of a faith that dares to negate and transcend itself. Tillich's "God beyond God" is not other than God, but other than the God who is simply given or ini-tially manifest in faith. A modern Christian Demythologizing can surely be no less than this, but can it be more? Has it in fact already been far more? And have the most radical ex-pressions of Demythologizing in the modern world succeeded in resurrecting a lost or hidden Jesus? If so, then a pure or radical Demythologizing could be known as a full expression of faith, and the negative movement and mode of Demythologiz-ing could be understood as an essential expression of faith.

II. THE THEOLOGICAL PROBLEM OF SPEECH

Nothing is more distinctive of the Biblical tradition or
traditions than the centrality therein of Word or speech.
Whether in its enactment of Creation, of Covenant, of Torah,
of Messiah, of Wisdom, or of Kingdom of God, we may observe
here the primacy of speech, and not simply the primacy of
speech but also the ultimacy or finality of speech. Nothing
truly parallel to this centrality and ultimacy of speech may
be found in other mythical and religious traditions, except
for its prefigurations in the ancient Near East and its later
expressions in Judaism, Christianity, and Islam. China and
India embody reverse parallels to this primacy of speech, for
here silence and emptiness effect and express a comparable
primacy and finality. While speech cannot be said to be primal or ultimate in the Greek religious and mythical traditions
as such, it is so in the Homeric epics and in Greek tragedy,
and the historical coming together of Classical culture and
the Bible in Christendom can give us a decisive clue to the
unique identity and role of literature in the Western tradition. Nothing comparable to Dante, Milton, or Blake may be
found in non-Western literary traditions, for nowhere else is
God, the sacred, or the ultimate fully spoken, nowhere else is
it truly realized or actualized in language itself. Here, God
is not simply the object of speech, but the subject of speech
as well, a subject which the Christian identifies as the Word
of revelation.

Word speaks in the Bible, and this is a unique historical
phenomenon, with the possible exception of the Koran. A distinctively Christian hermeneutics has good reason to identify
the prophetic oracle as the originating center of the Bible,
a center which is reenacted in the eschatological proclamation of the New Testament. But neither prophetic oracle nor
eschatological proclamation can be understood so long as the
theological identity of speech remains unveiled. We know that
the speaker or "I" of the prophetic oracle is Yahweh or the
Lord, just as we know that the speaker of eschatological
proclamation is Spirit, or Son of Man, or one who speaks
under the impact of the dawning or near advent of Kingdom of
God. But we have not taken with sufficient seriousness the
theological consequences of such an identity. Speech here is
divine speech or Word of God, or known in faith to be Word of
God. While Judaism and Islam can know Word of God to be a
lesser or even non-divine expression of God, this is not possible for orthodox or Trinitarian Christianity, and it is even
less possible for the radical forms of modern Christianity.
For Christianity can only be a reversal of its original ground
if it comes to know a God who is ultimately silent.

Christianity and Christianity alone knows a Word or speech which is the absolute antithesis of silence. Here, Word speaks finally, and Word speaks finally because Word became "flesh". Nowhere in the New Testament is the finality of speech more evident than in the synoptic parables. For we have come to see that the intention of the synoptic parable is to realize an enactment of speech wherein a totality of speakable or realizable identity is wholly present and immediately at hand. Therein the synoptic parable is pure parable, which is to say that it is the antithesis of allegory, and the antithesis of allegory because in its full expression it leaves behind all simile and metaphor. Not until the twentieth century with the advent of a literature of anti-metaphor or purely negative metaphor did this meaning of the New Testament parable become manifest. For the pure parable so centers the attention of its hearer upon its enactment as to end all awareness of a meaning or identity beyond its immediate arena of speech.

In this sense parable, or pure parable, is present only in its enactment, only in its telling or saying. Therefore it can pass into writing only with a loss of its immediacy, a loss which occasions a reversal of itself, a reversal effecting its fall into the language of simile and metaphor, a fall culminating in its full reversal in allegory. For writing stills the sound of speech by breaking up and dismembering its vertical immediacy into a horizontal presence. Then vertical presence recedes behind and before the impacting center of voice and in that expanding horizon an immediate identity passes into simile and metaphor. Nevertheless, a tension is present in the synoptic parables which gives witness to this process of dismemberment and reversal, a tension which is most evident in the chasm which opens up between the story or the anti-story of the parable and the allegorical interpretation which is sometimes present in the text. It is precisely in this tension that the original intention of the parable is manifest. Of course, that intention cannot be fully manifest in this tension, and cannot be so if only because of the silence of writing. Yet it is nonetheless true that a trace is present here of a primary process of reversal, and in that trace we can detect an echo of a now distant immediacy.

We must never lose sight of the fact that the early Christian communities created the gospel as a literary genre, and thereby made possible the conjunction or coinherence of action or plot and logia or saying. Nothing quite like this was previously present in either Greece or Israel, for only with the birth of Christianity does a speech appear and sound which is simultaneously praxis and voice. Christian anamnesis is not a mere remembrance or recollection, it is rather a renewal or re-presentation of an identity which was originally

act and voice at once. True, this original identity was dis-
membered by both the cultus of the churches and the text of
the gospels. But this dismemberment was not complete as witness the fact that the gospels establish an horizon of meaning
wherein logia can speak within the context of the actuality of
life and world. While the field of this actuality is repeatedly turned askew by the ecclesiastical motives and intentions
of the gospel writers, it is never wholly dislodged in the
parables, even if it often threatens to disappear from view.
The stark contrast between the parables and the legends in the
gospels is striking evidence of a dichotomous presence in the
New Testament which again and again tends to disrupt and de-
construct the text. Perhaps the continual if subterranean
presence of such a threat of deconstruction is a primary
source of both the power and the actuality of the gospel
texts.

What is most missing from the true parable is the vision
and language of myth. This is a striking phenomenon for both
myth and parable conjoin the world and the sacred and each establishes a continuum between human and cosmic identity. Yet
that continuum is horizontal in myth, it stretches out into a
visionary plane, whereas it is immediate and vertical in parable. Myth distances both the speaker and the hearer from the
moment or center of voice, a distance expanding in the horizon
of vision. But parable contracts attention into the presence
or moment at hand, a presence whose very immediacy resists and
opposes the horizontal movement of vision. Pure parable embodies an auditory as opposed to a visual presence, an immediate sounding which commands and effects a total attention.
One hears a parable, and does so even in reading, for parable
sounds or speaks an immediate presence. True, that presence
is the presence of world, and the presence of that world which
is immediately and commonly at hand. Yet in parable world
overwhelms the hearer, and overwhelms the hearer in its immediacy, allowing no room for the distancing of vision. Here,
world speaks only in its immediacy, only in its being immediately at hand, an at-handedness which itself is eschatological
judgment.

All too naturally parable expands into allegory in memory
and tradition, and is thereby transposed into a visual and
mythical language. However, in the synoptic Gospels, as opposed, for example, to the Book of Revelation, such language
is obviously derived and second-hand. No attentive reader
could possibly here confuse the language of allegorical interpretation with the speech of parabolic voice. The overwhelming difference between parabolic and allegorical language
not only bespeaks the distance between parable and allegory
but also the distance between memory and speech. While that

distance may well be crossed by the Gospel of John, it clearly
is not in the allegorical language of the synoptic Gospels,
and the very artificiality and second-handedness of that language gives witness to the loss or silencing of voice. With
and in that loss there is not only a loss of the original
speaker but a loss of world as well. No longer is world incarnate in the voice of speech, just as world is no longer immediately at hand. But this parallel distancing of both world
and speech gives witness to the original presence of an immediate continuum between voice and world.

The very everydayness of true parabolic language bespeaks
an immediate presence of world in voice. Parabolic enactment
occurs on earth and not in heaven, in "flesh" as opposed to
"spirit". Now is the time of decision, and this nowness reverses every trace of a beyond which is only beyond. So likewise there here occurs a reversal of a world which is merely
and only world. World now stands forth in its immediacy, and
that immediacy is itself the time of decision. Now voice itself is praxis, the praxis of a world come of age. At no
point in this immediacy is either world or voice only itself,
for each is charged with a total and eschatological presence.
In that presence there is an immediate continuum between the
actuality of both world and voice, and therein there is embodied a judgment which is simultaneously both eschatological
and here and now. This is a simultaneity which is lost with
the advent of metaphor and allegory. For metaphor and allegory break up the immediacy of a totally actual present by establishing a horizontal distance between language and world.

This is a distance which is absent in pure parabolic
speech. For pure parabolic speech does not speak about the
world if only because it does not speak of or about anything
whatsoever. On the contrary, here world speaks in voice itself, and as voice as well. True parabolic speech is the
speech of world itself, a speech wherein and whereby world is
totally actual and immediately at hand. Then speech is world
and world is speech at once. Such speech calls its hearer out
of a world which is silent and apart and into a world which is
embodied in the full actuality of voice. The silence of the
world ends in parabolic speech, and ends because parabolic
speech gives utterance to the actuality of time and world. It
is precisely the absence of metaphorical and allegorical distancing which makes possible the full and immediate presence
of speech. Then the act of speech is an incarnation of world,
an incarnation of world in the pure immediacy of voice.

III. SELF-EMBODIMENT

One of the most difficult problems posed by modern New
Testament scholarship is the identity of eschatological speech.
We now know that eschatological speech, or eschatological act
and speech, is the originating center of both Christianity and
the New Testament. But what is eschatological speech? It is
common to attempt to resolve this problem by way of establishing a dichotomy between eschatological speech and mythical
apocalyptic or Gnostic vision. In its Bultmannian expression,
this takes the form of posing a dichotomy between a subjective
or existential eschatological faith and an objective or cosmic
mythical vision. Then a consistent and comprehensive Demythologizing of an apocalyptic or cosmic vision is an eschatological or existential expression of faith. Thereby eschatological
becomes identified as existential and the incarnate or the
Christian Word becomes identified as the existential Word.
Then the center of the New Testament becomes eschatological
faith and its alien periphery either apocalyptic or Gnostic
mythology. Quite naturally this subjective or existential
form of Demythologizing has had an immense impact upon contemporary theology, for it seems to be our only way of bringing together a modern historical interpretation of the New
Testament with a contemporary meaning of its faith and Word.

But this option is closing as existential language is already receding into our historical past and mythical and cosmic language is being reborn in our midst. Language and speech
have also gained a new and comprehensive identity and surely
the time is at hand to conjoin the eschatological with a primal identity of speech. Once again our fundamental problem is
the theological identity of Kingdom of God. And here the synoptic parables must continue to remain at or near the center
of our analysis. Clearly the parables are parables of the
Kingdom of God, and thus they are an expression of Jesus' eschatological proclamation. But the Kingdom of God is not the
subject of these parables in an ordinary sense, for in that
sense they have no subject at all. That is to say they are
without a subject which can clearly be delineated or sharply
distinguished from anything else. The parables do not point
to the Kingdom of God in the sense of pointing at an object,
that is just the possibility which is hereby foreclosed.

In one sense the parables do point either to the presence
or to the immediately coming presence of the Kingdom of God.
Indeed, this very ambiguity makes manifest an essential identity of the Kingdom in the parables, for it is both present
and future and yet neither present nor future. Our temporal
distinctions break down upon impact with the parables, and so

likewise do our spatial distinctions. The Kingdom of God is neither "here" nor "there", neither above nor below, nor before or behind. Again and again the parables make clear that it is just such distinctions which divert our attention from the Kingdom of God. Yet the speech of the parables has a rich and even worldly immediacy which clearly speaks of the Kingdom of God. Thus a paradox is present here, and perhaps a pure paradox, for the parables seem both to speak and to be silent simultaneously. One might say that they speak with perfect clarity even while saying nothing which we can either define or repeat. There is a pure simplicity present here, a simplicity making the parable immediately understandable to everyone who hears it, and yet its meaning disappears when it is translated into another idiom.

Now we know or can imagine that the parable is intended to engage a total attention, an attention so total as to hear and be aware of nothing but this speech. Hence the immediate actuality of parabolic speech, an actuality making all meaning and identity incarnate here and now. This is the actuality which is diluted in metaphoric meaning and then lost in allegory. But it is an actuality which is also diluted and lost when the parable is transposed into anything which we can know as plot or story. The ending of the true parable is not simply a surprize, or even a shock, it rather shatters everything which is recognizable as meaning or identity to us. Yet the parable does not culminate in any kind of silence or emptiness. On the contrary, its ending evokes and embodies an actuality which is indubitable, and not simply indubitable but overwhelming to its hearer as well. Then the hearer can be understood to lose every identity and meaning which he or she initially brings to the parable. But that meaning is lost not simply by being negated but rather by being reversed. And it is reversed in the very context of the parabolic situation and by the very movement of the parabolic tale or image. So it is that the attention which the parable invites and commands culminates in an explosion of the hearer, and an explosion which is enacted by the hearer simply as a consequence of hearing this speech.

It is not difficult to associate such an explosion with eschatological judgment. But it is not only an existential or subjective judgment, it is a cosmic or objective judgment as well, or a judgment which transforms and reverses all actual and possible meaning. True, it is my identity which here comes under judgment. But it is my total identity which is assaulted by the parable, and this occurs through a reversal of a whole world of meaning. And that reversal occurs in the actual hearing of the hearer, a hearing in which the hearer is totally engaged. This is not a judgment which awaits the hear-

er, or falls upon the hearer, or even happens to the hearer.
It is far rather a judgment which is realized in the actuality
of hearing itself, and realized by the hearer in the hearer's
own act of hearing. Thereby hearing passes into speech, for
it realizes a new and total identity of the hearer, and does
so by way of the hearer's own act. Nor is that act simply a
self-destructive or self-negating act. On the contrary, it is
a self-realizing act, an act which realizes an actuality and
an immediacy which otherwise is absent.

Within the context of the world and sound of parabolic
speech it is possible to speak of speech itself as Demythologizing. And it is Demythologizing because it is pure speech,
a speech which is totally immediate and at hand. The silence
of distance vanishes in that pure immediacy, and it does not
simply vanish, it rather passes into speech. Then Kingdom of
God is not distant and apart, it speaks in the actuality of
voice. Then world is not simply and only world, it, too, is
embodied in voice. Then man is not simply the hearer of world
and Word, he speaks both Word and world in hearing this voice.
Thereby parabolic speech issues in a hearing whereby and wherein the Kingdom of God is immediately at hand. And it is at
hand in the actuality of hearing itself, a hearing transposing
the silence of both God and world into the immediate presence
of Kingdom of God. Therefore parabolic speech culminates in a
total hearing, a hearing whose own immediate actuality is the
self-embodiment or self-realization of speech.

Voice itself is the originating center of the New Testament, a voice which actually speaks an immediate and total
presence. That presence sounds in a purely parabolic speech,
and its sounding dissolves all boundaries between a "here" and
a "there", thereby fusing the "here" and the "there" into a
continuum of immediate actuality. But that actuality is a
spoken actuality, an actuality which fully speaks, and therefore it is worlds or aeons removed from the cosmic totality of
archaic myth. If myth in its purest expressions knows a center
which is everywhere, voice in its purest expression speaks a
center which is here and now. And that center is everywhere
only by being here and now, only by its actual embodiment in
speech. That embodiment shatters every mythical identity,
every speakable distinction, and does so by way of an eschatological or total judgment which is present in voice alone.
Here, voice is the self-embodiment of speech, and the self-
embodiment of a speech which is everywhere or all in all. But
it is all in all only by being a total disrupturing of silence,
only by bringing a final end to every identity which does not
or cannot speak.

In the presence of this judgment it is impossible to
speak of Kingdom of God. Impossible that is to speak of a
singular or particular identity of Kingdom of God. We might
say that here every mythical identity of Kingdom of God comes
to an end, and it comes to an end because here every mythical
or visual horizon is shattered by the pure immediacy of speech.
No longer does transcendence stand or appear apart, just as no
longer does world stand as world in our midst. Neither God
nor world is now speakable as God or world alone, and they are
unspeakable because it is now impossible to speak any identity
which is only itself. The fullness of voice or speech dissolves every identity lying beyond its own immediacy, and
thereby perishes every identity which is isolated and self-
enclosed. Here is Demythologizing in its purest form, in its
most radical expression, and it is so because it brings an end
to every possible mythical meaning. That end occurs in the
fullness of voice or speech, for in that fullness there is a
total absence of all silent identity. This can occur only by
way of the collapse of every horizontal or visual continuum,
and in that collapse is realized the advent of Word and Word
alone.

10

A THEOLOGY OF STORY: CROSSAN AND BEARDSLEE

John B. Cobb, Jr.

I.   FAITH AND HISTORY

Christian faith and a view of world history were once in-timately interconnected. The scriptural canon expressed this near identity, beginning with the creation of the world and the origins of human history and ending with the vision of universal destiny. Until the rise of critical, secular his-tory this union was rarely questioned, but once a secular his-tory arose which was in tension with the biblical one, Chris-tians were confronted by a critical problem.

The conservative response was to oppose the development of secular history. Since this was unsuccessful, it was nec-essary to accept secular histories alongside biblical history while insisting that they had no bearing upon the absolute truth and importance of biblical history. Hence, efforts were made to preserve the biblical record itself from secular criti-cism. When this failed, then a distinction was made between sacred history as the history of salvation and the secular history even of Israel and Christian origins.

The radical response to the challenge of secular history was to abandon the field of world history altogether. From the point of view of those Christians who have moved in this direction, world history is devoid of true meaning. What oc-curs in that sphere is irrelevant to our ultimate needs, that is, to salvation. Hence, they believe we can be grateful to secular historical study for forcing us to withdraw our atten-tion from this irrelevant sphere, and we can concentrate on that point at which our individual and inner lives are in fact touched by God. Rudolf Bultmann, who directed most of recent New Testament scholarship on this path, called the sphere of our encounter with God "Geschichte" in contrast to world his-tory or "Historie", thereby retaining for Christian faith an emphasis on the concreteness of the encounter with God in the midst of life. In an important sense Bultmann still main-tained the distinction between historical and mythical reli-gion and the custom of classifying Christianity normatively as historical. John Dominic Crossan, on the other hand, invites us

> to retire this distinction as irrelevant
> and to replace it with another. The more
> useful distinction might be between mythi-
> cal religion, a religion that gives one
> the final word about 'reality' and there-
> by excludes the authentic experience of
> mystery, and parabolic religion, a reli-
> gion that continually and deliberately
> subverts final words about 'reality' and
> thereby introduces the possibility of
> transcendence.[1]

A third response finds in Hegel its greatest exponent.
This response intends to accept without reservation the results of modern critical study and to build a new universal
history upon these results. In contrast with those who would
separate faith and world history, these Christians believe
that what is really taking place in world history is of fundamental importance to human beings and therefore has to do with
God's purposes and with human salvation. They also believe
that Jesus Christ is the key to the understanding of all
reality and that accordingly they have nothing to fear from
complete openness to all that is to be learned. In the twentieth century Teilhard de Chardin strongly revived this style
of theology. More recently Wolfhart Pannenberg has defended
the goal of universal history programmatically and has carried
it out in a way that retains a remarkable proximity to the
biblical record.

No New Testament scholar of our time has been more sensitive to the importance of the issues that are dealt with in
the second and third of these responses than is William Beardslee. In a series of books and articles he has gently criticized the extreme separation of the second response from all
efforts to make sense of ordinary life and the course of public events without supporting the full claims or program of
those who make the third response. In working out his alternative, which is indeed a fourth response, he has made use of
the philosophy of Alfred North Whitehead. In doing so he has
not only contributed to biblical scholarship and theology but
also to the understanding of the meaning and implications of
Whitehead's philosophy. In offering my tribute to his accomplishment, I am writing a companion essay supporting the
thrust of his own work.

Section II is a critique of Crossan's *The Dark Interval*.
Crossan is unusually explicit and vigorous in his support of

the second response and his rejection of the third. Section III proposes that the fourth response avoids what is legitimately offensive to Crossan in the third while opening itself to the public world. Section IV summarizes some of Beardslee's distinctive contributions to this fourth response.

II. CROSSAN'S POSITION

Crossan's position is that we live in our stories as fish live in water. He clarifies this over against three master-claims that we can get outside of our stories. First, there is the claim that science, unlike art, provides a neutral and objective grasp of reality as it is. Second, there is the claim that the changes that have occurred over the ages constitute progress. And third, there is the claim "that there is an external reality *out there* extrinsic to our vision, our imagination, and our intellect and that we are gaining objective knowledge and disciplined control over this extramental reality".[2] Against these master-claims he holds that science and art are both moments in all knowing, and that the relativity of art informs science as well; that the changes that have occurred are just that—changes; and that "reality is neither *in here* in the mind nor *out there* in the world; it is the interplay of both mind and world in language".[3]

For Crossan this raises the question of God acutely since he is not satisfied with locating God in his story. Since his story is his own creation, locating God within it would make God an idol. Hence, he can locate God only at the edges or limits of story or of language. It is where our language-world does not extend, or where it breaks apart, that God can be found.

Crossan distinguishes two basic types of story, those that establish the language-world and those that subvert it. The purest form of the former is myth; of the latter, parable. Jesus cast his message in parables. This means that the impact of Jesus' word was to shatter the language-worlds of his hearers. It is precisely at this moment of shattering that transcendence breaks through.

Whiteheadians such as Beardslee and myself find ourselves in agreement with much of this, and yet we are deeply troubled by what appears to us as one-sidedness and by the exclusion of much that is humanly important. We appreciate the point that the distinctive cut of much of Jesus' message of word and deed was the shattering of existing modes of thought and vision and

that also today, when we attend to him rightly, we find that
our new, supposedly Christian, systems are subverted in their
turn. But we are not persuaded that this insight exhausts all
that is important about Jesus. Indeed, we perceive this interpretation as another in a long series of modernizings of
Jesus, each of which has grasped an element of truth lost by
earlier ones, but each of which has also absolutized the frag-
ment of the whole which could be most easily assimilated at
that point in culture. We believe that Jesus' message will
be better able to challenge our culture when we refuse to
identify it too completely with what our culture wants to
hear--even when what our culture wants to hear is an opposition of faith to all culture.

The heart of Crossan's argument, I take it, is that
transcendence can be met only at the edges or limits of language. This means that God cannot be found in the ordinary
events of life or in our ordinary relations with one another.
Bultmann found God in the claim and call to authentic existence, but I gather that this would fall, for Crossan, in the
sphere of immanence. The reason for holding this position
seems to be that language cannot refer to something outside
of itself. It is a self-contained system in which words can
only refer to other words. Further, our experience does not
transcend language but is, instead, constituted by it. Hence,
to speak of an experience of God which I then try to put into
words would be to misunderstand language. The image of our
being in language as the fish is in the water is not strong
enough to express this doctrine. The fish is nothing but
water!

It may well be objected that I have exaggerated Crossan's
position. Indeed, many of his statements express a much more
moderate view. The problem is that the moderate view does not
drive us to the extreme conclusions which are so important to
Crossan.

Consider the quote above at the end of the first paragraph of this section. If, for a moment, we drop off the last
two words, "in language", and support this by the next sentence in Crossan's text ("Reality is relational and relationship"), we have a doctrine that is admirably suited for the
development of a quite different position, one for which there
truly is a real world made up of relationships, only a few of
which directly involve me. Many of those relationships are
beyond my ken and indeed beyond the ken of anyone, but there
are ways in which science and art together can extend our
understanding and our language to include more of them. In
this perspective some of those relationships can involve God.
But Crossan does not follow this line of thought. Instead he

adds the words "in language" to the first sentence and immediately follows the second with the unqualified affirmation that "even more simply, reality is language". The doctrine is not only the truth that all human relationships, such as a lover's caress, are informed by language through and through. The doctrine is that insofar as the lover's caress is real at all it *is* language. Hence the caress does not relate the lover and the beloved as two centers of extralinguistic feeling, for there are in reality no such centers. Any feelings that exist *are* language. Similarly if the lover tries to tell the beloved what he has felt, he cannot speak of feelings that are anything other than other language.

It may still be that I have misunderstood Crossan. By "language" he may not mean only human words. Perhaps we should read the connection of relationship and language the other way, interpreting language in terms of relationship rather than relationship in terms of language. But then again, the conclusions which Crossan draws would not follow. Relationships relate us to what is not ourselves, that is, to what transcends us. The other is given to us in the relationship as that which is more than the relationship to us. The wife to whom I am related is more than my relationship to her. Her life is made up of many other relationships as well. Thus she transcends me. But just this transcendence is what Crossan must exclude. He argues that "there's only story".[4]

It is still unclear how we are to take this. One possibility, supported by some of Crossan's statements, is that so far as *I* am concerned there is only *my* story. Now, of course, my story could include the reality of other stories, but I am the creator of my story and my story creates my world; so the other stories are real only as I choose for them to be real. My wife's story, then, or Crossan's is real or not only as I choose. If this were Crossan's position, then truly there would be no transcendence of story; and other people would exist only in my story, or at the edges, where my story breaks down! But Crossan never says this.

The fact that Crossan draws this kind of conclusion for God but not for other people (unless his fondness for Borges' "The Circular Ruins" is evidence to the contrary)[5] suggests that he does not mean to deny transcendence altogether. Perhaps it is acknowledged with respect to other stories. Perhaps, after all, the story of a Tibetan Buddhist master is "an external reality *out there* extrinsic to our vision, our imagination, and our intellect".[6] Perhaps there are elements in my story that refer to his story more or less accurately, and perhaps the relation is such that I can progressively reduce the inaccuracy of my first references. Perhaps, then,

other stories can be transcendent of ours, not our creations
but our discoveries.

What then about God? Crossan has said that if God were
in his story God would be his creation, whereas this does not
seem to be the case with respect to other stories. Is this
because only other stories can transcend our story and we know
that God is not a story? Perhaps, although this is certainly
not what Crossan says. It would be interesting also to learn
how language within one story can refer to other stories but
cannot refer to anything else, such as bodily feelings and
emotions. It would be interesting also to press the question:
Is the story that language does not contain a transcendent
reference itself but one of the stories we can create for ourselves, or does it have a privileged position in relation to
all other stories? But enough of this. I am convinced that
neither Crossan nor anyone else has been able to think consistently in the context of the dictum that language exhausts
reality. The very dictum presupposes a sense of reality as
something more inclusive than language.

There are, of course, other and more persuasive grounds
for the assertion that God cannot be spoken. Perhaps God is
not the sort of reality to which reference is possible. This
belief is probably the deeper basis of Crossan's conviction
that God is known only where language reaches its limits.
Hence my criticism of his brief excursus into philosophy does
not invalidate his interpretation of myth and parable or his
view that parable opens us to God by subverting our stories.
But since Crossan provides no consistent argument that God can
be met only at the edges of language, we can approach the literature of the New Testament with an open mind on this question.

Similarly, the rejection of the rigid, philosophical
identification of language and reality does not invalidate the
decisiveness of the category of story for understanding ourselves and our world. Whitehead shares with Crossan the denial
of a neutral, objective science that progressively builds up an
accurate picture of the world. For Whitehead as for Crossan
science and art operate together in the construction of theories which determine what is sought and how it is understood,
as well as being subject to alteration in light of the evidence. For Whitehead as for Crossan there is no human experience that is not already theory-laden. For Whitehead as for
Crossan human experience is penetrated by language through and
through so that we cannot exhibit actual human experiences that
are not informed by language. But for Whitehead it is equally
true to say that there is no language which is not penetrated
and informed by emotions and relations. These emotions and

relations would not be what they are apart from language, but it is at least equally true to say that language would not be what it is apart from them. It is because of emotions and relations that language can and does speak of what is not language or, at least, not only language.

A world of emotions and relations existed before human beings with their language appeared. That world has been transformed by language and transformed differently according to the diversities of language. But language does not create its world out of nothing. It expresses and thereby transforms a world that already exists. Since in expression it transforms, there is always more to the world than what has been expressed in language. Every story creates a world which transcends the story and calls for its improvement. No one way of expressing a world is *the* truth about the world; so there are many stories. And since each story tends to shape the world, each story tends to become more true of those who tell it. The Buddhist story, for example, is more true of Buddhist experience than of Christian experience. Even so, there are levels of Christian experience to which it applies before it is ever heard or known.

Crossan quotes Whitehead's famous saying to the effect that "in the real world, it is more important that a proposition be interesting than that it be true. The importance of truth is, that it adds to interest".[7] Crossan likes the first sentence but neglects the second. But Whitehead believes that truth *is* important. We will attend to theories or ideas longer if they have the ring of truth. As we discover with respect to any theory or idea more and more of its limitations, more and more ways in which it does not fit or illumine experience, we turn our attention elsewhere.

Crossan says that he has become bored with stories of universal history, but he recognizes that he rejects them also because they are in conflict with other stories that he finds exciting. He does not speak of truth since this would introduce transcendence and reference in ways he studiously, although unsuccessfully, tries to avoid. But I believe he finds the new stories exciting not only because they are new and different, but because they seem at least partly true. And I believe he is bored with the old ones at least partly because they do not seem to fit the world as he knows it. Whether or not this is true of Crossan, many moderns no longer find themselves persuaded by the universal histories of the past. Having rejected the encompassing stories of the tradition, they are likely to reject, as Crossan does, the idea that there could be some new all-encompassing story that would be final. In the absence of such a story, there is a strong disposition

to distrust any world-ordering story and to rejoice in those
which expose and undercut. This is the direction of much New
Testament scholarship, and it is to illustrate this that Crossan has been analyzed.

But the price of pursuing this direction to the end is
high. Crossan would agree, I think, that no one lives without
a story that makes some sort of sense of things, however limited. We cannot live by subversion alone! Christianity has
traditionally challenged the many stories with a master-story.
Crossan would have us challenge them only with myth-destroying
stories. It would not be the business of Christianity to
judge among stories which are better or worse, only to disrupt
every attempt to live in any world-establishing story or myth.
Crossan's "theology of story" is a theology of the limits of
story.

But if we all live by myths, then the judgment that only
the disruption of myth is important means withdrawal from in-
volvement in any effort to change the world by action. Such
withdrawal is appropriate if we believe that all our social
and political hopes and fears, all our ethical causes, and all
our liberation movements are pointless. If human effort can
accomplish nothing in human history, then indeed only as
people are torn from their illusions of historical meaning
can they know the one true meaning that is found in meeting
God. Perhaps this is the implication of Crossan's polemic
against progress. But is this the last word of the gospel
for the oppressed who long for justice?

III. THE FOURTH RESPONSE

It is against this conclusion that much of the theological community has sought to move in its new emphasis upon God
as the Liberator of the Oppressed. Instead of finding God at
the edges of each private story when that story is disrupted,
theologians have been trying to formulate a story that shows
God to be present in the efforts of the dehumanized to claim
their humanity. For this to occur, the disruptive word of
Jesus is absolutely essential, for the oppressed have inter-
nalized the myths by which they are held in bondage. Jesus'
word must be used against established Christian stories as
well, since dehumanization has often been sanctioned by such
stories. But when these oppressive myths have been exploded,
a story more appropriate to the struggle for liberation is
needed.

The effort to formulate this essay within Crossan's categories leads to difficulties in two respects. First, he places all of his stories on a single line from world-establishing to world-subversion. But this excludes the possibility that the story might transform world. Perhaps Crossan's world lacks the possibility of creative transformation because it lacks the possibility of real novelty. However that may be, to transform is neither to establish alone nor to subvert alone. It includes both moments. For a world to have its form altered is for it to be subverted. A world cannot be transformed without being shaken and disrupted, without losing its character of world. But this subversion in itself is not transformation, it is simply destruction. Transformation occurs only when a new world arises that takes account of the disruptive truth as well as of such truth as was present in the old world.

Crossan's own account of the parable of the Good Samaritan will serve as an example. In his view the function of the parable is to disrupt and subvert the world in which priests and Levites are expected to do deeds of justice and the despised Samaritan is not. But is it designed simply to subvert the entire world of the Jewish hearer? No, certainly not. The parable "takes it absolutely for granted that assistance is required in such a case".[8] That is a part of the inherited world of the hearer. But that belief, which far from being subverted is reinforced by the parable, has been bound up with self-righteous views of the superiority of the Jewish religion and its leadership. This is now confronted with a story that denies it. The effect will indeed be shattering if the story is truly heard. But is it only shattering? Can the hearer not enter a new world in which there is new openness to the Samaritan and new recognition of the distortions introduced by religious self-righteousness? If this is possible, then it is not enough to see the parable as subverting the world of the hearer. It can creatively transform that world.

The use of Crossan's categories creates confusion also in the use of "myth". I have been using the word "myth" for story that establishes world. But Crossan introduces another element into "myth", namely, that myth purports to give the one final word about reality. I am quite prepared to join Crossan in opposing mythical religion in that sense. But he does not offer us a term for story that establishes world without the claim to finality, a story that asserts its own limits but nevertheless provides the best organization of life it can. Perhaps we can call this "history". If so, then some of us believe that we have the task of formulating history so as to establish world while building into our formulation its own need to be superseded.

Such history is open in two ways. First, it is open-ended. It does not announce what must happen in the future although it tries to show that something new *can* happen and to draw people into the responsible shaping of events. Second, it is open in its account of the past. Its assertions, even if relatively true, turn out to be fragmentary and often to deal with fragments that in subsequent periods are not of greatest interest or importance. Histories written before we became aware of the environmental crisis or were sensitized to the universal oppression of women in civilized countries cannot now fulfill their world-establishing function. The histories we need have not yet been written, but we *do* need them even though they, in their turn, will be superseded. Furthermore, such histories will not serve us if they are parochial. They cannot establish a world for us if they deal only with modern times or only with the West. The call for inclusive history, when it is divorced from the tendency toward closure, is correct.

If we undertake to understand historically our drive for an inclusive and relevant history, we find that it comes to us from biblical faith. If our faith centers in Christ, then we can say that our drive for an inclusive history is shaped by our faith in Christ. For example, it is because of Christ that today we want to construct a history that energizes and appropriately directs the movements for liberation of the oppressed while developing a sustainable relationship to our environment.

This is a fourth response to the secular history which has destroyed the traditional identity of faith and history. It does not offer a final picture of how all things have been and will be. It is not a myth in Crossan's sense. But it does propose a story which seeks to be universal and which takes account of all that we know, as well as of our present needs, and which intends to be faithful to Christ.

IV. BEARDSLEE'S ACHIEVEMENT

A disturbing feature of our time is that while much of the theological community is attempting in some such way as this to move back into the public world where there is torture and starvation and subtle exploitation of the destitute by our middle class life styles, much of the community of New Testament scholarship points us to a Christ whose message seems to speak only to the individual at the periphery of her or his existence. Clearly a theology cut off from its roots in the

New Testament is a weak source of new histories! If in fact the message of Jesus in word and deed was iconoclastic only, then the efforts of theologians today to construct new liberating histories are poorly founded. But if the story which Crossan and others are now telling about Jesus is just one of the true stories that can be told about him, if there is also a true story about Jesus' concern for everyday people in the everyday world, for the healing of the sick and the feeding of the hungry, and if Jesus upheld belief in a God who relates to our bodily and earthy needs, then our present theological preoccupation with liberating histories is not misplaced.

William Beardslee has done more than any other New Testament scholar in recent times to call attention to this other story about Jesus and the New Testament. At a time when New Testament scholars were focusing their attention on the recovery and renewal of Paul's doctrine of justification by faith alone, Beardslee wrote a doctoral dissertation subsequently reworked and published as *Human Achievement and Divine Vocation in the Message of Paul*. He did not doubt the importance of the major emphasis on the primacy of God's act, but he did fear that a one-sided stress could lead to neglect of Paul's "intense concern for human achievement".[9] More recently, while recognizing the particular value of concentrating attention on Jesus' parables, Beardslee has chosen to devote considerable attention to the "Uses of the Proverb in the Synoptic Gospels".[10] He agrees with other scholars that Jesus' use of proverbs is often hyperbolic and disruptive of established world, but he does not accept the view that this disruptive note is all that is to be found. Jesus maintained continuities with ordinary human life as well as challenging established habits of mind. To be informed by Jesus in the telling of a larger story is not to oppose his spirit.

Turning to the parables themselves, Beardslee can make the same point. The disruptive element is there and primary. But it is not an absolute disruption. There are presupposed continuities with context and presuppositions. The new that has disrupted the old can also be integrated into a transformed version of the old. Instead of driving God out of the center of life, the parable can open us to seeing God in our midst.

Beardslee wrestles with this point with special force and clarity in "Parable, Proverb, and Koan". He rightly sees that Crossan attributes to the parable the function of the *Koan*. This is to open the hearer to "the transcendent as a creative negativity or emptiness".[11] Far from chiding Crossan for this, he commends this direction of interpretation and affirms its importance. But he insists that there are other

possibilities, equally true and equally valid. These depend
upon refusing to attend to form alone and insisting on the
importance of content as well. They lead us to view the
parables in relation to "the Kingdom of a God who creates,
judges, and renews the order of the world".[12] On this basis
Beardslee can relate the gospel to current social hopes as he
did in "New Testament Perspectives on Revolution as a Theological Problem".[13]

A similar pattern appears in Beardslee's contribution to
literary criticism. While most scholars devoted themselves to
the analysis of the Gospels into their parts and sought the
earliest form of Christian speech, Beardslee called attention
to the gospel narratives as such. He showed that the selection of the narrative form itself expresses an understanding
of existence and an establishment of a world. The gospel narratives use and develop this form so as to become stories "of
how something began that is still in process and moving toward its future and conclusion".[14]

These brief comments on Beardslee's particular emphases
barely identify his major contribution from the side of New
Testament scholarship. They hardly hint at this contribution
to process theology. What is now called "process theology"
developed out of the earlier Chicago school chiefly under the
influence of Charles Hartshorne and Alfred North Whitehead.
It focused on metaphysics and speculative cosmology as the
context for reworking the doctrine of God. In doing so it
largely cut itself off from the New Testament scholars, John
Knox and Amos Wilder, who continued to work with the categories and vision of earlier stages of the Chicago school.
Schubert Ogden showed how the new theism could supplement and
complement the anthropology of Bultmann, but process theologians did little work with the problems of history, language,
and hermeneutics. Biblical studies could be touched only tan-
gentially by such a philosophical theology.

Beardslee, however, perceived that there were resources
in Whitehead's vision which were too little developed by process theologians and which could renew the school of New
Testament studies which saw more continuities between nature,
history, and the divine, and between Christian faith and the
actualities of our cultural life. It was distinctively the
achievement of Schubert Ogden to build a bridge between Hartshorne's doctrine of God and Bultmann's anthropology, thus in
part restoring the relationship between process theology and
New Testament scholarship. But Beardslee's bridge-building
is more complex, for the pilings needed to support his bridge
were not in place. He has been required to do substantial,
original work at both ends of the bridge. Only gradually has

he succeeded in drawing others, both theologians and New Testament scholars, into his labors. In doing so he has significantly enriched process theology.

There are two ways in which, it seems to process theologians, Whitehead's conceptuality can contribute to New Testament scholarship. Beardslee has made use of both. Whitehead's categories can counter the tendency to absolutize a single hermeneutical method. From Whitehead's perspective we are not forced to choose between Crossan and Wilder, for example, despite their great differences. Both of their stories ring true and both can be included in a larger story. Second, Whitehead's categories can suggest fresh ways of viewing meaning in history, symbolism, language, the relation of language to experience, or the overcoming of apparent contradictions. Beardslee's contribution to the fourth response to the problem of secular history involves such fresh proposals.

Whitehead admired Plato's *Timaeus* in part because Plato put it forward as a likely tale. Whitehead, in his turn, has put forth another likely tale. Plato's tale was informed by the best science and art of his time. Whitehead's was informed by the best of his time. While his tale certainly is not true in any final sense, it has much truth which supports the possibility of much interest. But when it is viewed chiefly as a self-contained philosophical system standing to one side of the main philosophical movements of our time, it tends to lose interest. When it is tested and enriched in its application to the problems of many fields of inquiry, interest is quickened. Beardslee has done much to quicken interest.

NOTES

1. John Dominic Crossan, *The Dark Interval: Towards a Theology of Story* (Niles, Illinois: Argus Communications, 1975), pp. 127-128.

2. Ibid., p. 19.

3. Ibid., p. 37.

4. Ibid., p. 45.

5. Ibid., pp. 81-83.

6. Ibid., p. 19.

7. Ibid. The passage from Whitehead in *Process and Reality*, corrected edition, ed. David R. Griffin and Donald Sherborne (New York: The Free Press, 1978), p. 259.

8. Crossan, *The Dark Interval*, p. 108.

9. William A. Beardslee, *Human Achievement and Divine Vocation in the Message of Paul, Studies in Biblical Theology*, No. 31 (London: SCM Press, 1961), p. 7.

10. William A. Beardslee, "Uses of the Proverb in the Synoptic Gospels," *Interpretation* 24 (January, 1970): 61-73.

11. William A. Beardslee, "Parable, Proverb, and Koan," *Semeia* 12 (1978): 171.

12. Ibid., p. 168.

13. William A. Beardslee, "New Testament Perspectives on Revolution as a Theological Problem," *Journal of Religion* 51 (January, 1971): 15-33.

14. William A. Beardslee, *Literary Criticism of the New Testament*, in "Guides to Biblical Scholarship," ed. Dan O. Via, Jr. (Philadelphia: Fortress Press, 1970), p. 21.

PART III

LITERARY ANALYSIS OF BIBLICAL MATERIALS

11

PUNISHMENT STORIES IN THE LEGENDS OF THE PROPHETS

Robert C. Culley

The narratives about the prophets in the Books of Kings form a remarkable collection for many reasons. The purpose of this paper is to look at one aspect of narrative structure in six of these stories which tell of a wrong done which is subsequently punished, or at least a punishment is announced. The stories are: 2 Kings 2:23-25 (Elisha curses the boys); 2 Kings 1:2-17 (A sick Ahaziah sends messengers to Baalzebub); 2 Kings 5:20-27 (Gehazi deceives Naaman); 1 Kings 21 (Ahab gets Naboth's vineyard); 1 Kings 20:33-43 (The king of Israel makes a treaty with the king of Aram); and 1 Kings 13:7-30 (A prophet deceives a man of God).

Before moving on to the stories themselves, I will need to make some general comments to set the stage. What follows here continues the kind of work I have been doing over the past few years on narrative.[1] If recent approaches to the biblical text such as structuralist analysis,[2] discourse analysis,[3] and literary criticism (in the more general meaning of literary studies)[4] share in a broad sense an interest in the nature of the language and a consequent interest in the nature of texts as items of language, then I would see my work within this general perspective. And it is a new perspective. To be sure, everyone knows that the biblical texts are language; but only recently have scholars begun to probe this notion more deeply and explore its implications more extensively. If language is a system, then what is its structure? On how many levels can structure be perceived and described? How does language refer to things outside its system? Or can language only refer to language?

One of the topics within this broad perspective is the nature of narrative, and even more narrowly, action in narrative. What are some of the ways in which this can be examined and discussed? While I have learned a great deal from those who have applied Greimas' model to biblical texts, my preference has been to follow a strategy similar to that of Vladimir Propp, the Russian folklorist whose work lies behind so much recent structuralist and narrative analysis. Without trying to apply his set of functions directly to biblical texts, I have nevertheless worked with groups of stories in order to try to detect common structure.

One of the features of common structure that stands out in many of the short narratives in the Old Testament is a movement from complication to resolution. This movement has been widely recognized and discussed in connection with narrative. Nevertheless, this feature has not received a great deal of attention in Old Testament studies.[5] It may well prove useful to trace how stories move from complication to resolution and how similar movements may occur several times in more complex narratives. At least this point of view tries to take seriously the fact that Old Testament stories are narratives and do have a narrative structure which governs the shape and arranges the contents of these stories.

In very short narratives in the Old Testament, one can see that the movement from complication to resolution is realized in a number of ways. Miracle stories move from a difficulty to a removal of difficulty by means of divine intervention. Punishment stories move from a wrong to the punishment of that wrong. In previous discussions, I decided to use the term, "action sequence", for such movements; and I have spoken of a "difficulty-difficulty removed" action sequence and a "wrong-wrong punished" action sequence.[6] One can also speak of a "desired-desired taken" sequence. This refers to a story in which there is the opportunity or the desire to gain something not easily accessible so that a trick or deception is needed in order to get the desired object. These labels remain tentative and are intended merely as handy ways of identifying groups of stories which seem to share the same basic movement.

Such sequences also appear in longer and more complex stories in the Old Testament[7] not only as a dominant movement but also built in and around this main movement. In this paper, I would like to examine a group of stories which have the action sequence, "wrong-wrong punished", as the main movement in the narrative and indicate how this basic framework is filled out.

Much more needs to be said about the nature of "action sequences" than I am able to say at the moment. But at least the following can be noted. It is assumed that readers quite readily see a movement from complication to resolution in many Old Testament stories, not to mention narratives in general. This movement starts from an initial, incomplete or abnormal situation which implies or holds out the possibility of further action and passes on to a state of relative completeness or normality which suggests that the action begun as a result

of the earlier state is over. The fact that a number of punishment stories can be set side by side such that they appear
to have a basic common movement from "wrong" to "wrong punished" is taken as sufficient justification to speak of a
"wrong-wrong punished" action sequence. The two elements
"wrong" and "wrong punished" are not separate, independent
elements but must be defined in terms of each other. From
the point of view of narrative structure, a wrong is identified as a wrong because it is subsequently punished. In the
same way, a punishment is identified as a punishment because
it is related to a wrong.

2 Kings 2:23-25 Elisha curses the boys

Since this is a very brief story, the action sequence
"wrong-wrong punished" appears in a very simple form. As
Elisha goes on his way, some boys make fun of him. While
this may not strike us as a major crime, the prophet curses
the boys in the name of Yahweh. The curse is immediately
realized. Two she-bears come and attack the boys. Story
over. This appears to be a self-contained narrative, however
short it may be. To be sure, it is assumed that the reader
or listener possesses adequate information about the main actor and also Yahweh.[8]

This story may illustrate how a "wrong" is defined in
terms of the other element, "wrong punished". The action of
the boys does not appear to the modern reader to be a serious
matter. Perhaps it was to the earliest audiences. At any
rate, the fact that a curse is uttered and takes effect makes
it clear that the actions of the boys is taken to be a wrong
which requires punishment.

This is not to say that the "wrong-wrong punished" sequence is the most important feature of the story. Attention
may be focused on other aspects of the story. Here it may be
the power available to the prophet and the danger of trifling
with him. It would appear that stories with the same basic
action sequence may still be very flexible so that attention
may be drawn to the wrong, the punishment, the wrongdoer, or
the punisher. How stories are able to do this is a matter
which will require further investigation and it will be sufficient here to note that it happens.

2 Kings 1:2-17 Ahaziah sends messengers to Baalzebub

This story which begins in verse 2 and seems to end in
the first main clause of verse 17, displays the main action

of the story in a "wrong-wrong punished" sequence. The wrong is stated in only one verse (v. 2). The king, Ahaziah, fell and became ill. He sent messengers to a foreign god, Baalzebub, to inquire about his chances of recovery. In verse 3, a message comes to Elijah that he should deliver a word of Yahweh to the king. This word makes clear that the king has done wrong and announces a punishment (v. 4). The king will die. This word is repeated to the king by the messengers (v. 6). When Elijah finally confronts the king in person, he repeats the word again (v. 16). The announced punishment is reported as having happened in the first part of verse 17. While the "wrong" is simply stated, some elaboration can be seen in the presentation of the punishment. First, a statement is made by Elijah indicating that the king has done wrong, and this amounts to a declaration of guilt. This is followed by an announcement of a punishment. But the punishment does not occur immediately. This declaration of guilt plus announcement of a punishment appears three times in the narrative, once stated to Elijah and twice stated to the king. It is after the second statement of this to the king that the occurrence of the announced punishment is reported.

Between the first and second announcement of punishment to the king lies a section which seems to be a story in itself (vv. 7-15) and which, some have argued, may have had a separate origin from the main story.[9] Three times the king sends soldiers to Elijah, presumably to seize him, but the king's attempt ends in failure because of miraculous intervention. This segment is like some miracles stories in which danger is averted by means of the intervention of miraculous power.[10] But does this miracle story have any function within the framework of the punishment story? Perhaps a suggestion can be made in this direction. The hostile action of the king seems to function as a challenge to the announcement. It may be that the king did not accept the validity of the announcement or the authority of the prophet. The king has already sent abroad for advice, rather than consult a local prophet. Then too, when faced with danger, the prophet says: "If I am a man of God, let fire come down...", suggesting that a question of authenticity is involved. In any event, the failure of the attempt because of divine intervention is a sign of the truth of the announcement and the authenticity of the prophet who then confronts the king and restates the declaration of guilt and the announcement.[11] Whether or not the miracle story was at some time separate from the punishment story, it functions in the present form of the narrative as an embedded element in the main narrative.

In this story, then, the "wrong punished" element of the action sequence has been expanded. While in the previous story a curse was uttered which took immediate effect, this narrative presents a declaration of guilt, an announcement, a challenge, and a repetition of the announcement followed by a report that what was announced happens.

2 Kings 5:20-27 Gehazi deceives Naaman

There are two stories in this chapter, although they are very closely related. The first is a miracle story. Naaman comes to the prophet with a problem. He has leprosy. The prophet gives instructions for healing. When Naaman finally follows these instructions, he is miraculously healed, and the problem is thus removed. The second is a punishment story which flows from the first. In verses 15-19, the miracle story is finished off and the way is prepared for the punishment story to follow. In these verses, Naaman returns after being healed to offer the gifts he had brought with him, but Elisha refuses to accept them. In a real sense, this finishes the miracle story. It had been mentioned at the beginning of the story that Naaman had brought gifts; and this section indicates what happened to them. On the other hand, this section prepares for the following punishment story, since it provides information (the offering of the gifts and the refusal) that is important for the following punishment story.

In the "wrong-wrong punished" sequence of verses 20-27, the "wrong" element is not just a briefly-described action as in the previous stories, but an action sequence in itself. Gehazi sees an opportunity to gain something which is not readily accessible. The desire to gain something presents a challenge which creates a kind of tension in the story. How will he get what he wants in the face of the obvious difficulties? He employs a deception. Elsewhere, I have called this kind of sequence a "desired-desired taken" action sequence. In this kind of sequence, an opportunity is seen to gain something desirable, or there may simply be a desire to have something that is not easily accessible. In either case, special measures, usually a deception, are required. For example, Jacob gets Esau's blessing by means of a deception employed by himself and his mother. Ahab's desire to have Naboth's vineyard will be discussed below.

After this "wrong" element in the form of an embedded "desired-desired taken" action sequence, the punishment element follows. Elisha pronounces Gehazi guilty on the basis of knowledge gained through the prophet's special ability to know things at a distance. A punishment is announced and it happens immediately. Gehazi is stricken with leprosy, the disease of Naaman.

1 Kings 21 Ahab gets Naboth's vineyard

This story is similar to the previous one in that the "wrong" element is an embedded action sequence of the type "desired-desired taken". Ahab wants to have the vineyard of Naboth but discovers that he cannot get it by ordinary means. However, Ahab does nothing more than sulk. At this point, his wife takes over and employs the extraordinary means necessary to gain the desired object. She arranges a deception so that Naboth can be removed from the scene by apparently legitimate grounds, thus opening the way for Ahab to take possession of the vineyard.

While this section depicting the wrong (vv. 1-16) seems to flow fairly smoothly, the next section containing the punishment (vv. 17-28) betrays marks of unevenness and has drawn comment from several scholars.[12] It seems clear that later comments have been added, some of these stemming from the Deuteronomist or stages of the Deuteronomistic tradition. However, verses 17-20 seem to be accepted as original by most; and these contain the announcement of the punishment to Ahab for his wrongdoing, that is, his apparent willingness to allow his wife to proceed (although the story does not make clear that he knew what was going on) and his willingness to take possession of the vineyard after Naboth had been murdered. The prophet pronounces him guilty with the words: "Have you murdered? Have you also taken possession?" (v. 19). This is followed by an announcement of punishment indicating his violent death. A few verses later (v. 23), a similar punishment is announced for Jezebel. However, Ahab performs acts of mourning which are taken by Yahweh as suitable signs of repentance. The punishment is postponed. Whether or not verse 23 (Jezebel's punishment) and verses 27 to 29 (Ahab's repentance) are part of the earliest version of the story or have been added at a later time, they fill out the story in appropriate ways. The punishment of Jezebel parallels that of Ahab. The repentance of Ahab is similar to a variation sometimes found in punishment stories.[13] After a punishment has been announced or is in progress, an appeal may be made with the result that the punishment may be mitigated. This sort of additional segment is very much like a miracle story in which a difficulty is removed. The punishment becomes the difficulty. An appeal is made for help. It is granted. Here in the Ahab story, no miraculous intervention occurs beyond the promise of a postponement.

1 Kings 20:33-43 The king of Israel and the king of Aram

This "wrong-wrong punished" sequence comes at the end of
a longer narration. In the first part of the chapter, two
battle situations are depicted where victory is announced be-
forehand in each case by a prophet. After the last battle,
the king of Aram has to flee for his life. Following advice
from his aides, Benhadad meets the king of Israel. When Benhadad appears dressed in sackcloth, he is greeted warmly by
the king of Israel. The two kings make a treaty. It is at
this point that the punishment sequence begins. This generous
treatment of the foreign king, even though it gains trade con-
cessions, is considered a "wrong", and this is clear from the
following declaration of guilt and announcement of punishment
at the end of the chapter. Because the king of Israel let his
defeated enemy escape the ban, he must forfeit his life. What
is unusual here is that the punishment does not occur within
the story. The announcement of punishment alone seems to be
sufficiently definitive to allow the story to come to a satisfactory conclusion. Still, this narrative is one among a number associated with Ahab in the present text. The death of
Ahab depicted in a later chapter resumes and completes the
punishment story of 1 Kings 20. This story is thus woven into a cluster of stories about Ahab.

What is particularly interesting about this action sequence is the expansion and development of the declaration of
guilt. In almost all the stories under discussion here, a
short statement comes just before the announcement of punishment in which the guilt of the party to be punished is made
clear. Here, this declaration of guilt has been expanded into a couple of scenes, one embedded in the other. A prophet
prepares a disguise and goes to the king of Israel with a
story about having allowed a man to escape who had been put
into his charge. The king of Israel decides that he must forfeit his life for his negligence. At this point, the prophet
tears off his disguise. The king has judged his own case.
This device of having a king declare his own guilt is also
found in 2 Samuel 12 (Nathan before David). A further point
of interest is the embedded segment. It is a very brief
"wrong-wrong punished" sequence. When the prophet sets out
to prepare his disguise (vv. 35-36), he approaches a companion
and orders the companion to strike him. The companion refuses.
This refusal is taken as a "wrong". Guilt is declared: "because you did not obey". A punishment is announced. The companion will be killed by a lion. This happens.

1 Kings 13:7-30 A prophet deceives a man of God

1 Kings 13 contains a remarkable narrative and has been
the source of much scholarly discussion.[14] In spite of the
risks in dealing with this chapter at all and without becoming
too entangled in the difficulties, I think it is possible to
show that the part of the chapter involving the nabi and the
man of God is a punishment story with a "wrong-wrong punished"
action sequence as its base.

The nabi is first introduced in verse 11; and for many
reasons it could be argued that the punishment story begins at
this verse.[15] There is a change of setting and a new major
character is introduced. The king who was a major figure in
the previous story does not appear in this segment. Verses
7-10 appear to finish off the story about the encounter of the
man of God and the king. In these verses the king invites the
prophet to accept his hospitality. This gesture is still difficult to interpret within the story of the encounter. Perhaps it is a gesture of goodwill following the healing of the
king's hand by the man of God. However, the importance of
these verses for the following story is quite clear. They introduce the fact that a prohibition has been given to the man
of God, an important feature of the story to follow, even
though this prohibition is repeated later on within the punishment story itself (vv. 17-18). Thus, verses 7-10 bridge
both stories in the chapter, finishing off the first and providing a start for the second. The mention of a prohibition
holds out the possibility of transgression of that prohibition,
thus creating a wrong which must be punished.

The "wrong" then runs from the mention of the prohibition
in verses 7-10 up to verse 19 where the prohibition is transgressed. The "wrong" element is thus divided into two components very closely related to each other—a prohibition and
its transgression. Furthermore, the movement from prohibition
to transgression is made possible by an act of deception. The
nabi lies to the man of God in order to induce him to break
the prohibition by eating and drinking. No motive is mentioned for this deception. But the action is necessary for
the narrative in the sense that something has to happen to
get the man of God to break a prohibition which he clearly
takes very seriously. He has already refused the request of
a king. The serpent in Genesis 2-3 performs the same function
in that story by inducing the transgression of a prohibition.

The "wrong punished" element involves a declaration of
guilt ("because you rebeled") followed by an announcement of
punishment ("your corpse shall not go into the grave of your
fathers"). While this announcement of punishment is very

brief and very general, the punishment itself is depicted in
some detail. The man of God is killed by a lion and subsequently buried by the old prophet. A curious feature of this
story as opposed to the Genesis story is that the actor who
induces the transgression and the one who pronounces guilt and
announces punishment are one and the same.

SUMMARY AND COMMENTS

The chart provides a visual summary of how the basic action sequence, "wrong-wrong punished", is found in each of the
six stories and how in each case this basic sequence is expanded and filled out differently in each story.[16] With one
exception, each story moves from a wrong to the punishment of
that wrong. In one case the punishment is only announced.
With respect to the first element, the "wrong", three cases
state this very briefly while the other three expand it.
Twice we have embedded sequences involving a deception and in
one we have a prohibition which is transgressed because of a
deception.

The "wrong punished" element includes a declaration of
guilt in all but the first case and this is followed by an announcement of punishment. In the first story, the curse seems
to fill the role that the announcement does in the others. In
the second story, the movement from announcement to occurrence
is developed by a sequence which seems to function like a challenge. In the fourth story, there is an expansion in terms of
a mitigation. There is no description of a punishment in the
fifth example, although this story is expanded by developing
the declaration of guilt into a deception sequence with an embedded punishment sequence.

Since the aim of this study has been limited, the results
will also be modest. I have tried to consider one aspect of
narrative structure in relatively short stories from the Old
Testament. The use of a small group of stories has made it
possible to see a feature common to all the stories, the action sequence which I have called "wrong-wrong punished". At
the same time, it is also clear that each story has gone its
own way. Several possibilities of expanding and filling out
the basic sequence have been exploited with the result that
attention is drawn to different things in each story. Nevertheless, reading through these stories as a group, one hears
the repeated rhythm of "wrong-wrong punished" throbbing in
the background. The stories function both as individual narratives and as members of a group.

To explore narrative structure is to explore stories as items of language. One notices how strong the literary forces are in shaping these stories. This is not to say that historical and sociological factors do not have significant impact. Language does not exist in a vacuum, but functions along with other social systems and in some relationship with experience. However, just to pick up the historical question, it may be that the relationship between stories like the ones studied above and the historical events they appear to reflect may be much more indirect and complex than biblical scholars have on the whole been inclined to admit. It is not so much that history has been lost or distorted as that reality has been created or remade. These are, of course, old debates; but, perhaps the issues are being raised in a sufficiently different way so as to allow fresh discussion.

1. 2 Kings 2 Elisha and the boys	2. 2 Kings 1 Ahaziah and Elijah	3. 2 Kings 5 Gehazi and Naaman
WRONG		
action v. 23	action v. 2	⎡ embedded action sequence (deception) ⎣ vv. 20-24
WRONG PUNISHED		
	declares guilt v. 3	declares guilt vv. 25, 26
curse ⎤ v. 24 │ │ ↓	announced ⎤ v. 4 │ │ ↓ ⎡embedded sequence (challenge) ⎣vv. 5-15 announced again ↓ v. 16	announced ⎤ v. 27 │ │ ↓
happens ⎦ (immediately) v. 24	happens ⎦ v. 17	happens ⎦ (immediately) v. 27

4. 1 Kings 21 Ahab and Naboth	5. 1 Kings 20 Two kings	6. 1 Kings 13 Two prophets
WRONG		
embedded action sequence (deception) vv. 1–16	action vv. 33, 34	prohibition (deception) prohibition transgressed
WRONG PUNISHED		

declares guilt
v. 19
	embedded
	  vv. 35–42
	    embedded
	    sequence
	    (punishment)
	    vv. 35, 36
	sequence
	(deception)
		declares guilt
		v. 21

announced v. 19 (Ahab) v. 23 (Jezebel)	announced v. 42	announced v. 22
repents v. 27 (Ahab) mitigated v. 29		happens v. 24

NOTES

1. "Structural Analysis: Is it Done with Mirrors?"
Interpretation 28 (April, 1974): 165-181; "Themes and Vari-
ations in Three Groups of Old Testament Narratives," *Semeia* 3
(1975): 3-31; *Studies in the Structure of Hebrew Narrative*
(Philadelphia: Fortress Press; Missoula: Scholars Press,
1976); "Analyse alttestamentlicher Erzählungen: Erträge der
jüngsten Methodendiskussion," *Biblische Notizen* 6 (1978): 27-
39; "Narrative Sequences in Genesis 2-3," in the *Society of
Biblical Literature: 1978 Seminar Papers*, ed. Paul J. Achtemeier (Missoula: Scholars Press, 1978), 2:51-59.

2. For Old Testament, see by way of example these different approaches: Robert Polzin, *Biblical Structuralism:
Method and Subjectivity in the Study of Ancient Texts* (Philadelphia: Fortress Press; Missoula: Scholars Press, 1977);
Centre pour l'Analyse du Discours Religieux, "Rudiments d'analyse (X): La tour de Babel: exercise pratique," *Semiotique
et Bible* 10 (1978): 1-26; David Jobling, *The Sense of Biblical Narrative: Three Analyses in the Old Testament* (1 Samuel
13-31, Numbers 11-12, 1 Kings 17-18), *Journal for the Study
of the Old Testament, Supplement Series 7* (Sheffield: The
University of Sheffield, 1978).

3. For an Old Testament example, see Robert Longacre,
"The Discourse Structure of the Flood Narrative," *Society of
Biblical Literature: 1976 Seminar Papers*, ed. George MacRae
(Missoula: Scholars Press, 1976): 235-261.

4. See David Robertson, *The Old Testament and the Literary Critic*, in "Guides to Biblical Scholarship," ed. Gene
M. Tucker (Philadelphia: Fortress Press, 1977).

5. But see the recent discussion in Albert de Pury,
*Promesse divine et legende cultuelle dans le cycle de Jacob:
Genese 28 et les traditions patriarcales* (Paris: J. Gabalda,
1975), 2:473-502. He refers to Westermann's comments in this
regard and goes on to the work of Propp in order to attack the
difficult problem of determining what the basic narrative units
are. A related issue which interests de Pury is whether episodes are autonomous units used later to build larger narrative units or whether episodes have from the very start functioned within the movements from tension to resolution of
larger narratives.

6. See "Analyse alttestamentlicher Erzählungen," and "Narrative Sequences in Genesis 2-3" (note 1, above).

7. Ibid.

8. But note that the main actor is only designated by pronominal reference, pointing back to the name Elijah in the last clause of the previous story (2 Kg. 2:19-22, the restoration of the bad water). From the point of view of pronominalization, this story about the bears and the boys is linked closely to the previous one. A new mention of the subject is to be expected at the beginning of what is clearly a new segment on the basis of other evidence (verb of movement, change of place, new setting, new participants in relation to the main actor).

9. See for example the discussion by Klaus Koch, *Was ist Formgeschichte?*, 2nd ed. (Neukirchen-Vluyn: Neukirchener Verlag, 1967), pp. 223-238.

10. Compare the escape from danger by Lot's guests, Genesis 19:4-11, and possibly the attempt on Elisha, 2 Kings 6:8-23.

11. Perhaps a distant parallel of this might be Genesis 18:6-15. An announcement is made regarding the birth of a son. Sarah laughs, an expression of doubt. The announcement is repeated and thus affirmed.

12. For example, Martin Noth, *Überlieferungsgeschicht-liche Studien*, 2nd ed. (Tübingen: Max Niemeyer Verlag, 1957), pp. 82-83; O. H. Steck, *Überlieferung und Zeitgeschichte in den Elia-Erzählungen* (Neukirchen-Vluyn: Neukirchener Verlag, 1968), pp. 32-53; H. Seebass, "Der Fall Naboth in 1 Reg. XXI," *Vetus Testamentum* 24 (1974): 474-488.

13. See Culley, *Studies in the Structure of Hebrew Narrative*, pp. 101-108.

14. For a recent article with full references to the literature, see Walter Gross, "Lying Prophet and Disobedient Man of God in 1 Kings 13: Role Analysis as an Instrument of Theological Interpretation of an Old Testament Narrative Text," *Semeia* 15 (1979 in press).

15. See the remarks by Gross on the division of the chapter, ibid., 2.2.

16. In the chart, the embedded material has only been identified cryptically. The words in brackets do not describe the sequence, but simply draw attention to an important feature of its content.

12

ATTITUDINAL SHIFT IN SYNOPTIC PRONOUNCEMENT STORIES

Robert C. Tannehill

William A. Beardslee has led us to reconsider the function of proverbs and aphoristic sayings in the synoptic Gospels. While proverbs may identify repeatable aspects of experience, helping us to make a coherent whole of existence, the "intensification" of the proverb through hyperbole and paradox may shift its function "to that of jolting the hearer out of this hoped-for continuity into a new judgment about his existence".[1] Many of the striking sayings of Jesus occur in the setting of a pronouncement story; that is, they are found in a brief narrative setting, and the saying is a response to something said to Jesus or observed by Jesus on a particular occasion. While such sayings seldom provoke the complete "disorientation" which may result from encounter with the transcendent as "creative negativity",[2] they can introduce movement into human life. The words of Jesus in these settings frequently challenge certain attitudes and suggest others to replace them. These stories embody a tension between two attitudes (involving value commitments, emotional attachments, orientations of the will, and evaluative thought) and present an invitation to move from one attitude to another. The interpreter of such stories must catch this movement. The interpretation must attend to the shift *from* one position *to* another which the story invites. The tension which invites movement is apparent in some sayings even apart from a narrative context. Thus the antithetical aphorism[3] "The sabbath came for persons, not persons for the sabbath" (Mk. 2:27) clearly expresses the tension between two attitudes toward the sabbath and invites movement from the one to the other. This tension is dramatized and the sense of movement is heightened when such words are part of a pronouncement story. In a pronouncement story Jesus' words are a response to something said or observed, and this provoking factor is narrated as part of the story setting. The setting may present a person who assumes a certain attitude or a person who is likely to provoke a certain attitude from the reader. The response of Jesus may then challenge that attitude. Thus the story setting helps to express or evoke the attitude and make it available for challenge.

The reflections on tension and movement in this article arise from a careful study of the formal composition of pronouncement stories, based on observations concerning the relationship between the two necessary parts of such stories, the setting which provokes the pronouncement and the pronouncement which responds to the setting. Setting and saying are related as stimulus and response. Careful study of this relationship reveals six types of pronouncement stories in the synoptic Gospels:[4] 1. *Correction stories*, in which the climactic response corrects the views or conduct of the person or group provoking the response. 2. *Objection stories*, in which the behavior of the responder (the one who utters the climactic pronouncement) or the responder's followers is the cause of an objection and the climactic response is an answer to that objection. 3. *Commendation stories*, in which the responder commends or praises something said, done, or represented by another person. 4. *Quest stories*, which begin when someone approaches the responder in quest of something very important to the well-being of the quester. The suspense generated by the uncertainty of success in the quest is central to the story, and the story comes to an end with an indication of the quest's success or failure. The responder's pronouncement (sometimes accompanied by action) plays a crucial role in this success or failure. 5. *Test stories*, in which someone approaches the responder with a question, request, or proposal designed to test the responder. Like the objection story, the suspense in this type of story focuses on the responder, who must extricate himself or herself from a difficult situation. Unlike the objection story, this suspense does not arise from an objection against something already said or done by the responder. 6. *Inquiry stories*, in which the basic features of the other five types are absent and the responder simply responds to a question or request for information by supplying the information.

The two parts of a pronouncement story are correlative, i.e., the function of the stimulus part must correlate with the function of the response part or the story will be malformed and confusing. It is only by considering both parts in relation to each other that the type can be defined. The fact that Jesus is asked a question does not immediately tell us that the story is an inquiry, for Jesus may respond by correcting an assumption behind the question (a correction story), or the question may actually be a demand for justification of previous behavior (an objection story), or the question may announce a quest or pose a test. One of the values of this typology is that it requires us to look at the story as a whole, to consider the relation between the two major parts, and to define the type of narrative tension which is dominant in each case.[5]

"Hybrid" pronouncement stories, combining several of the types in a single story, are fairly common in the synoptic Gospels. Some of these will be noted below.

The movement from the provoking occasion to the response may also represent a movement from one attitude to another on important issues of religion and life. This can be demonstrated most clearly for correction, objection, commendation, and quest stories. I will concentrate on these four types in the remainder of this essay.

Correction stories are the dominant type of pronouncement story in such writings as Lucian's *Demonax*, Philostratus' *The Life of Apollonius of Tyana*, and Book VI of Diogenes Laertius' *Lives and Opinions of Eminent Philosophers*. They also have an important place in the synoptic Gospels, especially if we consider the role of correction in many hybrid stories. A correction story is a natural choice for inviting attitudinal shift. In correction stories the response corrects the views or conduct of the person or group causing the response. The response may clearly indicate the view or behavior which should be substituted for that which is being corrected, or the response may merely express disapproval in a forceful way, with the alternative left implicit. The occasion for the corrective response may be something observed, or it may be a statement, request, or question to the responder. In the case of requests or questions, the responder does not grant the request or answer the question but corrects an assumption on which the request or question was based. The cause of the response is a position concerning what is right or acceptable assumed deliberately or unthinkingly by someone, and the response is a correction of that position. Thus two attitudes are contrasted in a correction story. These two attitudes are usually represented by two characters in the story, one who has taken a position by action or speech and one who responds by correcting that position. This results in tension or conflict between the two characters. This tension is not apparent until the response is made, for the position corrected may represent a common practice, in society as a whole or in a certain part of society. It may seem reasonable, perhaps even laudable. The position corrected is not an attack upon the responder, requiring some defense, for this would lead to an objection story. Rather, the corrective response opens up distance between two positions in a situation where distance would otherwise not appear.

The words of the responder are placed in climactic position in the story. The story often ends with these words. Furthermore, the responder often speaks in a forceful and memorable way. It is clear from the way that the story is told that the climactic response is meant to make the dominant impression upon the hearer or reader. Thus the story tends to recommend the attitude of the responder, for the views of the other character do not share the advantages of climactic position and forceful expression. This also indicates that the story teller is recommending an attitudinal shift from the attitude being corrected to the attitude of the corrector.

Most pronouncement stories are brief, containing one or sometimes two exchanges of dialogue. While an extensive dialogue might permit reasoned discussion and careful argument, the pronouncement story does not. Some of the climactic pronouncements contain brief reasons for the judgment that is made, but generally there is less concern with reasons than with presenting an attitude in succinct and forceful language in order to arrest the hearer's attention and provoke new thought. The imaginative force of the language is important, for it must awaken new thought about an unconsidered or poorly considered possibility. A brief pronouncement need not put an end to thought. It can awaken imaginative thought by pointing to possibilities beyond the prison of old assumptions in which most of our thinking is trapped. For this purpose the impact of the words, their rhetorical power, is important. The climactic pronouncement is often carefully shaped to increase its impact, and in correction stories the setting of the pronouncement also increases its impact through contrast.

In synoptic correction stories the shift in attitude may simply involve a shift in the focus of concern, as when Jesus corrects the woman who blesses his mother, pointing to those who "hear the word of God and keep it" as the truly blessed (Lk. 11:27-28). However, there is a tendency in some stories to shift from seemingly reasonable expectations to a position which surrenders reasonable calculations and challenges basic social duties, as in Jesus' response to Peter's suggestion that he forgive seven times (Mt. 18:21-22) and to the disciple's request for permission to leave in order to bury his father (Mt. 8:21-22 par.). In some cases the response is paradoxical, as in Jesus' corrections of the disciples' desire to be the greatest (Mk. 9:35; 10:42-45 par.). This movement to the extreme and the paradoxical is useful not in replacing one social system by another system with clearly defined duties but in challenging basic assumptions and life goals while pointing to the overriding importance of a conflicting attitude. The task of applying the new attitude to daily behavior is left to the creative disciple.

In the correction stories Jesus is often (but not always) in dialogue with a disciple or with someone who, at the moment at least, seems to take a favorable attitude toward Jesus.

The response creates distance where we might expect harmony. These stories fight against the tendency of disciples and admirers to reduce Jesus' vision of God's will to the ordinary. The story opens up a choice and a new possibility by making the difference between the ordinary and Jesus' call stand out. A number of the correction stories speak to men and women attracted by security, status, and power. The conflict between Jesus' call and the security of home (Mk. 3:31-35 par.; Mt. 8: 19-22 par.; Lk. 9:61-62; 11:27-28) and the conflict between Jesus' way and the desire for status and power (Mk. 9:33-37 par.; 10:13-16 par.; 10:35-45 par.; Lk. 14:7-11)[6] are prominent themes in synoptic correction stories.

In objection stories there is also clear tension between two attitudes, but it is not a tension which the responder creates. The tension is caused by an objection to something said or done by the responder or the responder's followers, an objection to which the responder must reply. The position of the responder is called in question. Therefore, the tension focuses upon him or her. The objection story has three parts: 1. the cause of the objection, which is often narrated at the beginning of the story but which may be described as part of the objection; 2. the objection, which is often expressed as a question asking why something is being done; 3. the response to the objection. For example, in Mark 2:15-17 we are first told that Jesus and his disciples were banqueting with "many tax collectors and sinners". Then "the scribes of the Pharisees" object by asking why Jesus is doing this, and Jesus replies. In an objection story the responder must meet the challenge by giving an impressive reply, a reply that will make the responder's position attractive, if not to the objector then to the hearer or reader.

The response in objection stories does not create the tension but discloses what is at stake in a tension which already exists. Thus objection stories are useful in dealing with conflicts which are already part of public awareness. It is not surprising that the conflicts between the early church and outside groups are mirrored in the objection stories.[7] The scribes and Pharisees are the most frequent objectors. The responses to such objections defend the distinctive perspectives of the Jesus movement. Furthermore, the defense commonly discloses the basis for the objectionable action. The conflict may move to a fundamental level through the response. It becomes a conflict about basic priorities or about fundamental perceptions of the will of God. The conflict increases in significance through the response. For something fundamental is at stake. The objectionable action becomes indicative of a basic attitude, and the climactic pronouncement becomes a challenge for all (opponents and followers) to share that attitude. Thus many objection stories invite an important attitudinal shift, not only for the opponents of the early church but also for its members, who would seldom see the issue as clearly or be as firmly committed to the recommended attitude as the responder in the pronouncement story. The meal with the tax collectors and sinners (Mk. 2:15-17) and plucking grain on the sabbath (Mk. 2:23-28) are examples of objection stories in which the response opens issues of fundamental priorities, stories which not only challenge critics to new perception but also may move some of Jesus' followers to new or renewed attitudes.

To be sure, the objection story may become the vehicle of religious polemic in which one group, with a firmly fixed attitude, attacks another group with a contrary attitude. This may be the case in Mark 7:1-13 (or 1-15) and Luke 11:37-52. While these scenes begin with objections, they are not good examples of pronouncement stories, for the response is not a brief pronouncement but a rather long discourse. Furthermore, the response is primarily an attack upon the objecting group. The danger of such stories is that they will simply reinforce prejudices against the group being attacked.

We also find objection stories with objections from people who are closely connected with Jesus. In Mark 8:31-33 par. Peter objects to Jesus' announcement of the coming suffering of the Son of Man, and in Luke 2:41-50 (the boy Jesus in the temple) Jesus' mother objects to his behavior.[8] In these stories it is not the position of an outside group that causes the conflict. The objection arises from attitudes within the church or from general human expectations and desires. The response defends the path that Jesus has chosen against these attitudes.

Certain issues are prominent in the objection stories, being represented by several stories. Association with tax collectors and sinners is the cause of conflict in Mark 2:15-17 par. and Luke 15:1-32.[9] Three hybrid objection-quest stories deal with the same issue (Lk. 7:36-50; 19:1-10) or with the related issue of Jesus' authority to forgive (Mk. 2:1-12 par.). This suggests both that there was considerable public conflict over this attitude of openness to the outcast and that Jesus and his followers spoke out strongly to shift attitudes on this issue. The objection stories also emphasize the conflict between sabbath regulations and human need, with healing on the sabbath provoking objection on three occasions (Mk. 3:1-6 par; Lk. 13:10-17; 14:1-6), while plucking grain on the sabbath is the provocation on another occasion (Mk. 2:23-28 par.). The issue of eating with unwashed hands appears in Mark 7:1-15 par. and Luke 11:37-44. Two objection-

commendation stories deal with the issue of whether it is appropriate to praise Jesus as king (Lk. 19:37-40) and Son of
David (Mt. 21:14-16). The internal church problem arising
from conflict between family duty or household responsibility
and the call of God is reflected in Matthew 19:10-12,[10] Luke
10:38-42 (an objection-commendation story), and perhaps Luke
2:41-50.

In commendation stories, as in correction stories, the
responder evaluates a position taken by another person. In
other words, someone says, does, or represents something which
calls forth the evaluative comment of the responder. Unlike
the correction stories, this response is affirmative rather
than corrective. The responder commends or praises the person who is the occasion for the response. In doing so, the
response may disclose a previously hidden value or importance
in the person or quality being commended. The commendation
may be surprising in light of ordinary ways of judging. The
commendation story frequently presents the person commended
as a model to be imitated by others. In so doing, it seeks
to influence the hearer's or reader's attitudes.

In commendation stories the commender and the one commended are in basic agreement. It might seem inappropriate
to speak of attitudinal shift as a major concern in such
stories. However, the synoptic commendation story gains interest and importance because the responder often commends
someone or something that is *not* commendable by some other
standard of judgment. Thus tension appears in these stories
also, and we can see that the teller of the story is seeking
to move the audience from one way of judging to another. The
importance of this concern is shown by the fact that the majority of synoptic commendation stories are hybrids. They are
either correction-commendation stories or objection-commendation stories. These stories contain three characters (individuals or groups) and they emphasize the contrast between two
of them. The contrast is either between two ways of judging,
with Jesus commending and another party rejecting the third
person, or between two different ways of acting, with Jesus
commending the one and correcting the other. In commending,
Jesus is also rejecting a conflicting possibility, either another way of judging or another way of acting, and the rejected possibility is made explicit by the story teller, for
it is represented by a character within the story. The tension between attitudes is emphasized by dramatizing it, presenting the attitudes through persons in a situation of conflict. Here also the story teller seeks to influence the audience by inviting them to shift attitudes. The story presents the two possibilities which constitute the choice, and
the responder, whose words are placed in climactic position

in the story and therefore are meant to be dominant, evaluates the two possibilities, indicating to the audience how the choice should be made.

In the story of the widow's mites (Mk. 12:41-44), Jesus commends the poor widow by declaring that she put in "more than all". In doing so, Jesus compares the widow with the others who contributed "out of their abundance". In comparison with the widow, this group is not commended. This group is associated with a way of judging value which conflicts with Jesus' way. This way of judging is adopted in the introductory narration of the story. The narrator, by indicating that "many rich people put in much" while the widow put in only two *lepta*, allows the reader to judge the gifts in a way that will be corrected by Jesus. This represents the common way of judging, in which the economic value of the gift is primary. Thus the story commends the widow's offering and corrects another way of judging offerings, moving the reader from the rejected view at the beginning of the story to a contrasting view at the end. This story is more complex than it seems, for there is contrast between two ways of acting (the rich putting in much, the poor widow putting in a little) and also between two ways of judging those actions, expressed by the introductory narration and by Jesus' response.

Two contrasting judgments are also presented in the story of the blessing of the children (Mk. 10:13-16). The disciples and Jesus take different attitudes toward the children. Jesus both corrects the disciples and commends the children for what they represent. Thus the story seeks to move the reader away from the attitude of the disciples to the attitude of Jesus and to the characteristics of the children. Mark 14:3-9, the story of the anointing woman, is similar. Mark 3:31-35, Jesus' response to his mother and brothers, is also similar, except that the application of a favorable description ("your mother and brothers") is corrected by being shifted to another group, which is thereby commended.

Luke 17:12-19, the cleansing of ten lepers, does not present two contrasting judgments but two contrasting actions, the return of one healed leper to show his gratitude and the failure of the others to return. Jesus responds favorably to the grateful leper but criticizes the others. However, the story is primarily concerned with prejudicial attitudes toward Samaritans. The laudable gratitude of the Samaritan is used as a counterbalance to this prejudice, as is shown by the fact that we are told that he is a Samaritan only after his gratitude has been demonstrated (v. 16) and by the emphasis on the grateful leper's foreignness in Jesus' response (v. 18). The story attempts to shift attitudes by preventing quick, negative judgments about Samaritans.

Luke 10:38-42 is an objection-commendation story. It is similar to the correction-commendation stories, except that Martha not only makes a negative judgment about her sister but also objects to Jesus' behavior. Jesus' response is both a reply to Martha's objection and a commendation of Mary, whose behavior is thereby recommended to the reader.

Not only Jesus himself but those that he commends represent attitudes which the Gospels are recommending to their readers. These attitudes must compete with conflicting attitudes. This conflict is suggested by the tendency to select persons for commendation who otherwise might be judged bad or unimportant (the Samaritan leper, the children, the poor widow). It is even clearer in the strong tendency to form hybrid stories in which the commended action or quality is balanced by a contrasting action or quality or by a contrasting judgment about the one commended. Thus the choice is clarified for the reader, who is helped to see that the position recommended in Jesus' response involves a shift from attitudes which are common.

Quest stories are generally longer and more elaborate than most pronouncement stories. A pronouncement by Jesus occupies a prominent place near the end of the story, as in other pronouncement stories, and that pronouncement will determine the success or failure of the quest. Nevertheless, in a quest story the person who encounters Jesus stands out prominently. The story presents this person as a quester. He or she is seeking something very important for human well-being and comes to Jesus in hope that he will help. The story begins with an indication of this quest. It ends by indicating the success or failure of the quest. While many pronouncement stories end with a challenging word of Jesus, leaving unclear how other persons in the story may have reacted to Jesus' challenge, the outcome of the quest is a necessary part of a quest story. Thus the story is really the quester's story. Jesus has a crucial role as helper in the quest, and we are expected to judge the success or failure of the quest according to Jesus' words. But the story is shaped by the tension arising from the quester's need, indicated at the beginning of the story, and it comes to a resolution with the fulfillment or a clear failure to fulfill that need. Since the story focuses attention upon the quester's need and desire to fulfill that need, the reader becomes involved in the quester's concerns. This promotes sympathy for the quester on the part of the reader. This is supported by the "logic" of story, in which need calls for resolution of that need, even when, tragically, it does not come. This sympathy may be

further encouraged by indications of the quester's earnestness
and other attractive qualities. Suspense is increased by the
presence of obstacles to the quest. Jesus may pose a difficult condition, someone may object, or Jesus himself may object. Even when Jesus objects, the quest will be recognized
as valid in the context of the story as a whole. The condition for success or the objection to the quest is quite important to the story. It indicates the issue which will be
crucial for the outcome of the quest, which is also the issue
on which the story teller wishes to change attitudes.

Quest stories also are told in order to change attitudes.
Most of the quest stories contain elements likely to provoke
conflicting reactions on the part of the first hearers or
readers. The one quester who fails in these synoptic stories
has a characteristic which seems desirable (he is rich), while
most of the questers who succeed have characteristics that are
undesirable, at least to some groups. The outcome of the story
may bring about a shift in attitude toward those characteristics and the people who have them. The reader's concern with
the quester and his or her need will make the failure of the
quest seem tragic, emphasizing the danger in the factor that
caused that failure. On the other hand, the reader's concern
with the quester and Jesus' affirmation of the success of the
quest may require readers to reassess their attitudes toward
people who have characteristics that seem to disqualify them.

Mark 10:17-22, the quest of the rich man, begins with the
man indicating his quest: "What shall I do to inherit eternal
life?" Descriptive details suggest his earnestness (v. 17),
and his religious concern is also shown by the fact that he
has kept the commandments which Jesus lists. Furthermore, the
reader's sympathy is aroused by the statement that Jesus "loved
him". But Jesus poses a difficult condition, which the man is
unable to fulfill. At the end of the story there is a delayed
disclosure of the factor that causes the failure: the man had
great possessions. Through portraying the failure of the rich
man, the story changes riches from advantage to liability.

In Mark 7:24-30, the Syrophoenician woman, the woman approaches Jesus requesting healing for her daughter. At the
end of the story both Jesus and the narrator certify the success of her quest (vv. 29-30). Success comes in spite of a
seemingly insurmountable obstacle, for Jesus himself objects
to her request. The objection indicates the factor which dis-
qualifies her: she is not a Jew. The story teller has adopted
a daring but powerful strategy for dealing with negative attitudes toward gentiles. Jesus first affirms the negative view
but then, under the impact of this resourceful woman's words,
changes his mind. Those who share Jesus' first position find

Jesus deserting them. This story is like the previous stories with three characters, with two of them taking contrasting positions, except that Jesus occupies two positions within one story. The negative attitude toward gentiles is expressed so that it can be evaluated. It does not prevail. The story invites those who share this attitude to follow Jesus in his shift of position.

The story of Zacchaeus (Lk. 19:1-10) is also a quest story. The prominent role of the quester is especially clear in this story, for not only is Zacchaeus named but his characteristics and actions are described in some detail. His quest is introduced in disguised form. We are simply told that he wanted to see who Jesus was. His true need is disclosed by what he receives at the end of the story: "salvation", which includes both release from his greed and reaffirmation of his rightful place, as a "son of Abraham", among God's people. The emphasis on the fact that he belongs among the sons of Abraham comes in response to the crowd. The crowd has the role of a blocking force throughout the story, standing in the way of Zacchaeus' desire to see Jesus and objecting to Jesus' association with this man. This highlights Zacchaeus' isolation from his own people, and the resolution of the problem includes the affirmation that he rightfully belongs to the religious community. Thus the story not only affirms Jesus' right to "seek and to save the lost", but that through Jesus persons isolated from the religious community may be restored to it. The attitude of rejection of such persons is represented by the objecting crowd. The story speaks to this attitude and attempts to change it by helping the reader or hearer become interested in Zacchaeus and his problems and by affirming through Jesus that such a person may also share in God's salvation and be a part of God's people. Thus the story invites a shift from an attitude of exclusion to one of acceptance. This is a hybrid objection-quest story, for Jesus' final words respond both to Zacchaeus, disclosing the success of his quest, and to the objection of the crowd. This causes an awkward shift from Zacchaeus to the crowd as audience in mid-sentence (v. 9).

In Luke 7:36-50 we find another objection-quest story which deals with a sinner, this time a woman. The story of the paralytic in Mark 2:1-12 is also an objection-quest story that deals with a sinful person, though in this case the objection is more strictly directed against Jesus. In both the story of the Syrophoenician woman (Mk. 7:24-30 par.) and of the centurion (Mt. 8:5-13), we are presented with questers who are gentiles. All of these stories can bring about a shift in attitude toward those outside the religious community. All of them present the need of the quester in a way which can awaken

sympathy, and in all of them Jesus declares the success of the
quest, making clear that such persons rightfully share in the
salvation which he brings. Such stories can change the narrow
attitudes represented by the objections which appear in these
stories. These stories can both serve as invitations to the
religious outcasts and create openness for the outcasts on the
part of the religious community.

John Dominic Crossan has called attention to the frequency in parables of the reversal of expectations and values.[11]
While Crossan interprets this in terms of an eschatological
shattering of "world", many of the parables seem to be concerned with a reversal of specific values and attitudes. If
so, they share this concern with pronouncement stories that I
have discussed. In pronouncement stories Jesus commends those
who appear not commendable and announces the success of questers who seem to have disqualifying characteristics, thereby
reversing the expectations which arise from the usual judgments about such people. This suggests that parabolic and
non-parabolic stories, especially the pronouncement stories
most clearly concerned with attitudinal shift, may share some
common features.

A good story is interesting, but the stories we have
examined were not told merely for entertainment. Precisely
by being interesting these stories may involve the reader sufficiently to change attitudes. This concern to change attitudes is quite apparent when we study the relationship between setting and saying, or provoking situation and response,
in pronouncement stories, noting the different types of such
stories and recognizing the tension between two different attitudes which appears in them. These attitudes reflect the
world of Jesus and the early church. They are attitudes which
the first hearers and readers might share. Therefore, they
would recognize that *their* attitudes were being corrected,
that *they* were being invited to change. In the modern world
this may not be recognized. Tax collectors and gentiles no
longer arouse negative feelings in us. Because of this, the
function of the story may change. Instead of inviting us to
change our attitudes, the story may simply reinforce ideas
which we hold without passion or even reinforce prejudices
against people who could hold such narrow ideas long ago. We
are no longer the ones who are being attacked. Consequently,
the original purpose of the story may be lost. If the original story teller intended to bring about a shift in attitudes,
the story functions as intended only when this becomes a possibility. This happens only when the story speaks against
real resistance, when it challenges something in which some
readers, at least, have a real investment. Then the tension
of the original story reappears, and we recognize the impor-

tance of the movement from one attitude to another which is central to the story. Historical imagination can help us, for it can give us a sharp sense of how the story spoke to the problems of the past. But the interpreter who wishes to re-awaken the original function of the story may have to relate it to different but analogous attitudes in the modern world. If there is no resistance, there will be no shift of attitude. In such a situation it may be necessary to retell the story in order to preserve its original function.

In part this is already happening. There are certain standard ways of interpreting "tax collectors" and "gentiles" in sermons today. But the spark of imagination is usually missing, and it is this spark of imagination which can attract our interest. Story tellers once showed some imagination, even some daring, in telling these stories. This, too, must be recovered if the stories are to regain their power.

NOTES

1. "Uses of the Proverb in the Synoptic Gospels," *Interpretation* 24 (January, 1970): 72.

2. Beardslee has recently affirmed the importance of such encounters but has rightly cautioned against limiting the significance of the transcendent for the world to such disruptive encounters. See "Parable, Proverb, and Koan," *Semeia* 12 (1978): 151-177.

3. On antithetical aphorisms see Robert C. Tannehill, *The Sword of His Mouth* (Philadelphia & Missoula: Fortress Press & Scholars Press, 1975), pp. 88-101.

4. The following typology differs from Rudolf Bultmann's classification of synoptic apophthegms (equivalent to pronouncement stories). He divided them into controversy dialogues, scholastic dialogues, and biographical apophthegms. See *The History of the Synoptic Tradition*, rev. ed., trans. John Marsh (New York: Harper & Row, 1963), pp. 11-69. However, there is a connection between Bultmann's controversy dialogues and my objection stories.

5. In my article "Types and Functions of Apophthegms in the Synoptic Gospels," (forthcoming in *Aufstieg und Niedergang der römischen Welt*, ed. Hildegard Temporini & Wolfgang Haase, Band II.25.1) may be found more careful definitions of the six types and classification of synoptic pronouncement stories according to these types.

6. Of the listed stories, Mark 3:31-35 par. and 10:13-16 par. are hybrid stories which include correction and commendation.

7. Bultmann noted this when he described the setting of the controversy dialogues as the "apologetic and polemic of the Palestinian Church". See *History of the Synoptic Tradition*, pp. 40-41.

8. Martin Dibelius regards Luke 2:41-50 as an outstanding example of a legend. See *From Tradition to Gospel*, trans. Bertram Lee Woolf (New York: Scribner's, n.d.), pp. 106-09. It may have legendary features, but it comes to a climax with a pronouncement of Jesus which responds to the objection of his mother. Thus it has the essential features of an objection story.

9.   In Luke 15:1-32 three parables are presented as Jesus' response to an objection. This makes the response unusually long.

10.   Matthew 19:10 appears to be an objection against the severity of Jesus' teaching on divorce or against the limitation it places on married men who may leave their wives for the sake of the mission. The objection scene in 19:10-12 is dependent on 19:3-9, for the objection is provoked by Jesus' teaching in 19:6 and 9.

11.   See *In Parables* (New York: Harper & Row, 1973), pp. 53-78, 96-120.

13

STRUCTURE, CHRISTOLOGY, AND ETHICS IN MATTHEW

Dan O. Via, Jr.

Will Beardslee has made a significant and creative contribution to a number of areas of biblical and theological
scholarship, among them being the literary criticism of biblical texts, ethics, and reflection on Christology and Wisdom.
I should like to honor him and acknowledge my debt to him by
treating these issues in relation to the Gospel of Matthew.
It is not my purpose to deal with the structure of the Gospel
in a detailed or exhaustive way. I want rather, using broad
strokes, to consider three ways of grasping the main segments
of Matthew in relation to its Christology. Ethics will re-
ceive much briefer focal consideration, although more tacit
treatment along the way.

I. STRUCTURE AS THE ORGANIZATION OF THEMATIC CONTENT

Five times in Matthew (7:28; 11:1; 13:53; 19:1; 26:1) an
expression something like "And when Jesus finished these sayings..." occurs, each time at the end of a collection of teachings composing a unified discourse. On the basis of these dividing marks and other related material a characteristic approach to Matthew has developed, which I will describe briefly
and somewhat synthetically.

The center or substance of Matthew (3-25) is comprised of
five books, each one containing a narrative and discourse section. The birth narrative (1-2) and passion (26-28), therefore, serve as prologue and epilogue. This five-fold structure reflects the Old Testament Pentateuch, and Matthew thus
presents the Christian gospel as a new or revised law and Jesus as a new Moses or more authoritative law-giver.[1]

Let me now present one set of criticisms of this view of
Matthew and an alternative proposal regarding the governing
structure of the Gospel. Edgar Krentz[2] has argued that 4:17
and 16:21 are parallel verses, no less striking as dividing
marks than the five formula-statements noted above. Each

verse contains the words "from then Jesus began" plus an in-
finitive and a summary of the content of the material to follow. This suggests that 1:1 is the introduction to 1:1-4:16,
and Matthew is seen thus to have a fundamentally three-fold
structure: (1) Jesus as Son of David and Son of Abraham
(ideal Israelite) (1:1-4:16); (2) Jesus' proclamation of the
Kingdom (4:17-16:20); (3) Jesus' proclamation of his death and
resurrection (16:21-28:20).

More recently Jack Kingsbury has accepted this demarcation of the major sections of Matthew and has elaborated and
tightened the resulting understanding of the Gospel, with some
modifications. For Kingsbury, Matthew makes "Son of God" the
superior Christological term. Jesus is pre-eminently Messiah
Son of God. The three main sections deal with: (1) the person of Jesus Messiah; (2) the proclamation of Jesus Messiah;
(3) the suffering, death, and resurrection of Jesus Messiah.
The function of the structure is thus, not to present the gospel as law, but to set forth the claim of Jesus' person, ministry, and passion as ultimately significant.[3]

Among Kingsbury's reasons for rejecting the five-fold division as the principle of organization are the following:
(1) By placing the birth and passion narratives outside the
main structure it overlooks the climactic nature of the cross
and resurrection and the significance of salvation history.[4]
We might add that it also ignores the significance of Matthew's
narrative character for the nature and content of its Christology. (2) It is not clear that Matthew has only five discourses or that the Pentateuch presents the clear alternation
of narrative and discourse.[5] (3) Kingsbury[6] has observed that
two summary passages (4:23 and 9:35), both dealing with Jesus'
teaching and healing, press 5-7 (teaching) and 8-9 (healing)
together into one section. We might go on to observe that
the structural significance of this is that the "Pentateuchal"
division coming at 7:28 is relativized by the unification of
5-7 and 8-9.

Matthew may well have more than five discourses and the
Old Testament Pentateuch may not present a clear alternation
of narrative and discourse; nevertheless, the five-fold division is too obvious and unmistakable and the motif of the law,
too prominent in Matthew for this structure not to be an--if
not the--organizing principle. I am led to agree that the
(slightly) dominant pattern of the two is the three-fold one,
but the interpretive questions now become: why are there two
structural schemes on the surface of Matthew and what is the
meaning of their relationship?

Any narrative may foreground certain elements and background others. The foregrounded pattern is likely to express a deviation from a norm and the backgrounded pattern, the norm which has been surpassed. Both patterns belong to the synchrony (present meaning system) of the narrative, and the synchrony includes a diachrony (historical process) because the surpassed norm from the past is present as the backgrounded pattern.[7]

Let us begin provisionally by saying that Matthew foregrounds the three-fold Christological structure and backgrounds the five-fold legal one. The simultaneous juxtaposition of the two patterns has behind it and expresses a diachrony which is a part of Matthew's theological content. In the distant past God spoke in the prophets (1:22; 2:15, etc.) and law (5:21, etc.), but in the much more recent past the event promised by the prophets has been fulfilled (1:21-23; 2:14-15) and the real intention of the law has been brought to light (5:17; 5: 21-26; etc.) in Jesus Son of God.

But the picture in Matthew is more complicated than that. The backgrounded law is not as backgrounded as the foregrounded/backgrounded opposition might imply. Christological content is more prominent than legal content. But I would suggest that the five-fold Pentateuchal demarcation is more evident than the three-fold Christological one. The relative strength of the legal structure vis-à-vis the Christological structure reflects what might be considered a theological problem in Matthew: Jesus fulfills and transcends the law of Moses but not law in principle.[8]

II. STRUCTURE AS THE ORGANIZATION OF NARRATIVE PROCESS

The two competing structures thus far considered organize the content on the basis of two themes, respectively, the new law and Christology. But the surface structure of Matthew may also be grasped as the manifestation of a deep narrative structure, which will enable us to see how the themes are experienced as personal realities in the temporality of existence.

The structure in the light of which Matthew will be viewed *is* deep in that it is abstracted from narrative in general. But it is also broad, simple, and flexible. The governing category is Process, and any process has three moments, which constitute the functions or motifemes of a narrative. I am using the three functions as "macro-functions" for grasping the whole sequence of a more or less lengthy narrative. They are initial state as potentiality, process actualized or simply process, and goal (final state). The state quality can be directly expressed by descriptive statements or it can be the implication of an action: lack, for example, is implicit in an act of villainy. The initial (or final) state may be one of disequilibrium: a *surplus* of good (satisfactory state) or a *lack* of good (deficient state). Or the initial state may be a balance of good and bad. Any one of these states is a potentiality for change and thus the source of process. A satisfactory state can be degraded; a deficient state can be ameliorated; and a balanced state can be unbalanced for either good or evil. This, it seems to me, is more circumspect than the view which says that narrative always begins with stability and movement is introduced by disequilibrium or a negative equilibrium.[9]

Kingsbury is quite aware of temporal movement in Matthew,[10] but two benefits would accrue from more attention to the specifically narrative character of Matthew, to the Gospel as the manifestation of a structure derived from narrative in general. (1) It would enable us to compare Matthew carefully with other narratives (although that is not my purpose here). (2) It would be sensitive to the capacity of narrative to reproduce "the temporal tensions of experience", to reproduce "the very feel of lived time",[11] although, of course, no mode of interpretation is an adequate substitute for the story itself in this regard.

Initial situation. The initial situation (which precedes the initial state function) normally introduces the hero or enumerates the members of his family.[12] This morphological element is manifested in Matthew by the genealogy (1:1-17). He who is to be the Christ is preceded by a long line of "parents" who point to him.

Initial state. The birth of Christ is anticipated and then narrated. He is God with us (1:23) and Son (2:15) and thus potentially--future tense--Israel's savior (1:21). There are two factors in the initial potentiality--Jesus and Israel-- and thus we will be in the potentiality function until Israel and Jesus are brought together under the impact of Jesus' saving intention, which first occurs at 4:17. Both the birth narrative and the baptism-and-temptation belong to the initial state.

In the birth narrative Jesus is a passive figure; therefore, who he is at this stage does not emerge from his own actions. His birth and identity, however, provide the motivation for the actions of the other characters--Joseph, the wise men, Herod--and who he is comes to expression as descriptive and discourse material in the narration of the acts of others. He is generated by the Holy Spirit (1:18, 20), and his name is "God with us" (1:23). He is thus Son of God (2:15). He is also king and ruler of Israel (2:2, 6)--Messiah or Christ (1: 16-18). There is one further anticipation of his identity before he appears on the scene as an adult: He will be a judge (3:11-12). When he does appear, his submission to baptism fulfills all righteousness (3:15)--Matthew's comprehensive term for what God requires of all human beings (cf. 5:20; 6:1)--and his sonship is again affirmed (3:17). He is then tempted as Son (4:3, 6) but in the face of this test maintains his obedience (4:4, 7, 10).

The process function has not yet begun, for while Jesus has encountered John and the devil, he has not yet encountered Israel. The possibility has not yet begun to be actualized. Since he will be Son and savior in relation to Israel, he is not actually this until they meet (4:17ff.), although he is this in principle at least from the time of his conception. The implication of the narrative form of Matthew's interpretation of Jesus is that Christological identity is a dialectical process of inter-action between ontological possibility and different modes of actualization. Jesus is not who he is solely on the basis of principle. His identity is formed not only by his relation to God but also by his varying relations with human beings. At any point he is Son but not Son because any future event could add to the actual meaning of sonship. This is not only implied by the narrative form but is made explicit at least once by Matthew (cf. 28:18), as we shall see.

Israel's condition in the initial state is sinfulness. This is anticipated in the birth narrative by the fact that all Jerusalem, along with Herod, was troubled by the possibility of a new King (2:3; cf. also 1:21). Then in the Baptist section Israel is sinful and in need of repentance (3:2, 6) although also confessing (3:6). The Pharisees and Sadducees need to bear--and thus lack--fruit that befits repentance (3: 8); moreover, they trust presumptuously in their descent from Abraham (3:9).

For Matthew the eschatological time begins with John (11: 10, 12-15), and John and Jesus preach the same message: Repent, for the Kingdom of heaven is at hand (3:2; 4:17). And evidently John's preaching and baptism are able to effect the desired repentance (3:6, 11); but however eschatological John's time is, it is not as eschatological as that of Jesus (11:11b; 3:11). Again, eschatological salvation is not a point but a process. Israel's fully eschatological salvation awaits its conjoining with Jesus.

To sum up at this point in formal terms, in the initial state function a surplus of good is attributed to Jesus and a lack of good (i.e. bad), to Israel. The good and bad do not balance each other, for the good will ultimately outweigh the bad. We have then two disequilibriums, a surplus and a lack.

Process. A surplus of good can initiate a process of degradation or opposition, and a lack of good can be filled, this possibility inaugurating a process of amelioration. At 4:17 Matthew begins the process function with the latter. Note that the beginning of the second main part of the narrative according to the structural process scheme coincides with the beginning of the second part according to the Krentz-Kingsbury Christological scheme. Jesus appears as preacher calling for repentance and proclaiming the nearness of the Kingdom. When, somewhat later, a process of degradation, or opposition, also begins, it will have been initiated indirectly as reaction to the initial potential surplus and directly by the actual process of amelioration.

The purpose of the process function in Matthew is to present the events which effect a transformation in Israel's lack to change it to a surplus of righteousness and faith. The process of amelioration will present the progressive changes in the historical existence of Israel-church and also the progressive self-actualization of the Son of God, for just as human beings are renewed in various ways by their encounter with him, he is progressively defined by the enactment of his several roles in relation to human beings. And because of the place of the theology of the cross (not as predominating as in Mark but nevertheless present) the definition of the Son requires the process of degradation as well as that of amelioration. Jesus must be opposed in order to be who he is.

In narrative in general the most efficient means of producing transformations in a state is to introduce the supernatural.[13] Since Matthew so clearly qualifies Jesus as divine in the initial state function, our *a priori* expectation might be that once he appears on the scene as savior he will effectively change Israel for the good once and for all. But Matthew's narrative takes the recalcitrance and evil of history more seriously than that. The history of salvation will last "forever". The process of opposition does reach a goal in Jesus' death and the process of amelioration, in his resurrection. But the goal is the beginning point for a new, or continuing, process. The risen Son intends to extend his sovereignty to all peoples through the church as instrument (28:16-20), and this will continue until the end of the age.

It is appropriate at this point to indicate briefly the structural significance of Galilee for Matthew and its contribution to the scope of the Son's saving mission. In the initial state function the infant Jesus is taken to Galilee at the end of the Egyptian sojourn (2:22-23), and following his temptation it is emphasized that he resides in Galilee. Galilee is the place ordained by God through prophecy in which the light of messianic salvation is to shine, and it is Galilee of the *Gentiles* (4:12-16). The process function, then, begins in Galilee (4:18, 23) and later moves to Jerusalem (19:1; 20:17, 29; 21:1, 10). However, in the goal function the resurrected Christ reconstitutes his mission in Galilee (28:16, 17). It is a microcosm of all the nations, who are to be evangelized. Galilee is thus in a certain tension with Israel, a tension in which the former is finally victorious. At the beginning the people which Jesus will save is Israel (1:21; 2:6); and even during the public ministry it is Israel, and specifically not the gentiles, who are to be evangelized (10:5-6; 15:24). But the people of the resurrected Christ is the gentiles, all the nations (28:19).

Let us now look more concretely at the process function. Immediately after the programmatic summary of Jesus' preaching in 4:17, he encounters and calls two sets of brothers who leave their fishing and become members of his following (4:18-22). Now they are to be fishers of men. Recall that a similar commission is given at the end of the Gospel. Jesus has begun a community, a purpose which is further consolidated at other points in the narrative (10; 12:46-50; 16:18-19; 18).

In the summary statement of 4:23-25 three roles are attributed to Jesus--teaching, preaching, and healing. A collection of the teaching/preaching is presented in 5-7, and in 8-9 a number of miracle stories is collected.

Jesus teaches a radical righteousness of the heart (5:17-48), obedience to which gives his followers the identity of salt and light (5:13-15). The content of the greater righteousness which disciples must render (5:20) is defined by the Old Testament law reinterpreted by love (5:43-48; 9:13; 12:7; 19:19; 22:34-40), this reinterpretation of the law being effected both by Jesus' teaching (5:21-48) and action (12:1-14). The disciples are motivated by the desire to be children of God (5:43-45) and to lead others to acknowledge God (5:16) but also by the desire to escape judgment (6:14-15; 7:13-14, 19-20, 21, 24-27). Both Israel and the church face a future judgment (22:1-14). In Matthew radical obedience *is* a condition for salvation and human beings will be accountable for their deeds before the Son of Man (16:27-28; 25:31-46). Jesus' present ministry offers the opportunity for faith and

repentance for which persons must answer at the final judgment (10:32-33; 11:20-24; 16:1-4). Because of the great
prominence of teaching in Matthew, spread across the narrative in the five discourses and elsewhere, and because of the
eschatological content of much of the teaching (13; 24-25),
the role of Jesus as teacher-judge is strongly emphasized.
In relation to this actualization of the Son of God the saved
are those who have earned salvation by their obedience.

In the miracle stories of 8-9 (and elsewhere) Jesus appears as healer and rescuer. Often those who approach Jesus
with a need already have faith (8:2). The stories are told
so as to suggest that Jesus' very presence evokes faith, and
on occasion (14:14; 15:32) his compassion clearly initiates
the miraculous act. Human beings in relation to this manifestation of the Son are believers in Jesus' authority (8:
8-10), restored to spiritual, psychic, and physical wholeness.

In the midst of the miracle section another Christological role comes to expression, one which we might call Son of
Man as archetypal person. With no place to lay his head the
Son of Man actualizes the insecurity which typifies humanity
as over against the animals, who at least have some kind of
dwelling (8:20). He is also archetypal person in his association with all kinds of people, sinners and outcasts (9:11,
13), in his not requiring fasting of his disciples (9:14-15),
and in his non-ascetic eating and drinking (11:19). Sharing
the lot of humanity leads to suffering (10:38; 20:20-23).
Would-be disciples are called on to take up this exposed mode
of existence (8:19-22; 16:21-26; 20:20-23), trusting that
their well-being is in God's hands (6:25-33) and knowing that
death leads to life (10:39; 16:25). In the context of the
miracle stories, where Jesus' very presence elicits faith and
makes healing available, following Jesus' risky way is more
an enabled response to present salvation than a condition for
future salvation.

In an oracle (not a narrative) in 11:25-30 Jesus as Son
(and closely associated with Wisdom) is revealer of knowledge
of God and bestower of rest. The recipients are babes, lacking the wisdom of the world (cf. 18:1-3), and the heavy-laden
who need rest.

Following chapter 11 Matthew presents a great deal of
interesting and significant story and discourse material but
not fundamentally new types of material, material that requires additional interpretive categories or Christological
roles--with the important exception of the process of opposition. For Matthew Jesus' death is a divine necessity (16:21;
26:24) and the source of salvation (20:28); therefore, the

process of opposition or degradation becomes confluent with the process of amelioration, however foreign that may have been to the intention of Jesus' opponents. How does Matthew understand the death of Jesus within the process of opposition-amelioration?

That human beings are not what they should be—are in need of faith and righteousness—is implicit in the action and teaching from the beginning, but human opposition to Jesus becomes explicit and dramatic at 9:3, when the scribes tacitly accuse Jesus of blasphemy for pronouncing the paralytic forgiven. He is opposed for eating with tax collectors and sinners (9:11), for not requiring fasting (9:14), and for his loose attitude toward the sabbath law (12:1-14). The opposition becomes the intention to kill him (12:14) well before the beginning of the passion narrative.

Matthew's Jesus accepts the opposition unto death as necessary for his calling (16:21; 26:24, 36-46, 54-56), predicts his coming death and resurrection (16:21; 17:12, 22-23; 20:17-19; 26:2), and interprets his death as a ransom for the many (20:28). While here his death alone is spoken of as redemptive, the death and resurrection characteristically belong together (references above), and in 26:18 together they comprise the single eschatological event—Jesus' *kairos*.[14]

Jesus' purpose for going to Jerusalem, at least implicitly, is to die and be raised (16:21; 20:17-19). He comes into the city as humble king (21:4-5) but also to die. There in Jerusalem he continues to heal (21:14) and to be in conflict with the Jewish leaders (21:15-17; 21:23-23:39) as they plot to arrest him (21:46). Sometimes he is responding to their attacks and sometimes taking the offensive. At 26:3-5 the intention to arrest Jesus and to kill him becomes more focalized, but before the arrest he arranges to celebrate the Passover with his disciples (26:17ff.).

The last supper is then clearly a Passover meal for Matthew, and through the words over the cup Matthew's Jesus gives the Gospel's most explicit interpretation of his coming death. It is a ransom for the many (20:28) in the sense that it communicates the forgiveness of sins to the many (26:28). The cup is Jesus' blood of the covenant poured out for forgiveness. The note of forgiveness points clearly to Jeremiah's new covenant (31:31-34) and may refer to the servant of the Lord as God's covenant to the nations (Is. 42:6; 49:7-8).[15] There is surely a reference here to the blood with which Moses sealed the Sinai covenant (Ex. 24:8). The blood in the Old Testament passage may refer both to God's forgiveness and to the oath imposed on Israel.[16] In any case the fact that both altar and

Israel are embraced by the blood suggests the communion of God
and people. In Matthew the Son of God as Son of Man offers
his life as a sacrifice establishing the new covenant of forgiveness. This is expressly how Jesus saves his people from
their sins (1:21). But in addition to being a covenant sacrifice Jesus is also the slain Passover lamb (26:2), and the last
supper is the first Passover of the new covenant.[17] Obviously
the saved community in relation to this Christological role is
a body of forgiven sinners.

With the betrayal, arrest, abandonment, denial, trials,
scourging, and mockery (26:47-27:34) the process of opposition
has run its full course.[18]

Goal. In the crucifixion (27:35-49) and even more particularly in Jesus' death (27:50) the goal of the process of
opposition has been reached. When the Gospel account is
grasped through the narrative structure of potentiality-pro-
cess-goal, the beginning of the proclamation of the passion
at 16:21 is relativized to a stage in the process (part two),
and the third main part (goal) begins at 27:35 (or even 27:
50), not at 16:21.

Because the processes of amelioration and opposition have
become one, the death of Jesus cannot be the end of God's redemptive intention but is the way to new life and power (28).
The life that was there from the beginning outlasts death, although death defines the way to life. Because the two pro-
cesses--amelioration and degradation--are distinct in originating intention and yet confluent, their goals are also both
distinct and unified. The crucifixion and resurrection are
narrated as separate occurrences, but they are aspects of the
same salvation event for Matthew. This is seen not only in
the fact that the category of Jesus' *kairos* embraces them both
(26:18) but also in that immediately after the death (27:50)
the resurrection and some of its consequences are narrated by
anticipation (27:52-54), before even the burial is related
(27:57-61), not to mention the resurrection appearances (28).

In consequence of the resurrection Jesus is Son of God in
a fuller sense than he has been before because now "all authority in heaven and on earth" (28:18) has been given to him.
However much such power may have been a potentiality before
(11:27; 26:53), its present actuality contrasts vividly with
his actual helplessness (27:40-44) and abandonment by God on
the cross (27:46). But even this new accession is not naked,
miraculous power, for the church identified with (10:40) and
empowered by (18:18-20) the exalted Son will experience difficult times in the history of its mission (10:13-23, 34-39; 13:
18-22; 24:4-14, 23-24) and must finally face judgment itself

(13:36-43; 22:11-14; 25:1-12). It is the power to bring people
to the way of the cross.

The role of teacher-judge has been connected with the eschatological covenant sacrifice by attributing the commission
to the crucified exalted one (28:16-20). His authority under-
girds his teaching: persons become disciples through baptism
and observing his commandments (28:19-20). But his authority
is also the power of his presence among his people (28:20),
which is the presence of God (1:23).

In the goal function a goal is reached both by Jesus and
by Israel-church. Jesus is fully constituted as the one who
can save Israel because he now has all authority (28:18) and
is always present (28:20). And Israel, in the disciples, has
its lack of faith and righteousness filled. Jesus is acknowledged in faith as Son (27:54) and worshipped (28:9, 17) and
will be obeyed (28:20). The presence of faith, worship, and
obedience means that Israel, too, in some sense is resurrected
(27:52-53). But the goal is the initial state for a new process. Jesus' power will be exercised under the limits of historical existence. Even at the moment of the climactic resurrection appearance some disciples doubted (28:17). And as we
noted above, the redeemed community will have a problematical
history.

In summary, the Son is manifested as teacher-judge, archetypal human being, revealer of knowledge of God, healer and
miracle worker, and covenant sacrifice. The saved community,
correlatively, enters fully into the precariousness of the human situation, merits salvation by its righteousness but nevertheless is the graced recipient of healing, faith, knowledge
of God, and forgiveness. Demand for obedience and the gift of
grace seem to stand opposed in Matthew in unrelieved tension.

The Christological roles can be stated thematically and
systematically related even if the relationship involves conceptual tension. These roles as themes or concepts may be compared to vertical columns (paradigms). But because the roles
are manifested in the texture of a narrative process along with
their correlatives, modes of existence for the disciples, the
disciple-reader grasped by the story, is one who moves through
all the modes. He experiences himself as under the command to
forgive and perform works of righteousness in order not to be
judged. But he also experiences himself as one graced by
knowledge of God and forgiven without regard to his own righteousness, one from whom faith and righteousness are evoked by
a prior grace. Thus in the horizontal line of the plot (syntagm) the conceptual tension between the themes is transformed
into the personal or existential tension, which the disciple-

reader experiences in the movement of the narrative through conflicting modes of existence, but which is nevertheless given a form by the very existence of the narrative.

CONCLUSION: CHRISTOLOGY AND ETHICS

On the basis of his critical interpretation of Matthew 11:19b; 23:34-36; 23:37-39; 11:25-30 Jack Suggs concludes that for Matthew Jesus is identified with the heavenly Widsom, is Wisdom incarnate. Jesus does not just speak for Wisdom but as Wisdom. Because Wisdom and Torah are identified in Judaism as cosmic figures (cf. Sir. 24:3, 4, 7, 10, 11, 19, 23), and also because of the prominence of the law in Matthew, Jesus is also Torah incarnate. Evidently it is this identification which gives Jesus in Matthew the authority to say, in light of the love commandment, what is and what is not true torah.[19]

Suggs' argument is attractive, but if it turns out that the evidence does not reach as far as he takes it and Jesus in Matthew speaks only for Wisdom, there is still a cosmic--onto-logical--principle behind Jesus' teaching as the true law--heavenly Wisdom-Torah. It seems, then, that there are two op-posing ontological categories grounding Matthew's Christology: the Son as divine freedom or discontinuity (grace) and Wisdom-Torah as divine continuity or system (demand).[20] These two are opposed in principle, Matthew's (11:25-30) connecting of them notwithstanding. Now that we have recognized this dual Christology, the recognition should reflect back on our earli-er discussion. The Son can be manifested in the role of teach-er-law-giver-judge because the Son is also Wisdom-Torah. The tension observed in Matthew's Christology is expressed in his understanding of salvation and ethics as well. Salvation is based on the divine forgiveness demonstrated through the Son (1:21; 20:28; 26:28) and on the human extension of forgiveness and other good works (6:12, 14f.; 18:35; 7:13-14, 24-27; 16:27). The ethical life is response to the presence of salva-tion (4:23-9:38; 7:16b-18; 12:33-35) and condition for the re-ceipt of salvation (7:16-20; 12:33-37; 16:27; 19:17).

The opposition in Matthew's foundational Christology now requires further explication and placing in the narrative structure. We have already seen that in the birth narrative of the initial state or potentiality function Jesus is Son (2:15) and God with us (1:23). Matthew grounds this in Jesus' being born of a virgin, without human father, generated by the Holy Spirit (1:16, 18, 20, 22-23). The author makes use of a stylistic discontinuity which expresses an ontological-his-

orical discontinuity. The mode of expression in the genealo-
y is, for the most part: Abraham begot Isaac, and Isaac [now
father] begot Jacob, and Jacob [now father] begot Judah, etc.
he rhythm is partially disturbed at four points by the intro-
uction of a mother (1:3, 5-6)--for example, Boaz begot Obed
from Ruth. The four mothers--Tamar, Rahab, Ruth, and Bathshe-
a--are all foreign and/or morally questionable, which intro-
uces a moderate discontinuity. Salvation history is free to
ake turns unexpected from the standpoint of strict, legal
righteousness. In the case of the last three generations we
ave a more severe stylistic disruption and a much greater dis-
ontinuity (1:16): Jacob begot Joseph the husband of Mary,
from whom (Mary) Jesus was born. Not only is the mother intro-
uced; the husband is ruled out as father; the child is generated by the Holy Spirit (1:18, 20). God can act in history for
he salvation of his people, not only in freedom from moral-
religious expectations but in freedom from the human process
of generation. Attentiveness to the problem of mythological
language cautions us to recognize that if the language is/was
aken literally by interpreter or author, Matthew's intention
is undercut. Jesus' identity is made to rest on an identifi-
able divine cause which is assimilated to a human cause, the
ale principle in procreation.

The ontological possibility of freedom and grace is then
expressed in the potentiality function of the narrative. Is
he ontological possibility resident in law--continuity, sys-
em--also attached to Jesus' birth? Indirectly, yes. The
star announces Jesus' identity (King of the Jews) and place of
irth (2:1-2, 9) and brings the wise men (astrologers) who worship him (2:10-11). For Hellenistic astrology events on earth
re fixed because, according to the doctrine of "correspon-
ience", earthly affairs reproduce the movements of the stars,
which are determined by fixed laws.[21] Thus at least in an al-
lusive way Jesus' identity is brought within a fixed, continuous system analogous to the continuous system of demand-per-
formance-reward (Mt. 7:24-27; 16:27; Syriac Apocalypse of
Baruch 51:3-4, 7). I would not want to claim that Matthew
consciously drew the connection between the moral-religious
law and the law of fate. But the analogy is there--both are
means of security, and/or oppression--and Matthew is the only
Gospel which both makes an explicit astrological allusion and
emphasizes the positive value of law. And Paul did clearly
see a parallel between living under the law (Gal. 3:23-29) and
living under the cosmic powers (Gal. 4:1-7).

The question of the relationship between Christology and
ethics in Matthew has recently been posed in a very provocative
and stimulating way by Russell Pregeant. Based on his understanding of the Whiteheadian view of language, Pregeant makes

a distinction between the Matthean intention and the Matthean undercurrent, which expresses the Evangelist's presuppositions.[22] Matthew's conscious intention is to root salvation exclusively in Jesus' mission. But in the undercurrent Christology is a symbol for an original and primordial quality of human existence--existence in love--which is universally perceptible apart from the Old Testament law, salvation history, and Christ (cf. Mt. 5:45b; 25:31-46).[23]

The Matthean undercurrent in Pregeant's treatment of it makes Christology an empty symbol expressing the primordial human ethical possibility. But if the Christology is allowed an integrity of its own, is allowed to speak its own word, then the primordial ethical possibility becomes the eschatological ethical possibility. That Christology should be allowed its integrity in Matthew may be argued on two grounds, one exegetical and one hermeneutical.

1. Matthew's statements about love as a universal possibility (5:45b; 25:31-46) must be seen in the narrative context. Israel at the beginning of the story and, to an extent, at the end is lacking in love. The role of the process and goal functions is to show that this lack is filled from outside of Israel. Therefore, the possibility of love is seen to be only a possibility in principle and not a possibility in fact-- apart from Christ.

2. Here I would like to suggest that apart from the ontological (principle)/ontic (fact) paradox it is difficult, if not impossible to make sense of the Christology of the New Testament in general or Matthew in particular. In brief, this paradox, applied to the New Testament, says: faith and righteousness are possible in principle for human beings as such universally but possible in fact only through the Christ event. Pregeant rejects this distinction as vacuous. If what is true in principle is not actually effective, how can people be regarded as free or held responsible?[24] Pregeant also believes that the Matthean undercurrent has abolished the distinction. For Matthew's voluntaristic outlook it is not necessary that a vicarious sacrifice should rectify the divine-human relationship. The only grace necessary for obedience is given with the law itself, for the world is not so under the dominion of evil as to render the primordial possibility of faith actually unreal for human beings as such. What is possible in principle is possible in fact. Jesus represents or brings to full and definitive expression a possibility of existence before God always given in human experience.[25]

Does Pregeant's view that Jesus re-presents a possibility universally available fall back into the ontological/ontic par-

adox? He maintains that it does not, but it seems to me that
it does. He states that he has escaped the paradox because it
is a commonplace of human experience that we obscure by self-
deception, etc., what we know and therefore need to be reminded
in a disruptive way of what we already know. Jesus' representation is such a reminder.[26] For Pregeant there is a prior--
universal--revelation resident in human existence. But this
is shown to be ineffective by the fact that a new revelation--
the reminder--is necessary. The original revelation is therefore seen to afford only a possibility in principle. If people
must be reminded of what they already know, then they do not
know what they know. That is exactly what the New Testament
ontological/ontic paradox is about. Because we do not know
what we know and are responsible for, it must be reintroduced
into our lives from beyond us.

In Matthew's legal strain the Christological reminder is
necessary because in order to do the good words required for
salvation one must know what to do through the reinterpretation of the law (5:21-48). It is furthermore necessary because good fruits can only come from a tree made good through
renewal (7:15-20; 12:33-37). In the grace strain the Christological disruption is necessary because a sinful people (1:21)
can be restored to God only by the forgiveness extended in the
new covenant sacrifice (26:28).

NOTES

1. Benjamin W. Bacon, "Jesus and the Law: A Study of the First 'Book' of Matthew," *Journal of Biblical Literature* 47, nos. 3 and 4 (1928): 204, 207, 208, 223; *Studies in Matthew* (New York: Henry Holt and Company, 1930), pp. xvi, xvii; G. D. Kilpatrick, *The Origins of the Gospel According to Matthew* (Oxford: Clarendon Press, 1950), pp. 107-109, 135, 136.

2. Edgar Krentz, "The Extent of Matthew's Prologue," *Journal of Biblical Literature* 83 (December, 1964): 410, 411.

3. Jack Dean Kingsbury, *Matthew: Structure, Christology, Kingdom* (Philadelphia: Fortress Press, 1975), pp. x, 8-11.

4. Ibid., pp. 4-7.

5. Ibid.

6. "Observations on the Miracle Chapters of Matthew 8-9," *Catholic Biblical Quarterly* 40 (October, 1978): 556-567.

7. Cf. Frederic Jameson, *The Prison-House of Language* (Princeton: Princeton University Press, 1974), pp. 92-93.

8. Cf. Dan O. Via, Jr., "Narrative World and Ethical Response: The Marvelous and Righteousness in Matthew 1-2," *Semeia* 12 (1978): 140-142.

9. As in Tzvetan Todorov, *The Fantastic*, trans. R. Howard (Ithaca: Cornell University Press, 1973), p. 163. My scheme here is a synthetic adaptation of several related constructions. Cf. Todorov, pp. 163-166; Claude Bremond, "Morphology of the French Folktale," *Semiotica* 2 (1970): 247-252; Lubomír Doležel, "From Motifemes to Motifs," *Poetics* 4 (1972): 62; William O. Hendricks, "The Structural Study of Narration: Sample Analyses," *Poetics* 3 (1972); 101, 105.

10. Kingsbury, *Matthew*, pp. 7, 27-36.

11. Stephen Crites, "Angels We Have Heard, " in *Religion as Story*, ed. James B. Wiggins (New York: Harper and Row, 1975), p. 26.

12. See V. Propp, *Morphology of the Folktale*, trans. L. Scott (Austin and London: University of Texas Press, 1968), pp. 25-26.

13. Cf. Todorov, *Fantastic*, pp. 165-166.

14. Eduard Schweizer, *The Good News According to Matthew*, trans. D. E. Green (Atlanta: John Knox Press, 1975), p. 489.

15. Ibid., p. 491.

16. Brevard S. Childs, *The Book of Exodus* (Philadelphia: Westminster Press, 1974), p. 506.

17. Schweizer, *Matthew*, p. 489.

18. A full account would have to deal with opponents other than the Jewish authorities.

19. M. Jack Suggs, *Wisdom, Christology, and Law in Matthew's Gospel* (Cambridge: Harvard University Press, 1970), pp. 57-58, 60-61, 70-71, 96, 104-106, 114, 118-120.

20. This will be defended and elaborated upon below.

21. See W. W. Tarn and G. T. Griffith, *Hellenistic Civilisation* (London: Edward Arnold and Co., 1952), pp. 345-353; H. J. Rose, *Religion in Greece and Rome* (New York: Harper and Brothers, 1959), pp. 118-120.

22. Russell Pregeant, *Christology Beyond Dogma: Matthew's Christ in Process Hermeneutic* (Philadelphia: Fortress Press; Missoula: Scholars Press, 1978), pp. 30, 36-37, 57.

23. Ibid., pp. 48, 57-60, 81-82, 122-123, 127, 157.

24. Ibid., p. 147.

25. Ibid., pp. 89-90, 130, 145, 156, 158.

26. Ibid., pp. 156, 161.

14

LANGUAGE USAGE AND THE PRODUCTION OF
MATTHEW 1:18-2:23

Hendrikus Boers

I. THE FUNCTION OF LANGUAGE IN THE PRODUCTION OF A TEXT

It sounds trite to say that in the production of a text--
written or oral--an author makes use of language, until one
asks what is meant by "language". The distinction which
Ferdinand de Saussure made between "speech" (Fr. *parole*) as
the particular act of articulating one's thoughts in a written
or oral text, and "language" (Fr. *langue*) as the linguistic
ability of which one makes use in such particular speech acts[1]
should already be sufficient indication that the statement is
not trite. The most remarkable feature of our language usage
is that normally, i.e., except when we quote, and to a lesser
degree when we make use of idioms, no speech act is a repetition of a previous one, but a new realization of the wide
range of possibilities of linguistic expression provided to
us by our language competence.

But this also means that no speech act, new as each one
is, is arbitrary, since it is very precisely circumscribed by
the possibilities provided by language. Recognition of the
freedom of poets in this regard merely serves to affirm what
is commonly the case, but even poets probably merely make use
of previously unthought-of possibilities inherent in language
itself, which means that they too do not operate outside the
framework of the restraints provided by language. In any
case, it is the very fact of such precise circumscription,
i.e., of the restraints of language under, and by means of,
which a speaker or writer articulates her or his thoughts in
an act of speech which makes such an act of speech comprehensible. It is knowledge of the very same circumscription or
restraints of language which enables a listener or hearer to
order the words in syntactic structures, making it possible
for them to convey meaning. Anyone who has tried to master a
foreign language knows how much more takes place when we engage in language usage than of what we are conscious; that the
most difficult task is by no means to identify the meanings of
the words, but to place them in the appropriate syntactic
structures.

In order to understand a sentence such as "scrap that move" we need not only knowledge of the range of possible meanings of each of the words, such as are provided in a dictionary or lexicon, but also the syntax of the sentence in order to determine, e.g., which is the verb and which the noun, as the alternate sentence made up of the identically sounding words, "move that scrap", reveals. Different languages in many cases have different ways of disclosing such information, i.e., they are subject to different restraints. In normal language usage all of this takes place without much thought being given to it, especially to the syntactic features. We are frequently careful in the "choice of our words".

In oral language an additional difficulty has to be overcome, the separating of the flow of sounds into distinct words. For someone who is totally unfamiliar with English, the first sentence above would probably sound like "scra ptha tmove". The beginning student of Greek knows how difficult it is to distinguish words in an uncial manuscript, such as EPEIDHPER-POLLOIEPEXEIRHSAN, or how about SINCEMANYHAVEATTEMPTED (Lk. 1:1)?

In reality, however, even if one had the above-mentioned lexical and syntagmatic knowledge, she or he would still not be able to make sense of the above sentences, unless each occurred in a concrete setting, or in a discourse, which made their meanings clear. By itself, e.g., the sentence "move that scrap", says nothing. It is a mere linguistic potentiality of which an author may make use in order to say "get that stuff out of here", or "transfer that pile of rubbish to some other (specified or unspecified) place", or a number of other things. So also, as Chomsky points out,[2] the sentence "flying airplanes can be dangerous" is ambiguous only if it is not articulated in a concrete setting or in a discourse in which it would be abundantly clear whether "to fly airplanes can be dangerous" is meant, or "airplanes that fly can be dangerous".

All of this may seem obvious. That it is not should be evident from what has become a favorite endeavor of OT and NT scholars to interpret the thoughts of a biblical author by means of a study of his usage of certain terms, e.g., Paul's anthropological terms. However flexible one might be in such a study, it remains exceedingly improbable that the biblical writers had anything like the precisely worked-out systematic conceptualizations or even definitions of such terms that are presupposed by such studies. No word by itself conveys meaning. Meaning is conveyed by means of words only when they are used in actual settings, either concrete or provided by a discourse in which they occur. So for example, σάρξ in Paul, to use one of the favorite terms, probably did not mean anything

in particular to Paul, but was simply a word that had been
available to him and of which he made frequent use to give expression to his thoughts in a wide variety of ways, as the wide
range of uses of the term in his letters reveals. To say that
he was unsystematic in his usage of the term is merely to say
that he used it as one normally uses words in speech, and not
in the artificial way presupposed by such word studies.

The way in which meaning is conveyed in a text has been
described very well by Teun van Dijk with his concept of a
macro-structure, which he defines as follows: "...semantic
macro-structures are necessary to explain in sufficiently
simple terms how it is possible that throughout a text the
selection of lexical items and underlying formation of semantic representations is heavily restricted by some global restraint."[3] According to him, a text can have more than one
macro-structure: "Of course, everybody will construct the
macro-structure for a text which is relevant to him, personally, and these macro-structures will be different for the same
text."[4]

I propose that what van Dijk refers to in the latter
statement is not the macro-structure of the text itself, but
the hermeneutical structure by means of which a listener or
reader makes sense of a text by organizing the various elements of such a text into a meaningful whole. The multiplicity of hermeneutical structures is similar to the ambiguity in
the meaning of a sentence, such as "flying airplanes can be
dangerous". In the same way as ambiguity in a sentence is
normally resolved when it occurs in the syntactic structure
of a discourse, so, I believe, ambiguity in the meaning of a
text, reflected in a multiplicity of proposed hermeneutical
structures, will be reduced, if not resolved, as more aspects
of the text are considered. The choice from a number of ways
in which a text could make hermeneutical sense may be decided
by the recognition that what *does not* make hermeneutical sense
at all makes very good sense as a factor in the macro-structure of the text. So, e.g., an author's misunderstanding of
reality or of the situation she or he was addressing may have
been a determining factor in the production of a text.

The above remarks should not be taken to mean that the
macro-structure of a text is the same as the intention of the
author. M. A. K. Halliday identified the following macro-
functions that come to operation in a text: the *ideational*,
i.e., the communication of information in a text, the *inter-
actional*, i.e., the text as a means of interrelating between
author and readers/hearers, and the *textual*, i.e., the way in
which language functions as a factor in such an act of speech.[5]
The intention of an author can be an aspect of any one or more

of these functions, but it can never exhaust all that goes into a text as that which can "explain in sufficiently simple terms how it is that throughout a text the selection of lexical items and underlying formation of semantic representations is heavily restricted by some global restraint". Only when all factors are taken into consideration can such an explanation be given.

All of this is relatively simple when dealing with the text of a single author. It is already more difficult when an author quotes another, e.g., in support of what she or he is trying to say. In such a case the author in effect temporarily suspends her or his own act of linguistic performance in favor of such an act in the past by the quoted author or the tradition, in the sense of the author herself or himself becoming temporarily a reader/hearer, as if saying: "Let us hear what so-and-so has to say in support of the matter."

In reality, however, there is no way in which such a quotation can really speak for itself as long as it is left within the context in which it is quoted, because that context demands a certain reading/hearing of the quoted text. It is similar to the case of a word being restricted to a single meaning out of a range of possibilities when it occurs in a sentence in a particular setting or as part of a discourse. Similarly, a particular reading of the quotation out of a range of possibilities is circumscribed by the context in which it is quoted.

This is not only true in an extreme case when an author states the sense in which she or he intends a quotation, in that way clearly circumscribing its meaning in the context in which it is quoted, e.g., when Paul interprets Genesis 12:7 in the sense of distinctively a single "seed" in Galatians 3:16, a possibility he *argues* is inherent in the formulation, even though we know that it is not the sense of the passage from which he quotes. It is also true when no *specific* reading is suggested, e.g., when Paul quotes a number of OT passages in Romans 3:10-18 with the intention of drawing certain conclusions from them. Whatever else the quotations may say individually, in the context in which they are quoted only a single, common meaning is primarily intended, that which is suggested in v. 9, and clearly specified in vv. 19f.

The original meaning of a quoted text does not necessarily have to make sense in the context in which it is quoted. The only sense it makes is that to which it is restricted by the context in which it is quoted, however removed that may be from the original meaning of the quotation. In some cases an author may change the quotation in order to let it convey her or his intended meaning. So, e.g., the Synoptics change Isaiah 40:3c, "(make straight the paths) of our God" to "of him" (Mk. 1:3, parallels) in order to allow the quotation to apply to Jesus which the original formulation could not. The difficulty is that the earlier meaning is frequently not excluded, and it is quite possible that a reader may pick up that meaning even though the author of the quotation may not have been aware of it. The original is there as a potential meaning, and in that regard the text is ambiguous; the meaning of the text is not coordinate with the meaning intended by the author. The ambiguity in such a case can be removed only when it becomes possible to distinguish between the original meaning of the quotation, and the meaning intended by the author who quotes it.

It is still relatively easy to distinguish between these meanings when the quotation is clearly distinguishable. A case in point is Galatians 3:16 where it is easy for a reader to recognize that the singular "seed" could also have been intended in the sense of a collective noun, i.e., of a plurality of seeds, in the passage from which Paul quotes. The meaning intended by Paul with the quotation nevertheless remains clear, even though it may not be what had been intended originally.

It is already much more difficult to determine how much of the original meanings of the passages quoted by Paul in Romans 3:10-18 are also intended by him, even if only in a secondary way. In a case such as Romans 1:18-32, however, where Paul apparently freely quotes anti-gentile polemics for the sake of the point he wants to make in 2:1ff., probably at least partly formulating the arguments himself, it is well-nigh impossible to distinguish clearly between which meanings are also intended by Paul, and which are included simply as part of the argument. It would be safe to assume that Paul does not knowingly disagree with anything he quotes in the passage, but it is another question how much he *really* intends. The same probably applies to Romans 13:1-7, from which one cannot learn what Paul's attitude was toward civil authorities.

Thus, when an author quotes in such a way that it remains unclear which meanings express what she or he intends, and which are included simply as part of the quoted material, her or his text remains ambiguous, i.e., more than one meaning is possible. Although what the author intends is *not the entire meaning of a text*--other factors also determine its meaning-- it is *one factor among others*, and unclarity about it leaves the text itself unclear. It is of course possible that in the context of the writing as a whole such ambiguity becomes insignificant in the same way as the ambiguity in the meaning of a word in a single sentence may become insignificant in a discourse in which the sentence occurs. This is a very strong argument against the typical biblical commentary which attempts to clarify the meaning of every detail of the biblical text.

In this regard a comparison of Matthew and Mark can be very revealing. Neither of these Gospels is a new speech act, i.e., neither evangelist himself selected the "lexical items and underlying formation of semantic representations", i.e., the words and the syntactic structures into which they were ordered. Most of this was given to them by tradition and even written sources. But whereas Mark's Gospel, e.g., the parable chapter (Mk. 4), is in many respects an incoherent and even contradictory compilation of traditions, Matthew, with a minimum of editorial alterations, changed this into a meaningful whole that gives expression to what he himself had in mind (Mt. 13). Even though Matthew himself, similar to Mark, did not select most of the lexical items and the underlying formation of semantic representations, he made sure that they gave expression to what he understood to have been their meaning.[6] So smooth is his version of the chapter that it would have been very difficult, if not impossible, to distinguish between sources and his own formulations if we did not have Mark's Gospel. In a sense one can say that Matthew made use of given material to produce his own text, whereas Mark's text is an ambiguous combination of quotations and his own formulations. The fact that it may be possible to distinguish between quotations and his own formulations is not much of a help since such a distinction does not clarify how Mark understood the material he quoted, i.e., which meanings of the quoted material also give expression to what he meant, and which do not.

II. THE PRODUCTION OF MATTHEW 1:18-2:23

The way in which Matthew makes use of existing material to give expression to his own, intended meaning can be investigated very easily in a case such as chapter 13 where it is possible to distinguish between quoted material and his own formulations. In that regard a passage such as 1:18-2:23 is a greater challenge, since we do not have independent access to his sources. Charles T. Davis, however, succeeded in making at least a beginning of distinguishing possible sources.[7] It would thus be an interesting enterprise to attempt to distinguish how quotation and personal linguistic expression interrelate in this passage.

A. *The Cycle of Joseph Stories*

A number of conclusions that are relevant for us can be drawn from Davis' study.

1) A number of formal characteristics reveal a close relationship between 1:18-25, 2:13-15 and 2:19-21. A genitive absolute construction which links the story in each case to what precedes (1:20a, 2:13a and 2:19a) is followed first by the formal announcement of the appearance of an angel in a dream to Joseph, introduced by ἰδού, then by the command of the angel, in each case with an added motivation introduced by γάρ (1:20c-21, 2:13c-f, and 2:20); and finally by the carrying-out of the command in virtually the same words as those in which the command was given (1:24f., 2:14-15a and 2:21). The stories are enumerated I, II, and III, in the accompanying text.

It will be noted that the formal similarity is much closer in the second and third stories, especially the formal parallelism of command and carrying-out is much closer. Furthermore, 1:18f. is introductory, not a part of the formal narration of the story. It is thus possible that 1:18-25 was subjected to considerably more editorial adaptation than were the other two stories. However, to try to reconstruct the possibly original story is futile. Such an effort merely satisfies the expectations of the scholar who engages in it.

Reconstruction is a form of *authorship*, rather than of *research*, in which given material is dislocated and then put together in accordance with a new conception of what is structurally appropriate. This applies not only to what is explicitly presented as such, but also in large part to what we NT scholars engage in as in effect the *reconstruction* of the history of fragments of tradition, identifying where in the line of development each piece belongs.

2) There is also a material parallel to these stories in 2:22f.; but, formally it is very different. The scene is also introduced with a participle, but not a genitive absolute construction, and the appearance of the angel is referred-to only indirectly, if at all--χρηματισθεὶς δὲ κατ' ὄναρ, and a command is at the most implicit in the story. It is more closely similar in formulation and motif to 4:12-16 to which it is also closely-related topically: 2:22f. tells how Jesus came to Nazareth; 4:12-16 tells how he moved on from there to Capernaum. In each case, news of danger or evil is introduced by ἀκούσας δὲ ὅτι, which is followed by a change in locality, the setting in the new locality being formulated with ἐλθὼν κατῴ-

κησεν. Both stories are concluded with formula quotations.

Because of these stylistic features of 2:22f., its similarity to 4:12-16 (which is considered a formulation by the
redactor), and also because it is dependent on 2:19-21, whereas the latter does not require a continuation in it, Davis concludes that it is a product of the redactor. In reality, however, there is nothing which excludes it from having been another Joseph story that was reformulated by the redactor--even
if that is less probable--or even a separate tradition which
he quoted. The important thing is what he effected by the way
in which he used these stories. By linking the return from
Egypt to the move from Nazareth to Capernaum via the move to
Galilee and Nazareth in order to avoid Judea, the redactor
shifted the emphasis of 2:19-21 from its original function as
one of the Joseph stories, to one of clarifying the moves of
the infant, and subsequently adult, Jesus. The same shift is
also effected by the formula quotations as we shall see below.

3) That the first scene is not constructed from the quotation of Isaiah 7:14, notwithstanding many similar features,
is indicated by the fact that it does not fit the story in
every respect. The prophecy focuses on the pregnancy, the
birth and the naming of the child, whereas the story concerns
the fact that the pregnancy was by the Holy Spirit, and the
way in which this was resolved for the father through the appearance of an angel in a dream. It is not improbable that
some of the features of the story in the present version were
influenced by the prophecy, but it is highly improbable that
it was developed from it.

What is particularly important--and a further indication
that the story was not a product of the biblical passage--is
that the prophecy is introduced after the announcement of the
angel, and not after the actual incident to which it refers.
In this way the focus of the story shifts from Joseph's re-
ceiving a command in a dream and carrying it out ὡς προσέταξεν
αὐτῷ ὁ ἄγγελος κυρίου to the facts of the birth of Jesus as
announced by the angel. The quotation from Scripture gives a
clear indication how the story is to be understood in its present context. From a Joseph story, the focus has shifted to a
story of the birth and the naming of the child as the one in
whom "God is with us". Although the name which Joseph was com-
manded to give the child is not the same as that to which
Scripture refers, they may be considered semantically equivalent.

A similar concern about the naming of the child comes to
expression in 2:23, although in this case the story has every
indication of being etiological. It is important to note fur-

thermore that the latter story and the formula quotation, for which in this case an actual scriptural passage cannot be found, also give expression to another, a geographic concern.

The Joseph story, concerning the move to Egypt to escape Herod (2:13-15) received a new focus by means of the quotation in verse 15 in Jesus' being called from Egypt as God's Son. This shift does not eliminate the original focus, leaving the story in its present context with two foci. It is nevertheless clear which meaning the redactor had in mind. Noteworthy is the introduction of the quotation not at the return *from* Egypt, but after the story of the flight *to* that land. This shift in focus is similar to the one which occurred when the Joseph story of the return from Egypt (2:19-21) became a story which clarified the geographic moves of Jesus when it was linked to the move to Nazareth and subsequently to Capernaum in 2:22f. and 4:12-16. There is no formula quotation after the story of the return from Egypt which may indicate that it was taken with the move to Nazareth as a single semantic unit. The focus thus shifts from the command to Joseph and his carrying it out as he was directed to the localization of the child Jesus in Nazareth. That may be the greatest significance of the story of the move to Nazareth, whether it was newly constructed or, less probably, a reformulation of an existing Joseph story, namely, that by the way it is formulated it focuses less sharply on Joseph, presenting his fear of Archelaus merely as the circumstance of the move to Nazareth.

The original meanings of the Joseph stories have not been lost, even though they have been reduced in some respects. The main point is that they now fulfill a new function in the overall structure of Matthew. The culmination of the meaning which the redactor wanted to communicate may very well be expressed in 4:15f.: "The people sitting in darkness saw a great light, and to those who sit in the land and the shadow of death a great light rose up." As will be seen, the geographic concern which links these stories is also brought into focus in the quotations in those parts of Matthew 1:18-2:23 which we have not yet discussed.

In a preliminary way, thus, we may conclude that Matthew 1:18-2:23 contains an original cycle of three, possibly four, Joseph stories telling how the pious father of Jesus received instructions in dreams which he carried-out ὡς προσέταξεν αὐτῷ ὁ ἄγγελος κυρίου. Formally, the stories are introduced by a genitive absolute construction, connecting the story with what precedes by referring back to it. The appearance of the angel is announced with ἰδού. In each case a motivation for the angel's command is introduced with γάρ. Finally, Joseph's carrying-out of the command is described with virtually the

same words as those with which the command was given. This
formal structure appears to have been preserved more precisely in the second and third stories than in the first.

The genitive absolute of the second story now refers back
to the visit of the magi (2:13a), which means that one would
probably have to assume that it is an adaptation. If the
fourth story also belonged to the original cycle, it appears
to have been reformulated completely in accordance with the
requirements of the present text.

In Matthew's text these Joseph stories are used to function in a very different way. They now describe the birth
and early movements of the infant Jesus in accordance with
what had been prophesied about him in Scripture. In this new
function the emphasis on Joseph, originally the central figure, has shifted to Jesus. This is achieved by the interpretation of the events by means of the formula quotations, including their placement, and also by the linking of the return
from Egypt to the move of the adult Jesus from Nazareth to
Capernaum via the story of the move to Nazareth.

There is no reason to assume that the redactor intentionally tried to suppress the original meanings of the cycle of
Joseph stories; but, it would also be a mistake to interpret
them as meanings which he specifically intended. The meaning
of the text, thus, its macro-structure, includes more than
what was specifically intended by the author. It also includes meanings that were not specifically intended by him,
but are nevertheless present as meanings that were brought
along with the material out of which he formulated his text.

Davis also tried to reconstruct an additional story,
formally structured in the same way as the first three Joseph
stories, from 2:1-11. That does not need to concern us here.
As will be seen, there are compelling reasons to believe that
the story of the magi was originally independent of the Joseph
cycle.

B. *The Story of the Magi and Herod*

An investigation of the structure of Matthew 2:1-12 reveals the following:

1) The story is divided into five clearly-marked paragraphs, in three cases by beginning with a participle and δέ
(vv. 3, 9, and 10), and in the fourth more sharply with τότε
and a participle (v. 7). The τότε marks a hinge. The first

two paragraphs concern the search of the magi for the newborn
Jewish king, climaxing in verse 5a with the disclosure that he
is born in Bethlehem. The last three paragraphs then turn to
their proceeding to Bethlehem, climaxing with their finding
him there and worshiping him. However, one may also note an
alternation between the magi and Herod in paragraphs one and
two (vv. 1f., and 3-5b, respectively) and between Herod and
the magi in paragraph three and paragraphs four and five (vv.
7f., and 9, 10-12, respectively), revealing the following
scheme AB BAA. The final A appears to stand on its own as
the climax of the story when the magi achieve what they had
come for.

2) However, it should be noted that the one remaining
passage in Matthew 1:18-2:23 which we have not yet discussed,
2:16-18, also begins, as 2:7, with τότε Ἡρῴδης and a participle. It stands in contrast with the last paragraph of the
magi story. The magi whose activity culminates in worshiping
the infant are contrasted with the deceitful Herod, who, although he also said that he wanted to worship the child, commands the murder of the children. Matthew 2:1-12, 16-18 is a
story in which the devout behavior of the magi is contrasted
with that of a deceitful and vengeful Herod. This gives us
the scheme AB BA AB, as indicated in the accompanying text.

3) Once more the redactor has introduced scriptural
quotations which focus on geographic factors, Bethlehem in
vv. 5a-6, and Rama in vv. 17f., but also on those who are in
need of the salvation which was to be brought by Jesus, as in
1:23 and especially 4:16. Note also the emotional coherence
of 4:16 and 2:18.

4) It should also be noted, however, that this story,
too, is introduced with a genitive absolute, which connects it
with the previous one to which it refers back, followed by
ἰδού which introduces the key fact of the story. This is what
led Davis to attempt a reconstruction of another story, formally similar to the Joseph stories. The evidence for such a reconstruction is insufficient. The genitive absolute construction is used frequently in the Gospel, also followed by ἰδού,
e.g., in 9:18, 32; 12:46. (The same actually applies to many
other such stylistic features in these stories, e.g., τότε
which also occurs frequently elsewhere in the Gospel, which
should make one very cautious in drawing conclusions from
such factors.)

One cannot be sure, however, whether there were only the
three (possibly four) Joseph stories, or whether the cycle included more which the evangelist did not use. Did the story
of the flight to Egypt, for example, follow on the story of

the birth in the source, possibly introduced with the genitive absolute of 2:1, Τοῦ δὲ ᾽Ιησοῦ γεννηθέντος ἐν βηθλέεμ τῆς ᾽Ιουδαίας ἐν ἡμέραις ᾽Ηρῴδου τοῦ βασιλέως, or was there another story between them? The story of the magi and Herod, on the other hand, is so well rounded-off that one may presume it to be complete--which does not mean that it is quoted unedited.

In the present text, the flight to Egypt was placed at the only place where it could fit, after the visit of the magi but before the murder of the children. The effect of its introduction at this point in the story of the magi and Herod is that it de-emphasizes the significance of Herod in the latter story. Separated from the story of the murder of the children, Matthew 2:1-12 has now become a story of the magi, with Herod merely an unsavory accessory in their achieving the goal of finding the child and worshiping him. In the original story he was their evil counterpart. Even his cruel action of having the children murdered is now not much more than a transition between the flight to and the return from Egypt. The present text, thus, is no longer a sequence of stories about Joseph, the pious father of Jesus, and of the magi and Herod, but stories about the birth and infancy of Jesus.

C. *The Function of these Stories in Matthew*

By means of the stories of the move to Nazareth (2:22f.) and subsequently to Capernaum (4:12-16) these stories have become linked with those about his relationship to the Baptist (3:1-17) and his temptation (4:1-11), culminating with the quotation in 4:15f. This close linkage is also indicated by the confirmation of Jesus' sonship of God at his baptism in 3:17. There is a great deal to be said, thus, for the view of Jack Dean Kingsbury that the first part of the Gospel is a unity up to 4:16, and that 4:17 introduces the second main part.[8] This may very well be the structuring that was intended by the evangelist.

However, in producing this first part of the Gospel as the background to the public ministry of Jesus, the material of which the evangelist made use left him with three distinguishable sections, a genealogy (1:1-17), the infancy narratives (1:18-2:23), and Jesus and the Baptist (3:1-4:16). There is no indication that he tried to mask these divisions. They are actually clearly marked in the Gospel. Indeed, the infancy narrative section is divided into two further subsections, the birth of Jesus (1:18-25), introduced with ᾽Τοῦ δὲ ᾽Ιησοῦ Χριστοῦ ἡ γένεσις οὕτως ἦν, and the infancy stories (2:1-23), introduced with the genitive absolute construction

of 2:1 which refers back to the birth story, Τοῦ δὲ 'Ιησοῦ
γεννηθέντος, κ.τ.λ.

Out of a cycle of Joseph stories, thus, and a story about
the magi and Herod, Matthew produced a new, coherent account
about the infancy of Jesus, his birth and those incidents that
were decisive as revelations of his significance. This account
itself became part of an even larger whole, beginning with his
genealogy and concluding with the stories about his relationship to the Baptist, culminating in the quotation from Scripture in which he stood out as the one who had appeared for the
sake of the salvation of those who were in dismal circumstances.

Unlike Mark, thus, Matthew is not a redactor but genuinely an author who made use of materials even where they were
preformulated to give expression to the meaning he intended,
similar to the way in which the specific meanings of words are
determined by their functions in syntactic structures. Something similar also happens, of course, partly by default, in
the case of a redactor. But Matthew is a master of his material, which is especially evident in the fact that he produced
a new, coherent whole without suppressing all the meanings
that were already present in his materials, in this way producing something like a bouquet of flowers in which the pleas-
ing whole is achieved, not by subduing the individual beauty
of the flowers, but by benefiting maximally from it. An interpretation of Matthew thus cannot ignore that the Gospel is
a coherent whole, by dissecting it into individual traditions
and sources; but, it also cannot ignore the individual meanings
out of which this whole has been constituted.

Nothing has been said in this paper of the meanings that
anteceded even the formulation of the stories which Matthew
used as his material, the influence, for example, of rabbinic
traditions,[9] or different sources which may be implied by the
contradictory conceptions of the function of the star in 2:1-
12, as an astrological sign in 2:2, εἴδομεν γὰρ αὐτοῦ τὸν
ἀστέρα ἐν τῇ ἀνατολῇ, but as a star which leads in 2:9. For
an exhaustive interpretation of Matthew's text, these factors
also will have to be taken into account. Only then would its
macro-structure become clear, explaining "in sufficiently simple terms how it is possible that throughout (it) the selection of lexical items and underlying formation of semantic
representations is heavily restricted by some global restraint", which in this case includes being able to distinguish which of the underlying semantic representations actually function as lexical items, i.e., which meanings are quoted.

The Text of Matthew 1:18-2:23,
Showing its Structural Features

Formula quotations are indented to allow the structural
features to stand out more clearly.

Τοῦ δὲ Ἰησοῦ ἡ γένεσις οὕτως ἦν.   1:18

μνηστευθείσης τῆς μητρὸς αὐτοῦ Μαρίας τῷ Ἰωσήφ,
πρὶν ἢ συνελθεῖν αὐτοὺς εὑρέθη ἐν γαστρὶ ἔχουσα ἐκ πνεύ-
ματος ἁγίου. Ἰωσὴφ δὲ ὁ ἀνὴρ αὐτῆς, δίκαιος ὢν καὶ μὴ   19
θέλων αὐτὴν δειγματίσαι, ἐβουλήθη λάθρα ἀπολῦσαι αὐτήν.

I.   ταῦτα δὲ αὐτοῦ ἐνθυμηθέντος, ἰδοὺ ἄγγελος κυρίου   20
κατ' ὄναρ ἐφάνη αὐτῷ λέγων·

        Ἰωσὴφ υἱὸς Δαυίδ, μὴ φοβηθῇς παραλαβεῖν Μαρίαν
τὴν γυναῖκά σου. τὸ γὰρ ἐν αὐτῇ γεννηθὲν ἐκ πνεύματός
ἐστιν ἁγίου.

        τέξεται δὲ υἱόν, καὶ καλέσεις τὸ ὄνομα αὐτοῦ Ἰη-   21
σοῦν· αὐτὸς γὰρ σώσει τὸν λαὸν αὐτοῦ ἀπὸ τῶν ἁμαρτιῶν
αὐτῶν.

            Τοῦτο δὲ ὅλον γέγονεν ἵνα πληρωθῇ τὸ ῥηθὲν   22
            ὑπὸ κυρίου διὰ τοῦ προφήτου λέγοντος· ἰδοὺ   23
            ἡ παρθένος ἐν γαστρὶ ἕξει καὶ τέξεται υἱόν,
            καὶ καλέσουσιν τὸ ὄνομα αὐτοῦ Ἐμμανουήλ, ὅ
            ἐστιν μεθερμηνευόμενον μεθ' ἡμῶν ὁ θεός.

        ἐγερθεὶς δὲ ὁ Ἰωσὴφ ἀπὸ τοῦ ὕπνου ἐποίησεν ὡς   24
προσέταξεν αὐτῷ ὁ ἄγγελος κυρίου,

        καὶ παρέλαβεν τὴν γυναῖκα αὐτοῦ· καὶ οὐκ ἐγίνω-   25
σκεν αὐτὴν ἕως οὗ ἔτεκεν υἱόν·

        καὶ ἐκάλεσεν τὸ ὄνομα αὐτοῦ Ἰησοῦν.

A.　　Τοῦ δὲ Ἰησοῦ γεννηθέντος ἐν βηθλέεμ τῆς Ἰου-　　2:1
δαίας ἐν ἡμέραις Ἡρῴδου τοῦ βασιλέως, ἰδοὺ μάγοι ἀπὸ
ἀνατολῶν παρεγένοντο εἰς Ἱεροσόλυμα λέγοντες· ποῦ　　2
ἐστιν ὁ τεχθεὶς βασιλεὺς τῶν Ἰουδαίων; εἴδομεν γὰρ αὐτοῦ τὸν ἀστέρα ἐν τῇ ἀνατολῇ, καὶ ἤλθομεν προσκυνῆσαι
αὐτῷ.

B.　　ἀκούσας δὲ ὁ βασιλεὺς Ἡρῴδης ἐταράχθη, καὶ πᾶσα　　3
Ἱεροσόλυμα μετ' αὐτοῦ, καὶ συναγαγὼν πάντας τοὺς ἀρχιε-　　4
ρεῖς καὶ γραμματεῖς τοῦ λαοῦ ἐπυνθάνετο παρ' αὐτῶν ποῦ ὁ
χριστὸς γεννᾶται. οἱ δὲ εἶπαν αὐτῷ· ἐν βηθλέεμ τῆς　　5
Ἰουδαίας·

　　　　οὕτως γὰρ γέγραπται διὰ τοῦ προφήτου· καὶ　　6
　　　　σὺ βηθλέεμ, γῆ Ἰούδα, οὐδαμῶς ἐλαχίστη εἶ
　　　　ἐν τοῖς ἡγεμόσιν Ἰούδα. ἐκ σοῦ γὰρ ἐξε-
　　　　λεύσεται ἡγούμενος, ὅστις ποιμανεῖ τὸν
　　　　λαόν μου τὸν Ἰσραήλ.

B.　　Τότε Ἡρῴδης λάθρα καλέσας τοὺς μάγους ἠκρίβωσεν　　7
παρ' αὐτῶν τὸν χρόνον τοῦ φαινομένου ἀστέρος, καὶ πέμψας　　8
αὐτοὺς εἰς βηθλέεμ εἶπεν· πορευθέντες ἐξετάσατε ἀκρι-
βῶς περὶ τοῦ παιδίου· ἐπὰν δὲ εὕρητε, ἀπαγγείλατέ μοι,
ὅπως κἀγὼ ἐλθὼν προσκυνήσω αὐτῷ.

A.　　οἱ δὲ ἀκούσαντες τοῦ βασιλέως ἐπορεύθησαν· καὶ　　9
ἰδοὺ ὁ ἀστήρ, ὃν εἶδον ἐν τῇ ἀνατολῇ, προῆγεν αὐτοὺς
ἕως ἐλθὼν ἐστάθη ἐπάνω οὗ ἦν τὸ παιδίον.

A.　　ἰδόντες δὲ τὸν ἀστέρα ἐχάρησαν χαρὰν μεγάλην　　10
σφόδρα. καὶ ἐλθόντες εἰς τὴν οἰκίαν εἶδον τὸ παιδίον　　11
μετὰ Μαρίας τῆς μητρὸς αὐτοῦ, καὶ πεσόντες προσεκύνη-
σαν αὐτῷ, καὶ ἀνοίξαντες τοὺς θησαυροὺς αὐτῶν προσή-
νεγκαν αὐτῷ δῶρα, χρυσὸν καὶ λίβανον καὶ σμύρναν. καὶ　　12
χρηματισθέντες κατ' ὄναρ μὴ ἀνακάμψαι πρὸς Ἡρῴδην,

232

δι' ἄλλης ὁδοῦ ἀνεχώρησαν εἰς τὴν χώραν αὐτῶν.

II.   <u>Ἀναχωρησάντων δὲ αὐτῶν, ἰδοὺ ἄγγελος κυρίου</u>   13
<u>φαίνεται κατ' ὄναρ τῷ Ἰωσὴφ λέγων·</u>
     <u>ἐγερθεὶς παράλαβε τὸ παιδίον καὶ τὴν μητέρα</u>
<u>αὐτοῦ</u>, καὶ φεῦγε εἰς Αἴγυπτον, καὶ ἴσθι ἐκεῖ ἕως ἂν
εἴπω σοι· μέλλει <u>γὰρ</u> Ἡρῴδης ζητεῖν τὸ παιδίον τοῦ
ἀπολέσαι αὐτό.
     <u>ὁ δὲ ἐγερθεὶς παρέλαβεν τὸ παιδίον καὶ τὴν</u>   14
<u>μητέρα αὐτοῦ</u> νυκτὸς καὶ ἀνεχώρησεν εἰς Αἴγυπτον, καὶ   15
ἦν ἐκεῖ ἕως τῆς τελευτῆς Ἡρῴδου·

          ἵνα πληρωθῇ τὸ ῥηθὲν ὑπὸ κυρίου διὰ τοῦ
          προφήτου λέγοντος· ἐξ Αἰγύπτου ἐκάλεσα
          τὸν υἱόν μου.

Β.   <u>Τότε Ἡρῴδης ἰδὼν</u> ὅτι ἐνεπαίχθη ὑπὸ τῶν μάγων   16
ἐθυμώθη λίαν, καὶ ἀποστείλας ἀνεῖλεν πάντας τοὺς παῖ-
δας τοὺς ἐν Βηθλέεμ καὶ ἐν πᾶσι τοῖς ὁρίοις αὐτῆς ἀπὸ
διετοῦς καὶ κατωτέρω, κατὰ τὸν χρόνον ὃν ἠκρίβωσεν παρὰ
τῶν μάγων.

          τότε ἐπληρώθη τὸ ῥηθὲν διὰ Ἰερεμίου τοῦ   17
          προφήτου λέγοντος· φωνὴ ἐν Ῥαμὰ ἠκούσθη,   18
          κλαυθμὸς καὶ ὀδυρμὸς πολύς· Ῥαχὴλ κλαί-
          ουσα τὰ τέκνα αὐτῆς, καὶ οὐκ ἤθελεν παρα-
          κληθῆναι, ὅτι οὐκ εἰσίν.

III. <u>Τελευτήσαντος δὲ τοῦ Ἡρῴδου, ἰδοὺ ἄγγελος κυρίου</u>   19
<u>φαίνεται κατ' ὄναρ τῷ Ἰωσὴφ ἐν Αἰγύπτῳ λέγων·</u>   20
     <u>ἐγερθεὶς παράλαβε τὸ παιδίον καὶ τὴν μητέρα αὐ-</u>
<u>τοῦ</u>. καὶ πορεύου εἰς γῆν Ἰσραήλ· τεθνήκασιν <u>γὰρ</u> οἱ
ζητοῦντες τὴν ψυχὴν τοῦ παιδίου.
     <u>ὁ δὲ ἐγερθεὶς παρέλαβεν τὸ παιδίον καὶ τὴν μητέρα</u>   21
<u>αὐτοῦ</u> καὶ εἰσῆλθεν εἰς γῆν Ἰσραήλ.

ἀκούσας δὲ ὅτι 'Αρχέλαος βασιλεύει τῆς 'Ιου- 22
δαίας ἀντὶ τοῦ πατρὸς αὐτοῦ 'Ηρῴδου ἐφοβήθη ἐκεῖ ἀπελ-
θεῖν· χρηματισθεὶς δὲ κατ' ὄναρ ἀνεχώρησεν εἰς τὰ
μέρη τῆς Γαλιλαίας, καὶ ἐλθὼν κατῴκησεν εἰς πόλιν 23
λεγομένην Ναζαρέθ·

ὅπως πληρωθῇ τὸ ῥηθὲν διὰ τῶν προφητῶν
ὅτι Ναζωραῖος κληθήσεται.

NOTES

1. Ferdinand de Saussure, *Cours de linguistique générale* (Paris: Payot et Cie. 1st ed., 1916, 2nd ed. 1922), pp. 27-33; Eng. tr. *Course in General Linguistics*, trans. Wade Baskin (New York: McGraw-Hill, 1966), pp. 11-15. Cf. also the similar, but not identical, distinction which Noam Chomsky makes between "performance" and "competence" e.g., Noam Chomsky, *Aspects of the Theory of Syntax* (Cambridge, Mass.: M.I.T. Press, 1965), pp. 3-15.

2. Cf. Noam Chomsky, *Aspects of the Theory of Syntax*, p. 21.

3. Teun van Dijk, *Some Aspects of Text Grammars. A Study in Theoretical Linguistics and Poetics, Janua Linguarum*, Series Maior 63 (The Hague/Paris: Mouton, 1972), p. 160.

4. Ibid., p. 161.

5. M. A. K. Halliday, *Explorations in the Functions of Language* (London: Edward Arnold, 1973), pp. 22-45.

6. Cf. in this regard my *Theology Out of the Ghetto* (Leiden: E. J. Brill, 1971), pp. 9-17.

7. In an Emory University dissertation, the essential part of which was subsequently published under the title "Tradition and Redaction in Matthew 1:18-2:23," *Journal of Biblical Literature* 90 (December, 1971): 404-21.

8. Cf. Jack Dean Kingsbury, *Matthew: Structure, Christology, Kingdom* (Philadelphia: Fortress Press, 1975): 7-17.

9. Cf., e.g., Paul Winter, "Jewish Folklore in the Matthaean Birth Story," *The Hibbert Journal* 53 (October, 1954): 34-42.

15

A STRUCTURALIST ANALYSIS OF JOHN 6

John Dominic Crossan

*If it recedes one day, leaving behind its
works and signs on the shores of our civi-
lization, the structuralist invasion might
become a question for the historian of
ideas, or perhaps even an object. But the
historian would be deceived if he came to
this pass: by the very act of considering
the structuralist invasion as an object he
would forget its meaning and would forget
that what is at stake, first of all, is an
adventure of vision, a conversion of the
way of putting questions to any object
posed before us, to historical objects--
his own--in particular. And, unexpected-
ly among these, the literary object.*

Jacques Derrida[1]

What would one see if one took John 6 as a unity and of-
ficially omitted any historical questioning of the text? What
would happen if one attempted by looking at *how* the text means
to see *what* the text means? An historical vision could legitimately explain disjunctions in terms of sources and redactions, of additions appended by an initial author, an intermediate redactor, or even a final editor. But a structuralist
vision will want to know, even granting all that is true, how
did such an appender add it here rather than there, now rather
than earlier or later? The adventure of vision is to see John
6 as a whole and to study how it holds together as such.

I. Narrative

The terms "Narrative" and "Discourse" distinguish between
deeds and *words* within the text. The normal line between Narrative and Discourse is indicated by the quotation mark. I do

not intend any other more profound differentiation at the moment.[2]

A second distinction is that between Actant and Action.
Actants are the personae who cause certain effects, or Actions,
within the text.

A. NARRATIVE ACTANTS

(1) *6:1-15.* Between the external index of space in 6:1 and
the external index of time in 6:4, the three major Narrative
Actants are introduced, separately and pointedly.

(a) Jesus is introduced first in 6:1, as if he was cross-
ing the sea by himself ("Jesus went"), although, of course, the
Disciples are with him. But the principal Narrative Actant may
be appropriately introduced first and alone.

(b) Crowds are introduced in second place in 6:2, and
they have "followed him".

(c) Disciples finally appear in 6:3 and they are simply
"with" Jesus.

Later, with a deliberateness similar to their introduction in 6:1-3, the three Narrative Actants separate and go
their different ways in 6:15-16.

(2) *6:16-21.* Only two Narrative Actants reappear here; the
Disciples alone (6:16-18), then Jesus and the Disciples (6:
19-21).

(3) *6:22-24.* Although the other two Narrative Actants are
mentioned (6:22, 24) the Crowds are alone in this unit.

(4) *6:25-59.* The Disciples are *textually* absent, with only
Jesus and the Crowds explicitly mentioned. It is clear from
6:60, of course, that the Disciples were actually present
throughout 6:25-59.

But there is a strange development between 6:25-40 and
6:41-59. Prior to 6:25-40 the Crowds have been frequently
identified with various terms (6:2, 5, 10a, 10b, 14, 22, 24).

That is, four times in 6:1-15 and twice in 6:22-24. Now, suddenly, they become nameless. Throughout the fairly long section in 6:25-40 they are identified only indirectly, remaining hidden behind such words as "they" or "them". But, again suddenly, they are termed "the Jews" in 6:41 and 6:52 and it is "the Jews" who speak with Jesus throughout 6:41-59. The Crowds of 6:1-40 become "the Jews" of 6:41-59.

(5) 6:60-71. Once again only two Narrative Actants are textually present, but now it is Jesus and the Disciples.

But a similar, strange development takes place between 6:60-66 and 6:67-71 as previously between 6:1-40 and 6:41-59. In 6:60-66 the Disciples are named three times (6:60, 61, 66). Then in 6:67-71 there appears a group not heretofore either distinguished or named. And as with the Disciples in 6:60-66, so now this new group, the Twelve, is named three times once they appear (6:67, 70, 71).

B. NARRATIVE ACTIONS

There are two main Narrative Actions to be considered in the text: Moving and Feeding.

(1) NARRATIVE MOVING

For Narrative Moving I wish to distinguish between Moving in terms of Space and Moving in terms of Narrative Actants.

(a) Narrative Moving and Space

In terms of Space the Moving is rather homogeneous. First, Jesus explicitly (6:1), the Disciples implicitly (6:3), and the Crowds explicitly (6:2, 5), "went to the other side of the Sea of Galilee" (6:1). So also, again with Jesus and the Disciples in first place (6:17, 21), and the Crowds in second place (6:24), there is a recrossing of the sea to Capernaum.

(b) Narrative Moving and Narrative Actants

But Moving is much more significant not just in terms of who is Moving to where but in terms of who is Moving to which other Narrative Actant.

1. Jesus and the Disciples

Coming. Jesus comes to the Disciples but the Disciples do not come to Jesus. Thus, Jesus comes to the Disciples in 6:16-21 and this advent is emphasized by the rather awkward comment in 6:17b. After having noted that the Disciples had embarked, it is then said that Jesus had not arrived. "When evening came, his disciples went down to the sea, got into a boat, and started across the sea to Capernaum. It was now dark, and Jesus had not yet come to them" (6:16-17). It should be noted that when Jesus comes to the Disciples in 6:21 they are immediately where they want to be. The Disciples, on the other hand, never come to Jesus; they are always simply there (6:3). Compare, in contrast, Mark 6:35 with John 6:5.

Going. Jesus leaves the Disciples in 6:15. Although the primary withdrawal here is from the Crowds, the terminal presence of Jesus on the mountain alone (6:15) reflects back on the initial one on the mountain with his disciples (6:3). So also do the Disciples leave Jesus in 6:16 (compare, in contrast, Mark 6:45), and (some of) the Disciples leave him in 6:66.

2. Jesus and the Crowds

Coming. Jesus never comes to the Crowds. It is twice stressed, most emphatically, that they come after him. They move after him, first in 6:2 ("a multitude followed him") and 6:5 ("a multitude was coming to him"), and again later in 6:22-25 ("seeking" in 6:24, "found" in 6:25). Thus, once on each day and once on each land, the Crowds move after Jesus. Compare, for contrast, Mark 6:33-34 with John 6:2, 5, and note that the Crowds precede Jesus in Mark so that he comes to them.

Going. Jesus, of course, leaves the Crowds in 6:15. It would also seem that he is leaving them, textually, in 6:59. But nowhere in the text are the Crowds explicitly described as Moving away from Jesus.

In summary: Jesus never comes to the Crowds but they always come to him; Jesus comes to the Disciples and they never come to him; Jesus leaves them both but the Disciples and not the Crowds leave him.

(2) NARRATIVE FEEDING

The Narrative Action of Feeding in 6:1-15 is totally dominated by Jesus. In terms of Action, he himself distrib-

utes the food in 6:11, in contrast, for example, with Mark 6:
41 where the Disciples do this.

(3) NARRATIVE MOVING AND NARRATIVE FEEDING

The twin Narrative Actions are closely linked together
in that the Crowds come to Jesus, the Feeding ensues, then
Jesus and the Disciples leave, and the Crowds follow. Thus
the feeding is at the center of the Moving and the Moving is
to and from the Feeding.

II. Discourse

The simplest reading of the text reveals how the predominance of Narrative in 6:1-21 gives way to the predominance of
Discourse in 6:22-71. But before turning attention to that
situation, it will be useful to study the interaction of Narrative and Discourse in 6:1-24.

A. NARRATIVE AND DISCOURSE

(1) 6:1-15. In this unit there is a section of Discourse (6:
5-10) framed by two Narrative sections (6:1-4, 11-15). The
Narrative is quite conceivable by itself, as if one read from
6:1-4 into 6:11-15. But the interaction of Narrative and Discourse in this small unit of 6:1-15 effects certain very significant results.

(a) The Discourse in 6:5 stresses, just as did the Narrative in 6:11, the complete dominance of Jesus over this entire event. Compare, in contrast, Mark 6:35, where the Disciples initiate the Discourse.

(b) The Discourse here establishes the pattern of (i) a
dialogue composed of (ii) questions which (iii) are not really answered. This will be much more important in 6:25-71.

(c) The predominance of Narrative over Discourse in 6:
1-15 prepares the way for the opposite situation in 6:25-71.

(d) In 6:5-10 the three Narrative Actants become Discourse Actants, that is, they talk about themselves. Thus in

6:5 Jesus asks the Disciples about the Crowds: "How are *we* to buy bread, so that *these* people may eat?" This will also be of future importance.

(e) The Discourse between Jesus and the Disciples in 6: 5-10 contains a single Discourse Actant who, unlike the preceding case, is never a Narrative Actant. Yet this Discourse Actant is the necessary basis for the continuance of both Narrative and Discourse. In 6:8 Andrew says, "There is a lad here who has five barley loaves and two fish." When one notices that this Discourse Actant is absent in Mark 6:38, one might well wonder if it has a function here in John. At very least, it is a first alert to the possibility of Discourse Actants who are not Narrative Actants, who appear only in the Discourse and yet on whom the whole Narrative and Discourse may depend.

(2) *6:16-21.* In this unit there is again Discourse (unanswered dialogue) in 6:20 within Narrative frames in 6:16-19 and 6:21. Once again the Narrative is conceivable without the Discourse and once again Narrative Actants cross the quotation marks to become Discourse Actants. Jesus talks about himself to the Disciples and about them to themselves.

But now, in contrast to 6:1-15, the Discourse is extremely important. In Mark 6:49-50 the frightened disciples "thought it was a ghost, and cried out; for they all saw him, and were terrified". In such a situation the phrase ἐγώ εἰμι may well be translated by the reassuring, "It is I." But not so in John where there is no mention of non-recognition. There is, of course, fear which is the proper response of numinous awe. In such a context, then, the phrase must be given full transcendental value. Given absolutely, without any qualification or addition, it breaks the rules of grammar and must be taken precisely as such a breach. Jesus says: I AM.

B. NARRATIVE ACTANTS AND DISCOURSE ACTANTS

A distinction was noted above between Narrative-Discourse Actants and pure Discourse Actants, between Actants appearing in both Narrative and Discourse and those appearing only in Discourse. These latter now require further study.

(1) THE PRESENCE OF DISCOURSE ACTANTS

The following are the major Discourse Actants to be noted in 6:25-71.

(a) Jesus introduces God under various titles. The first mention is of "God the Father" (6:27) and thereafter one finds "God" (6:29, 33, 46), "my Father" (6:32, 40), "the Father" (6: 37, 44, 45, 46 twice, 57, 65), "the living Father" (6:57), and "Him Who Sent Me" (6:38, 39).

The Crowds refer to God, once as "God" (6:28) and once as "He" (6:31).

The Disciples do not mention any Discourse Actant but the Twelve mention God in addressing Jesus as "the Holy One of God" (6:69).

(b) Jesus speaks of the "Son of Man", once to the Crowds, once to "the Jews", and once to the Disciples (6:27, 53, 62). He also refers to "Him Whom He Has Sent" (6:29), and to "the Son" (6:40).

There are no such references for either Crowds or Disciples, but the Twelve address Jesus as "the Holy One of God" (6:69).

(c) Jesus refers to "Moses" (6:32), "the prophets" (6: 45), and "your fathers" (6:49). The Crowds also refer to "our fathers" (6:31).

The Crowds refer to the parents of Jesus: "Jesus, the son of Joseph, whose father and mother we know" (6:42).

(d) Finally, and most importantly, there is a group designated repeatedly by Jesus, and nobody else, with such expressions as (i) "he who..." (6:35, 47), or (ii) "all who..." (6:37, 39, 40, 45), or (iii) "anyone who..." (6:50, 51), or "no one... unless..." (6:44, 65).

(2) THE DOMINANCE OF DISCOURSE ACTANTS

There are two facets to this domination. First, once certain Discourse Actants appear they dominate not only the succeeding Discourse but even the preceding Narrative as well. These Discourse Actants *absorb* and *consume* (the verbs are not innocently chosen) the Narrative Actants themselves. Second, the apparent exception to that generality is Jesus. In this case all the mediator Discourse Actants are absorbed along with the Narrative Actant Jesus into the Narrative-Discourse Actant, the "I" of Jesus. Here it is this Narrative-Discourse Actant which continues to dominate the text and which *absorbs* and *consumes* the Narrative Actant Jesus himself.

(a) *God*. The domination of this Discourse Actant over the entire text, both Narrative and Discourse, will be discussed below under C.

(b) *Jesus*. After the supreme and unqualified revelation of "I AM" in 6:20, it is not very surprising that the "I" of Jesus should dominate the Discourse. This is effected in two ways. First, of course, only Jesus uses "I" within the Discourse. The Disciples/Twelve (6:68-69) and the Crowds (6:28, 30, 34, 52) use "we". Second, and more important, all other mediating Discourse Actants are absorbed into this "I" of Jesus. Thus, anything said of Discourse Actants such as "Son of Man", or "Son", or "Him Whom He Has Sent" is repeated also in terms of the "I" of Jesus, with one very important exception:

1. Son of Man. In 6:27 it is the "Son of Man" who "will give" them "the food which endures for eternal life". But in 6:50-51, "I shall give" (51) this bread "that a man may eat of it and not die" (50). Again, what is said of the "Son of Man" in 6:53 is repeated of the "I" of Jesus in 6:54: "unless you eat the flesh of the Son of man and drink his blood, you have no life in you; he who eats my flesh and drinks my blood has eternal life".

2. Son. In 6:40 it is a question of "every one who sees the Son and believes in him...". But in 6:36, "you have seen me and yet do not believe".

3. The Sent One. In 6:29 Jesus refers to "him whom he has sent"; but, in 6:38 it is a case of "him who sent me".

4. Finally, there is the statement in 6:62, "What if you were to see the Son of man ascending where he was before?" Nowhere in John 6 is there any mention of the "I" of Jesus ascending to heaven. This leaves an unfulfilled expectation reminding us that John 6 is part of a wider unity and 6:62 will be repeated in terms of the "I" of Jesus only much later in 20:17: "I am ascending to my Father."

In summary, then, the Narrative Actant Jesus and also the mediator Discourse Actants such as "Son of Man", "Son", and

"Sent One", are absorbed into and consumed by the Narrative-Discourse Actant, the "I" of Jesus.

(c) The Crowds & "The Jews". One could imagine three types of pronominal interaction within Discourse:

1. "I-You": speaker and hearer interact as reciprocating "I" and "You" in their mutual Discourse.

2. "I-He": speaker interacts reciprocally with another than the hearer in his own Discourse.

3. "You-He": speaker has the hearer ("you") and another ("he") interact reciprocally in his own Discourse.

In the light of these possibilities, there is a very strange change between Jesus' dialogue with the unspecified Crowds in 6:25-34 and the specified "Jews" in 6:35-38.

In dialogue with the Crowds (1) there is not a single instance of "I-He" Discourse but (2) "I-You" (6:26, 30, 32a, 34) and (3) "You-He" (6:27, 29, 32 twice) are about evenly distributed. Note, for example, how 6:26 ("I-You") shifts to 6:27 ("You-He"), or again how 6:32a ("I-You") moves to 6:32b ("You-He").

But in dialogue with "the Jews" all of this changes completely. (1) Now "I-He" dominates completely (6:35b, 37, 38, 39, 40, 44, 45b, 54, 56, 57) so that (2) only three uses of "I-You" (6:36, 47a, 53a) and (3) only one use of "You-He" appear (6:53b). Note, for example, how 6:53-54 move from "I-You" (53a) to "You-He" (53b) to "I-He" (54).

This means, in summary, that the "You" of the Crowds/ "Jews" disappears almost completely. It is displaced and absorbed by the reiterated mentions of the new Discourse Actant, "He who..." (see B*(1)(d)* above).

(d) The Disciples. There is a rather similar development in the case of the Disciples. Although there is no such sheer numerical predominance of "I-He" as previously in 6:25-59 for the Crowds and "the Jews", it is clear, in 6:60-66, that (1) "I-He" gets the last word in 6:65b ("no one can come to me unless it is granted him by the Father") despite about even usage of (2) "I-You" (6:63, 65a) and (3) "You-He" (6:62).

Like the Crowds and "the Jews", the departing Disciples lose their "You" into "He who..." ("no one...unless...").

(e) *The Twelve.* In 6:67-71 the dialogue is exclusively
"I-You" with nothing of either "I-He" or "You-He". But I am
not inclined to read this as a terminal exaltation of "I-You"
over the other forms of dialogue in John 6. First, there is
the evident and supreme approbation contained in the reiterated "I-He" expressions noted above. Second, there is the
fact that 6:67-71 is very deliberately open to the future of
the Gospel as a whole. This derives not only from the insta-
bility effected by the positive and negative poles of *"Simon
Peter"* in 6:68 and "Judas the son of *Simon* Iscariot" in 6:71,
but also from the fact that, at this stage, we do not know
what it might mean "to betray him".

In conclusion, then, the Narrative-Discourse Actant, the
"I" of Jesus has taken over the Discourse completely; but, the
most important recipient of this dialogue is "I-He", so that
it is the "He who..." that is the counterpart of the "I" of
Jesus.

C. NARRATIVE ACTIONS AND DISCOURSE ACTIONS

A very similar process takes place between Narrative and
Discourse Actions as that just seen for Narrative and Discourse Actants.

(1) THE PRESENCE OF DISCOURSE ACTIONS

There were two Narrative Actions considered earlier:
Moving and Feeding. In the Discourse two new Discourse Actions are introduced. But these are not new in the way that
the added Discourse Actants (God, Son of Man, etc.) were new,
that is, not previously mentioned in the Narrative. They are
new because they are the transcendental equivalents of the
earlier Narrative Actions of Moving and Feeding. The Discourse Actions are transcendental Moving and transcendental
Feeding. But, as with the Discourse Actants, once these Discourse Actions are introduced they dominate both the Narrative
and the Discourse by absorbing and consuming the Narrative Actions within themselves.

(a) Narrative Moving and Discourse Moving

In discussing the Narrative Action of Moving above, I
distinguished between Moving in Space and Moving between Actants. So also here with Discourse Moving.

1. Discourse Moving in Space

Narrative Moving in Space was rather uniform: Jesus and
the Disciples (6:1-3), and then the Crowds (6:2, 5) crossed
the sea; the Disciples and Jesus (6:16-21), and the Crowds
(6:22-25) crossed it back again.

But the new Discourse Moving separates Jesus from all
the others, intersecting, as it were, all such horizontal
movements with its own radical verticality. This Discourse
Moving involves Jesus' descending and reascending back to
heaven:

descending: 6:33, 38, 41, 42, 50, 51, 58
                   (see also 46)

reascending: 6:62

This then becomes the primary Moving and it overshadows completely any geographical movements by Jesus or the others.

2. Discourse Moving among Actants

In similar fashion another and superior Moving subsumes
the movements of either Crowds to Jesus or of Jesus to the
Disciples. Any Moving to Jesus must be a "coming" (6:35-37,
44, 65) which is "given" (6:37, 39) or "drawn" (6:44) or
"granted" (6:65) by God. Only one who has "heard and learned
from the Father comes to me" (6:45). Even more significantly,
not even a choice by Jesus himself precludes this imperative:
"Did I not choose you, the twelve, and one of you is a devil?"
(6:70). Neither the Crowds' coming to Jesus nor Jesus' coming
to the Disciples is what counts since all such Narrative Moving is controlled absolutely by a far more profound and transcendental Discourse Moving.

(b) Narrative Feeding and Discourse Feeding

The second major Narrative Action was Feeding. As one
moves into Discourse one is prepared for a rather obvious
parallel between feeding and teaching, between bread and
revelation. This would be an obvious development of 6:1-15
(feeding, bread) and 6:16-21 (teaching, revelation). One is
quite prepared for a relationship between Narrative and Discourse along the following lines. In Narrative: (1) Source
of Food, (2) Feeder, (3) Feeding, (4) Food, (5) Consumption of
Food, (6) Consumer, (7) Bodily Life, will beget a parallelism
in Discourse of: (1') Source of Revelation, (2') Revealer,
(3') Revealing, (4') Revelation, (5') Belief, (6') Believer,

(7') Eternal Life. But this is not all that happens. Still, what does happen is in complete continuity with the fundamental process whereby Discourse has been steadily absorbing and consuming the Narrative and where the only Narrative element (Actants and Actions) not already thus consumed is the Narrative-Discourse Actant, the "I" of Jesus. But it would be impossible to emphasize too much the paradoxical nature of this final consumption since it is the "I" of Jesus that demands that the "I" be consumed. Thus even, or especially, here the absolute and unqualified "I AM" of 6:20 is still dominant, even over "I AM to be consumed" in 6:51-58.

The steps of the process whereby the Feeder becomes the Food are both deliberate and obvious:

1. The first step is 6:25-34 and the message is soothingly acceptable. God will give you the true bread from heaven which insures eternal life. What can anyone respond but: "Lord, give us this bread always" (6:34).

2. The second step is 6:35-48 (in a giant chiasm between 6:35a and 6:48 with the center at 6:42a) and now the Discourse turns problematic but not yet as problematic as it will be later. This bread is now identified with the "I" of Jesus. Feeder and Food are equated. The response now is murmuring and questioning (6:41-42). But the situation is not yet desperate. At this point it is still possible to hear Jesus metaphorically. If he is heavenly bread, one could see it as a metaphorical expression that he is not only Revealer (Feeder) but Revelation (Food). The call for *consumption* would still be metaphorical and would mean *acceptance* of the Revealer as the Revelation.

3. The third step is in 6:49-58 and it may be summarized as follows:

6:49-50		Bread/Eat
6:51-52		I/Bread/Eat/My Flesh
6:53-56		Eat/Flesh//Drink/Blood [four times]
6:57	I/	/Eat/Me
6:58		Bread/Eat

The outer frames of 6:49-50 and 6:58 do not really go beyond the development of the second step in 6:35-48. The next inner frames of 6:51-52 and 6:57 already go beyond this by insisting outside metaphorical tolerances that the bread, which is Jesus, must be *eaten*. But it is the inner core of 6:53-56 that makes it clear that something beyond metaphor is happening.

In a formulaic, hypnotic, and almost rhapsodic repetition the phrases, Eat/Flesh//Drink/Blood, move the Discourse beyond any interpretation in terms of merely *accepting* (eating) the Revealer.

I would summarize the total development so far as follows:

6:25-34   Bread

6:35-48   I/Bread

6:49-58   I/Bread/Eat Me
           Eat/My Flesh//Drink/My Blood

Two questions must now be asked. First, what is the meaning of this fourfold repetition of Eat/Flesh//Drink/Blood? Second, why is it placed precisely here in John 6?

The language of 6:49-58 is explicable only in terms of eucharistic formulae known from outside this chapter but it is even more startling than the similar formulaic repetitions in I Cor. 11:27-29 (eat/bread//drink/cup). This furnishes four main points: it is formulaic, eucharistic language; it is extremely more *realistic* than is usual elsewhere for such formulae; it is addressed to the murmuring and debating Crowds/"Jews"; it is not reacted to by them but by the Disciples among whom it causes a division (6:60-66).

It is the reaction of the Disciples that must come first in interpretation since John omits here any reaction from the Crowds/"Jews". To the murmuring Disciples Jesus says: "'Do you take offense at this? Then what if you were to see the Son of man ascending where he was before?'" (6:61b-62). At first glance the logic of this question is not very compelling. If one presumes that *ascension* means some sort of great triumphant manifestation, then belief would be rendered easier rather than harder by witnessing it. But if ascension means crucifixion, then the logic is clarified. So also is the basic meaning of 6:51-58. Jesus is announcing there that to accept him is to accept the one who must die, who must die by the violent separation of body and blood, that is, as we shall only know later, by crucifixion. But it is also to insist that such acceptance is the only way that acceptance will ever after be possible. In other words: I am always the one to be consumed. Hence, of course, the double mention of betrayal (6:64, 70-71) follows the mention of crucifixion-ascension (6:62).

Thus the primary function of the eucharistic language is to indicate a split in eucharistic understanding, that is, in

the permanent acceptance of crucifixion, among the Disciples.
Jesus must always be accepted as the Crucified One. What the
alternative to crucifixion-eucharist might be is not indicated
within this chapter (parousia-eucharist?).

But the unit in 6:51-58 is expressly addressed to the
Crowds/"Jews" who do not react to it after 6:59 while the Disciples to whom it is not specifically addressed are the ones
who respond to it, both negatively and positively. For John
"the Jews" are those who will deny and reject the divine necessity of this crucifixional destiny and by so doing render it
inevitable. *The supreme irony is that, for John, those who
reject crucifixion theoretically will thereby effect it po-
litically*. Hence, although addressed to "the Jews", their
final reaction is not recorded yet. But it is reacted to immediately by some of the Disciples now because even though
they will not effect the crucifixion, they will deny its permanent and enduring, that is, its eucharistic necessity.

NOTES

1. Jacques Derrida, "Force et Signification," *Critique*
193-94 (June-July, 1963) was the opening essay in his *L'écriture et la différence* (Paris: Seuil, 1967), a collection of
essays all, save one, published separately during 1963-1966.
The collection has been translated by Alan Bass as *Writing and
Difference* (Chicago: University of Chicago Press, 1978), and
this opening essay, "Force and Signification," (pp. 3-30) has
been reprinted in *Structuralist Review* 1, 2 (Winter, 1978):
13-54. My quotation is that essay's opening sentences.

2. I am aware that the terms "Narrative" (deeds) and
"Discourse" (words) are not entirely satisfactory. They may
cause confusion with the much more technical distinctions between Story (the content, the what) and Discourse (the expression, the how) suggested by Seymour Chatman, *Story and Discourse: Narrative Structure in Fiction and Film* (Ithaca,
N.Y.: Cornell University Press, 1978). I have not been able
to adapt Chatman's excellent categories to John 6 (although
it may well be possible to do so with future study) primarily
because of the very special relationship between what Jesus
does (my "Narrative") and what Jesus says (my "Discourse") in
John 6. But, for future reference, see Chatman's section on
(his term) "Discourse" (pp. 146-262) and especially his comment that, "When we know more about textual and semantic analysis, it may be possible to develop viable taxonomies of dialogue types" (p. 177). He cites Maurice Blanchot's three-way
distinction of dialogue, exemplified from Malraux, James, and
Kafka, and notes that, "Kafka's characters, for their part,
are doomed forever to talk at cross purposes, past each other"
(p. 178). The application of that concept to the "non"-dialogue in John 6 is quite obvious.

INDICES

INDEX OF SCRIPTURE REFERENCES

I. Old Testament

254

II. New Testament

III. Apocrypha and Pseudepigrapha

INDEX OF MODERN WRITERS